DUE TO
ENEMY
ACTION

DUE TO ENEMY ACTION

The True World War II
Story of the USS *Eagle 56*

Stephen Puleo

Based largely on research by
Attorney and Naval Historian Paul M. Lawton

THE LYONS PRESS
Guilford, Connecticut
An imprint of The Globe Pequot Press

The Lyons Press is an imprint of The Globe Pequot Press.

10 9 8 7 6 5 4 3 2

Printed in the United States of America

Designed by Kirsten Livingston

ISBN 1-59228-739-5

Library of Congress Cataloging-in-Publication Data is available on file.

For the entire crew of the USS *Eagle 56 (PE-56)*—those who
died and those who survived on April 23, 1945; especially for
John Breeze, Harold Petersen, John Scagnelli, and Joseph Priestas,
survivors who learned the truth.

And for World War II veterans James R. Lawton,
and my father, Anthony W. Puleo.

Brave heroes all.

✪ ✪ ✪

April 3, 1946

"This office has been informed that, in view of the fact the investigating officers conducting the Board of Inquiry into the loss of the USS *Eagle (PE-56)* stated that the loss of this vessel was due to the explosion of its boilers, there is no authority for changing the status of the personnel from 'dead or injured not the result of enemy action,' to 'dead or injured as the result of enemy action.'

"In view of the above, favorable action cannot be given to your request for the award of the Purple Heart to the personnel listed . . ."

Captain H. G. Patrick,
Navy Department Board of Decorations and Medals
To Lieutenant John P. Scagnelli, USNR,
lone surviving officer of the USS Eagle PE-56

May 1, 2001

TO: Secretary of the Navy

FROM: Director of Naval History

Subj: Request for correction of historical record ICO [in case of] USS *Eagle (PE-56)* and recommendation of award of Purple Heart medals

"I have determined compelling evidence and facts that support the correction of the historical record in the case of the loss of the USS *Eagle (PE-56)*, sunk on 23 April 1945, by enemy action. It is further strongly recommended that . . . a blanket authorization for the 49 crew members of the USS *Eagle (PE-56)* killed and those 13 eligible survivors, be awarded the Purple Heart Medal for death and wounds suffered in combat. . . ."

Contents

DUE TO ENEMY ACTION

Prologue
Honor and Redemption

Saturday, June 8, 2002
Quincy, Massachusetts
aboard the USS *Salem*

Under a piercing blue sky, bright late-morning sun splashed across the main deck of the moored USS *Salem* and danced upon her gray anti-aircraft guns. High above the ship, white seagulls glinted as they wheeled in lazy circles amid faint cloud wisps. Light traffic thrummed across the short drawbridge nearby that traversed Quincy's inner bay, and the *Salem*'s American flag whispered in the soft wind. A hushed crowd aboard the *Salem* listened as eighty-two-year-old John Scagnelli read the names of his former comrades, men who had perished on another warship, the USS *Eagle PE-56*, nearly six decades earlier. After each name, Scagnelli's fellow *Eagle 56* survivors, Johnny Breeze and Harold "Pete" Petersen, took turns tolling the ship's bell in memory of men they had known in another lifetime, shipmates who would remain forever young.

Flanking Scagnelli, the invited VIPs sat ramrod straight, their chairs lined across a low platform stage, facing the families of the deceased *Eagle 56* crewmen, loved ones who, in many cases, had traveled thousands of miles to attend this special ceremony aboard the *Salem*. A sprawling canopy shielded these relatives from the hot sun, protecting

3

them as surely today as their fathers, brothers, grandfathers, and uncles were left vulnerable and exposed fifty-seven years earlier.

As the lone surviving officer of the *Eagle 56*, Scagnelli's job was to read the names of the forty-nine men who had gone down with their ship in the final days of World War II, but as he neared the end of the list, his strong, clear voice caught in his throat and he blinked back tears. In his mind's eye, he saw each of these young men, their faces flashing one after another, some smiling, most still in their twenties, and he was overcome with emotion. With Scagnelli literally unable to speak for a few moments, Breeze and Petersen struck the clapper against the bell again and again, pausing a respectful two seconds between each. The clarity and resonance of each peal reverberated across the *Salem*'s decks and into the harbor beyond, until finally the forty-ninth clang faded like a memory in mournful tribute to those crew members of the *Eagle 56* who never returned home from World War II.

On April 23, 1945, just two weeks before Germany's surrender, the *Eagle 56* had sailed from the U.S. Naval Frontier Base in Portland, Maine, at 8:15 A.M., with sixty-two men aboard. She had been towing a target buoy at the end of a 500-yard line for naval aircraft bombing exercises. With the war in Europe nearly over, Navy and Marine pilots practiced to stay sharp in case they were needed to fight the Japanese in the Pacific.

Shortly after noon, with the *Eagle 56* at a dead stop less than five miles southeast of Cape Elizabeth off the rocky Maine coast, she suddenly exploded amidships, sending a geyser of steam and water two hundred feet skyward. She broke in half and sank within minutes. Forty-nine men perished in the terrible blast, either from the explosion itself or from drowning in the frigid waters of the North Atlantic. Of the "Lucky Thirteen" who survived, only Scagnelli, Petersen, and Breeze were still alive in 2002. Each of them, along with their ten shipmates who had been pulled from the water by rescue ships, had testified in 1945 as part of a hastily convened and clearly biased Court of Inquiry (COI) investigation, which ultimately concluded that a faulty boiler had caused the explosion. Soon afterward, the Navy modified its findings, officially attributing the destruction of the *Eagle 56* to "undetermined causes."

The "Lucky Thirteen" knew otherwise. As they plunged into the icy North Atlantic to save themselves, their ship torn in two, several men spotted a German U-boat that—against all rules of engagement—had surfaced near the wreckage of the *Eagle 56*. Even those men who did not see the U-boat testified unanimously that the rocking, concussive power of the blast left little doubt in their minds that it was caused by an external force, either a torpedo or a mine, but certainly *not* by a ruptured boiler. The thirteen survivors also knew, and many testified, that the *Eagle*'s boilers and engines had been completely overhauled two weeks earlier, and were in perfect working order.

Yet, their accounts were ignored by the Court of Inquiry and the Portland commander. The Navy brass, while skeptical of the COI's findings, was reluctant to overturn the official ruling and went along with the decision. Top-secret U.S. intelligence intercepts that showed a German U-boat, the *U-853*, prowling in the Gulf of Maine during April of 1945 were not declassified until many years later. Scagnelli, as the *Eagle*'s lone surviving officer, wrote condolence letters to the families of his dead comrades, but was prohibited from mentioning a cause for the explosion.

The 2002 ceremony aboard the USS *Salem* signified that everything had changed. A year earlier, the Navy had grudgingly acknowledged its mistake, fifty-six years after the *Eagle 56* was sunk, thanks primarily to the efforts of one man, attorney and naval historian Paul M. Lawton. His dogged persistence revealed the truth about the *Eagle 56* and convinced the Navy to alter its official history. For the first time ever, the Secretary of the Navy had overturned a Court of Inquiry decision and revised the official cause of the *Eagle*'s sinking to "due to enemy action." The ruling entitled most of her crew to Purple Heart medals, awarded by the military to servicemen wounded or killed in action. The Navy awarded those medals posthumously to the forty-nine sailors who died on April 23, 1945; many of their family members accepted them with reverence at the ceremony aboard the *Salem*, eloquently sharing their feelings about the importance of the emotional day.

Scagnelli and Petersen also received Purple Hearts for injuries they sustained when the *Eagle 56* was torpedoed. Breeze, who spent twenty minutes in the freezing water and suffered hypothermia, was not awarded the Purple Heart, nor were the other ten members of the "Lucky Thirteen" who had died since; the Navy apparently believed that their ordeal was not sufficient to earn the medal. Johnny Breeze, however, had little concern about a medal and an abiding passion for the truth. To him, the ceremony aboard the *Salem* was a vivid testament to that truth, albeit a half-century too late.

The Navy's reversal vindicated Scagnelli, Petersen, and Breeze. Scagnelli served as the *Eagle 56*'s engineering officer, and thus had responsibility for the vessel's operation and maintenance. He supervised the boiler-room crew, and the Court of Inquiry's findings haunted him for years afterwards. Petersen and Breeze were proud members of the ship's "Black Gang" who reported to Scagnelli, the men who worked belowdecks in the boiler and engine rooms. All three believed that the Navy had perpetrated a miscarriage of justice when it blamed the explosion on faulty boilers; all three took the 1945 decision personally. They had always known that their shipmates had not died due to carelessness. Now the families of the deceased *Eagle 56* crew members knew it, too.

The *Salem*'s bell tolled as a solemn reminder of a forgotten World War II story that began in the 1940s and did not conclude until 2002, a story that is told in its entirety here for the first time.

It is much more than a story of a small subchaser, the *Eagle 56*, caught in the crosshairs of the *U-853*, whose brazen commander doomed his own fifty-five-man crew in a desperate, last-ditch attempt to record final kills before his country's imminent defeat. Rather, the *Eagle 56* (officially the *PE-56*—for Patrol Escort—one of sixty "Eagle-class" boats built in the World War I era) and the *U-853* were the major players in the final chapter in the Battle of the Atlantic, an epic struggle that began with dramatic U-boat attacks against hundreds of defenseless merchant ships off American shores in 1942. The tide of this great sea battle turned in 1943, thanks to an unprecedented American industrial effort that produced vast numbers of ships and planes, coupled with the astonishing intelligence-gathering, analysis, and sub-tracking capabilities of the British at Bletchley Park and the Americans at the Navy's "Secret Room" in Washington, D.C. By 1945, when the *U-853* sunk the *Eagle*, superior Allied air and sea power had rendered any U-boat maneuver in Atlantic waters perilous, virtually suicidal. Yet, the *U-853* had managed to creep shockingly close to the Maine coast to destroy the *Eagle 56*, the last American warship sunk by a German U-boat in World War II. Eleven days later, on May 5, 1945, after eluding surveillance along the East Coast, the *U-853* sunk the final American freighter of the war, the *Black Point*, off the coast of Rhode Island. American warships hunted the *U-853* and destroyed her one day later, the last German U-boat that the Allies destroyed in the war, just hours before Germany surrendered.

The Battle of the Atlantic, and the war against Germany, both finally ended with the "kill" of the *U-853* just off America's East Coast.

But the story did not end there; Paul Lawton would not let it. More than a half-century later, he began a quest to right an injustice that had affected the lives of so many for so long. Inspired by his own father's bravery in World War II, and his friendship with the sons of a deceased *Eagle 56* crew member, Lawton dug tenaciously for the truth and refused to take no for an answer, despite encountering one bureaucratic obstacle after another. Through his commitment and dedication, he achieved what the mere passage of time could not. He brought peace to the *Eagle 56* family: to the three living survivors, Scagnelli, Breeze, and Petersen, part of the "Lucky Thirteen," who lived with painful memories for nearly sixty years; to the widows and children of the deceased *Eagle* crew members who wondered what really happened on that fateful April day; and perhaps even to the sailors who died in 1945, whose frozen bodies sank below the roiling Atlantic waves and never resurfaced.

All of them were forgotten at war's end, their stories lost amid a flurry of stunning headlines in the spring and summer of 1945: the death of President Franklin D. Roosevelt, the liberation of the Nazi death camps, the suicide of Adolf Hitler, the fall of Berlin, the German surrender, V-E Day celebrations, the dropping of the atomic bombs on Japan, and finally, the Japanese surrender and the end of the war. In the wake of these events, which would reshape the world in the twentieth century, the full story of the USS *Eagle PE-56* remained buried in archives and memories for more than fifty years—until Lawton unearthed the truth and changed history.

Now, in a new century, even as John Scagnelli's voice broke with sadness during the solemn Purple Heart ceremony aboard the USS *Salem*, the souls of those who had perished could finally rest. For the young *Eagle 56* officers and crewmen who had died so unexpectedly and so violently in 1945, and for old sailors like Scagnelli, Petersen, and Breeze, who remembered their shipmates with each toll of the *Salem*'s bell, World War II was finally over.

Part I

The Hunters and the Prey

1

As much as Lieutenant Commander John L. Barr Jr. loved these men, he knew in his heart that it was now time to leave them.

The skipper of the USS *Eagle PE-56* was relinquishing command of the 200-foot subchaser. Barr was finished with the boredom of stateside duty, the sluggishness of Portland, and the predictability of the *Eagle*'s role since she had arrived in Maine seven months earlier. He had requested a transfer to the Pacific, where the real action was for an experienced naval officer.

The *Eagle 56* had a noble World War II record. Early in the war, before Barr had assumed command, her crew had rescued survivors from the USS *Jacob Jones II* after the destroyer had been sunk by torpedoes from a German U-boat, the *U-578*, off the Delaware coast. The date was February 28, 1942, less than three months after Pearl Harbor; the *Jacob Jones* was the first U.S. warship sunk by a German U-boat within American coastal waters in World War II. She would be far from the last vessel sunk along the country's eastern seaboard in the war's early stages. More than six hundred merchant and war ships totaling three million aggregate tons went to the bottom between January and August of 1942, with thousands of crewmen lost. Yet, the destruction of the *Jacob Jones*, an elite destroyer of the U.S. Navy's Atlantic fleet, less than twenty-five miles from the U.S. shore, was a powerful message that German U-boats were operating with impunity and little fear of retaliation along America's Atlantic coast in the months following Pearl Harbor. Of the nearly two hundred crew members aboard the *Jacob Jones*, only about two dozen escaped the doomed ship in life rafts, and several of those men were killed when their ship's depth charges exploded as she sank.

The other surviving crew members were spotted by an army observation plane in the early morning hours of February 28, 1942. The pilot reported their position to the *Eagle 56*, which was then stationed at Cape May, New Jersey, as part of Inshore Patrol. Her crew fought rising seas—and the knowledge that a U-boat was in the area—to reach the stranded *Jones* crewmen, and two hours after the plane had spotted the life rafts, the *Eagle 56* radioed back to Cape May: "Am picking up survivors from the USS *Jacob Jones*—details later." The details were few; the *Eagle 56* had rescued twelve survivors, and one of them died on the way back to shore. For the next two days, planes and ships searched without success for other *Jacob Jones* survivors.

The *PE-56* did other important work, too. In May of 1942, she reported to Key West, Florida, as a sound training school-ship conducting exercises in anti-submarine warfare tactics. In 1943, with Barr at the helm, she had participated in the development of the Navy's top-secret "homing mine" (or anti-submarine torpedo) by acting as an acoustic target during testing trials.

Since Portland had become the *Eagle*'s home base in late June of 1944, though, the "old girl," or the "tub" (as the crew affectionately referred to the twenty-five-year-old vessel) had been relegated to towing a green cylindrical target float, which was mounted on a sled at the end of a 500-yard cable, off the coast of Cape Elizabeth. The green float, nicknamed "the pickle" by Barr's men, was used for bombing practice by Navy "Avenger" torpedo bomber aircraft from the Naval Air Station in Brunswick, Maine. The Navy and Marine flyboys needed the practice before they shipped out to battle the Japanese in the Pacific.

Barr would soon join them. The war in Europe was drawing to a close, which would snuff out any remote chance the *PE-56* had of ever seeing combat. It was only a matter of time before Germany surrendered; the Allies had just repelled the Reich's massive last-gasp counteroffensive through the Ardennes Forest that had begun just before Christmas of 1944. Hitler's final gamble, the Battle of the Bulge, had failed, and American, British, and Russian troops were all converging on Berlin. For Barr to feel he was truly contributing to the war effort, he would have to transfer to the Pacific Theater to fight against the Japanese, seeking not glory but the fulfillment of his own sense of duty. Some of the guys thought he was crazy, giving up a cushy command on America's shores and *volunteering* to ship out to hostile waters to face a tenacious enemy ten thousand miles away. But his decision was final.

Now, he prepared to read the change of command order, with the entire crew assembled before him as part of the formal ceremony, including Lieutenant James G. Early, who would become the new skipper of the *Eagle 56*. Barr believed he was leaving the old girl in good hands. His officers were competent: Lieutenant Early, Lieutenant (junior grade) John Scagnelli, and especially, his executive officer, Jack Laubach, with whom he was particularly close; and the crew was as skilled and well trained as any in the Navy. Bidding farewell to shipmates who had become friends was difficult, but Barr felt the war was passing him by. Many other good men had sacrificed far more than he had in this war; for their sakes, and his, he needed to venture into harm's way.

"Almighty God has blessed our land in many ways," President Franklin D. Roosevelt had said in his fourth inaugural address just a few days earlier. "He has given our people stout hearts and strong arms with which to strike mighty blows for freedom and truth."

The time had come for Barr to strike his own blows for freedom and truth, to leave the snugness of Portland Harbor and the safety of the *Eagle 56*.

2

One month after John L. Barr relinquished command of the *PE-56* in Portland, Maine, Helmut Froemsdorf, twenty-three-year-old commander of the *U-853*, maneuvered his boat out of Germany's alternative operational center, one of five U-boats with orders to proceed to America's New England coast and wreak as much havoc as possible with Allied shipping.

Froemsdorf's orders had been issued by *Grossadmiral* (Grand Admiral) Karl Dönitz, formerly head of *Unterseeboote*, the German U-boat service, and now commander in chief of the *Kriegsmarine*, the German Navy. Froemsdorf was well aware of Dönitz's swift rise in the German high command, and knew the *Grossadmiral* was a trusted adviser of the Führer, Adolf Hitler. Like most U-boatmen, Froemsdorf admired and respected Dönitz, and would do most anything to please him.

Remarkably tall for a U-boatman—nearly six feet, five inches—Froemsdorf was bright and strong, an athlete, a skier, and a dancer. He was neither a member of the Nazi Party nor a fanatic, but he had great pride in the Fatherland, a brashness to accompany his ascendance to U-boat commander at such a tender age, and a determination to carve out a reputation for himself in the U-boat service, whose ranks were replete with Germany's most celebrated heroes.

One of those was the *U-853*'s previous commander, Helmut Sommer, whose heroics helped him and the boat achieve near legendary status when, on May 25, 1944, the *U-853* happened upon one of the most prized targets in the Atlantic, according to authors Henry C. Keatts and George C. Farr. While the *U-853* was surfaced to transmit a weather report, Sommer sighted the enormous profile of the *Queen Mary* filling the horizon, transporting American troops and goods to England. Usually, large ocean liners required no escorts; they were so fast that no U-boat could get into attack position unless she happened to be in the right spot. Immediately, Sommer had ordered the *U-853* to submerge and pursue, but the fast ocean liner easily outran it.

The *U-853* surfaced again to complete her interrupted weather transmissions. German intelligence believed these reports could help anticipate Allied plans to invade Europe from across the English Channel—an invasion the Germans knew was imminent by May of 1944, and one which would be heavily influenced by weather conditions. The *U-853* was suddenly attacked by three rocket-firing British planes. Instead of diving immediately, Sommer ordered his anti-aircraft guns into action, a daring strategy that briefly confused the attacking pilots. While the three planes regrouped for a second attack, the captain took the *U-853* down to safety.

Three weeks later, June 15, 1944—nine days after the Allied invasion on the beaches of Normandy, France—a hunter-killer group, comprised of the carrier USS *Croatan* and six destroyers, pursued the *U-853*. The Allied ships had located the U-boat by intercepting radio transmissions using high-frequency direction-finding (h/f-d/f, or "Huff-Duff") detecting equipment. For seventy-two hours, according to Keatts and Farr, aircraft from the carrier combed the area while the carriers waited for the U-boat to surface, which it would have to do sooner or later. Men on the waiting surface ships named the elusive *U-853* "Moby-Dick" after the great white whale that the fictional Captain Ahab pursued in Herman Melville's classic novel. During this same period, the *U-853* crew, in admiration of Sommer's skill in eluding attackers, nicknamed their boat *Der Seiltaenger*, or "Tightrope Walker."

Finally, on June 18, *Croatan*'s Huff-Duff equipment intercepted a weather transmission from the *U-853* only thirty miles distant. Within minutes, fighter planes from the carrier were strafing the deck of the surfaced U-boat. This time, the *U-853*'s anti-aircraft gun crews were less fortunate. Two crewmen were killed, and several others were wounded, including Sommer, who was riddled by slugs and fragments that ripped into his head, stomach, and arms. In all, Sommer was hit twenty-eight times, but he managed to stay alert long enough to give the order to submerge just seconds before bombers arrived to finish off the *U-853*. The act became folklore in the U-boat service, and Sommer became a hero to his men.

The *U-853* limped back to her base in Lorient, France, on July 4 of 1944, sixteen days after the attack, but was forced to leave the base as the Allies advanced on the port city. With a temporary commander at the helm, she was transported to Germany, where she underwent repairs and was fitted with a *schnorchel* (snorkel), a retractable air intake and exhaust pipe that would permit operation of her diesel engines while submerged. The new device reduced the dangerous periods the U-boats had to spend on the surface charging their batteries. Soon thereafter, on September 1, 1944, Froemsdorf, the *U-853*'s twenty-three-year-old former executive officer who had performed well on the previous mission, assumed command of the 252-foot-long Type IXC/40 U-boat.

Though young, Froemsdorf understood that the world had changed dramatically in three short years.

In the first few months of 1942, German U-boats had operated boldly and with little resistance off the East Coast of the United States, inflicting physical and psychological damage on the Americans by sinking hundreds of ships just miles from her shores. German U-boat commanders dubbed it the "Great American Turkey Shoot" and the "Second Happy Time," a sequel to the resounding success U-boatmen had against British shipping in the summer and fall of 1940.

By mid-1943, though, the tide had turned, and the situation deteriorated quickly for the U-boats. The American president, Franklin Roosevelt, had called the United States home front to action. Her people and her factories responded by building ships and airplanes at astounding rates. The U.S. Navy soon developed a sophisticated convoy system whereby merchant ships were protected by warships both across the Atlantic and along the eastern seaboard. American fighter planes and bombers became the nemesis of the U-boats, which had operated in the early days primarily on the surface, submerging to stay hidden for a short time or to slip away undetected if enemy ships were in the area. Now, remaining on the surface was near suicide. The *U-853*'s snorkel meant it could remain submerged at periscope depth for most of the trip across the Atlantic—with just the top of the snorkel tube protruding above the surface—but the trade-off was that travel was unbearably slow. A slight miscalculation by the operator who controlled the boat's depth, or even a moderate amount of extra surface turbulence, would cause water to cover the snorkel cap, closing its valve suddenly and shutting off the flow of air. At that point, the U-boat's diesels, which needed a large amount of air, would suck the air from the inside of the hull unless they were immediately switched off. This could result in a dangerous buildup of carbon dioxide that could prove toxic to the crew. Froemsdorf and his men were protected from Allied planes while submerged, but the trip across the Atlantic would take them the better part of two months. The U-853 would only be about halfway through its Atlantic crossing when Froemsdorf celebrated his twenty-fourth birthday on March 26.

Though they were now more the hunted than the hunter, the crew of the U-853 possessed a strong sense of pride. The men had adorned the U-boat's black conning tower with the insignia of a trotting red horse on a yellow shield, which was technically against German Navy regulations, but a remnant of the boat's glory days under Sommer. Froemsdorf would try to recapture some of that glory for the U-853, though he knew his efforts would ultimately be in vain. With the Russians bearing down on Berlin from the East, and the Americans and British advancing from the West, the outcome of the war was no longer in doubt. Germany would keep fighting, but she could not win, and with each passing day, her options narrowed. Dönitz hoped that these recently dispatched U-boats could disrupt Allied supply lines enough to convince American president Franklin D. Roosevelt and General Dwight D. Eisenhower to reconsider their position—that only the "unconditional surrender" of Germany would be acceptable to end the war.

For Germany, the fighting was all but over. The intent of Froemsdorf's mission was to improve the prospects of the Fatherland's postwar future.

As the U-853 headed westward toward the American coast in late February of 1945, Helmut Froemsdorf knew the chances for survival were slim for him and his crew. The U-boat service suffered casualty rates approaching 85 percent, the highest of all the military branches, Axis or Allied. In the last three years, thousands of brave U-boatmen had met their deaths in watery graves, pummeled by bombs from Allied airplanes or depth charges from their ships. Not only was Froemsdorf's mission difficult, it was perilous; even if the U-853 managed to record any kills, she would be hard-pressed to return to Norway safely.

Froemsdorf, a member of the U-boat class of 1939, hoped for some success, but in his last letter to his parents, even while expressing his pride at commanding the *U-853*, he portended a sense of doom: "I am lucky in these difficult days of my Fatherland to have the honor of commanding this submarine and it is my duty to accept . . . I'm not very good at last words, so good-bye for now, and give my sister my love."

3

Early March 1945
Phyllis Westerlund
Brockton, Massachusetts

Rain drummed on the roof and plinked into the metal pails that Phyllis Westerlund had set out under her leaky ceiling, the repeating *clink-clank-clink-clank* the only sounds in the house as midnight drew near. All four children had been asleep for hours, and Phyllis had turned off the radio so she could collect her thoughts; turned off every light, too, except for the overhead in the kitchen, where she sat now rereading her husband's poems, missing him desperately. The loneliness was always worse at night. It was bad enough that Ivar had been away from home with the Navy for nearly a year, but America was now more than three years into this war, and on nights like this, Phyllis wondered if it would ever end.

She pictured him every day: the brown hair, the hazel eyes, the warm sense of humor, and the cocksure attitude that had taken her breath away from that first moment in 1935, when he had pulled his car up to the Brockton bus stop where she and her friend had been waiting for the Stoughton bus. He had rolled down his window and asked, "Can I give you girls a ride?" The women looked at each other, shrugged, and because there were two of them, decided to accept the offer. On the short ride to Stoughton, Ivar talked mostly to twenty-year-old Phyllis, both of them laughing often. She knew then that Ivar Westerlund would become her husband; they were married on June 6, 1936, during the heart of the

on. Ivar worked as a clerk in a feed store and they were dirt-
, but as Phyllis always said, "very happy with nothing."

The children had followed quickly; Carol first, and then the three
boys: Robert, Frederick, and finally, Paul, in 1943, with America at war.
Their fortunes improved as the family grew. An elderly couple and friends
of Ivar's parents, the Nelsons, had been unable to afford their home any
longer, and told Ivar and Phyllis that the house was theirs if they could
pay the back taxes and mortgage. The Nelsons' misfortune provided a big
break for the Westerlunds; Phyllis and Ivar bought the house on Belair
Street and took over the $59 annual property-tax bill and the $28
monthly mortgage. Phyllis felt like a millionaire when she walked through
her new home—two floors, a beautiful walk-in basement, and a garage.
By the time Paul was born, Ivar had switched jobs, too, and was earning
considerably more money as one of 51,000 workers at the enormous and
bustling Quincy Fore River Shipyard, building America's warships.

Life had been good, even in the aftermath of Pearl Harbor, with the
shortages and endless rationing of meat, sugar, coffee, butter, paper,
gasoline, and what seemed like hundreds of other items. Ivar, her first
love, was a wonderful husband and father, her best friend, a joy to be
around. He was a strong man with a boyish sense of humor, an animal-
lover who brought home one pet after another for the children: chickens, a billy goat, dogs, cats, turtles, parakeets, and finally, a baby pig
that had grown to three hundred pounds, which they kept in a backyard
pen near the woods. Phyllis had scolded Ivar gently for bringing so
many animals home, insisting that the City of Brockton would not look
kindly on the pig, especially; Ivar just laughed and said it was important
for their children to love and enjoy animals.

His sense of humor was his most endearing quality, and sometimes
his most infuriating. The only time Phyllis remembered being truly
angry with him was when she returned home from grocery shopping
one summer day and discovered that he had shaved every last hair off
the heads of two of their sons. She had always loved her sons' beautiful
hair, and was initially devastated, but she couldn't stay angry with Ivar
for long. He took to calling the boys "Eight Ball" and "Cue Ball," said
it would be cooler for them in the summer, and claimed that their hair
would grow back thicker than ever.

She considered herself lucky to have shared so much time with Ivar
before he entered the Navy. The draft boards took the single men early,

nearly all of them, before claiming the married men without children first, and finally, those with children. By the time Ivar's number had come up in the spring of 1944, he probably could have petitioned for a deferment, but he chose not to, even at the age of thirty-one. So many men had been called up and sent to faraway places to fight, and Ivar had felt a sense of duty to join them. He had entered the Navy on Good Friday, leaving Phyllis with the four children. She remembered the sense of despair she had felt two days later, on Easter Sunday of '44; she and the children had been dressed in their finery, but the family felt incomplete without Ivar's solid presence.

He was assigned to the USS *Eagle PE-56*, which was then based in Key West, Florida. For Phyllis, it might as well have been Egypt. She longed for him, especially on D-Day, June 6, 1944, their eighth wedding anniversary. City Hall closed early and churches remained open late as prayer services took place around the city. At the nearby Eaton Shoe Company factory, a moment of silence was called throughout the building at 11:30 A.M. on June 6, and 600 men and women offered prayers for the safety of American troops landing in France. "Many with tears streaming down their faces prayed aloud for loved ones 'over there,'" the *Brockton Enterprise* reported. At Brockton High School the next day, students stood at attention for several moments during the normally festive end-of-year "Class Day" ceremonies, while their parents again observed several moments of silence from the stands. For those families who had servicemen stationed overseas—and that was virtually every family—no one really knew if their loved ones had been part of the massive invasion force that had crossed the English Channel into the teeth of Hitler's "Fortress Europe."

Phyllis had been thankful that Ivar was stationed in Key West, and took some solace in the fact that he was not landing on the beaches of Normandy facing withering German machine-gun fire; still, she felt desperately alone and frightened on D-Day, and while the fear had subsided in the months that followed, the loneliness persisted. A recent *Enterprise* survey had asked men and women what they missed most during the war. Nearly everyone insisted that their sacrifices were small, but since the paper *had* asked, the men said they missed regular access to rationed items like good cigars and gasoline. The women said, indisputably, that they missed their men the most, an answer Phyllis would have echoed immediately had the paper contacted her.

Phyllis had been thrilled when, shortly after D-Day, in late June of 1944, the *Eagle 56* had been reassigned to Portland, Maine. Ivar was now close enough to visit on weekend furloughs, and by the early months of 1945, she knew that the war in Europe was nearly over, a day for which she longed. Ivar would return home soon, much sooner than GIs stationed overseas, and they could get on with their lives. For that, she realized she was one of the fortunate women in Brockton.

But at this late hour, just before her mother came over to be with the children so she could go to work, Phyllis felt most alone.

With the raindrops the only sound on this quiet night, she read his poems. He was a warm, loving man, but it was not like him to write poetry. He had sent two, one entitled "To My Wife and Children," and one just to her, called "Remember." He signed them both, "Daddy." Both had been written from the heart and both contained a wisp of melancholy that sent a chill through Phyllis each time she read them. To Phyllis and the children Ivar had written:

> *Each night before I go to bed*
> *I say a prayer with low-bowed head.*
> *Praying to God that he will keep*
> *watch o'er my family while they sleep . . .*
>
> *So good night my love and my children, too.*
> *One more night to dream—if my dream could come true*
> *I'd hope and I'd pray there would come a day,*
> *When I'll come home safely to you.*

And to Phyllis in "Remember," Ivar had written:

> *Remember the hours we spent, dear*
> *The happiness we knew*
> *The peaceful hours in the parlor*
> *In the house I once knew.*
>
> *Oh darling, everything we did*
> *I will never forget.*
> *And I always thank my star*
> *For that lucky day we met.*

Phyllis was no poet, either, but she felt like she needed to respond in verse. If Ivar had taken the time to bare his heart, she would, too. She had been thinking for a long time, reading and rereading Ivar's words, growing more saddened than reassured, feeling that her husband seemed further away rather than closer. She tried to shake these thoughts; maybe the rain or the late hour was causing her this intense melancholy. She titled her poem "Miss You," and began to write:

> *Hon, this isn't much, as you can see,*
> *But I want you to know I am thinking of thee.*
> *The days are so dreary, the nights are so long,*
> *If God only knew, he would send you along—*
> *Home to your family, your children, your friends,*
> *But God only knows when this thing will end.*

There would be more, Phyllis knew, but she had no time to finish tonight. Her factory job was much too important. Ivar was able to send home a small amount of money, but she was the family's main bread-winner.

As the raindrops tapped into the metal pails and midnight approached, she put down her pen, and went to check on the children and get ready for work.

4

Around the same time that Phyllis Westerlund was reading her husband's poetry in the quiet of her own home, Helmut Froemsdorf was reading the latest secret radio dispatch from Berlin. *Grossadmiral* Dönitz's message exhorted U-boat commanders to remain steadfast in their loyalty to the Third Reich's cause.

"Let us fly into the face of all those who want to give up, who adopt the silly motto 'It is no longer any use.' Those are the greatest weaklings. They are the ones who let themselves be led to the slaughter like patient cattle," Dönitz's message read. "Let us fly into the face of any German who now becomes the least bit shaky in his loyalty to the Nazi state and to the Führer. The motives for this are only fear, cowardice, and weakness. We are the strong and the faithful."

Froemsdorf, who would soon celebrate his twenty-fourth birthday in the cramped quarters of his U-boat, never publicly questioned his crew's loyalty, but was aware that he had two things working against him as a commander of men: his tender age, and former Commander Sommer's stellar reputation, which would be difficult for him to emulate. This alone would make it difficult for him to command the respect of his crew, a relationship "based squarely on the concept of a benign autocrat who is all-powerful but who nevertheless requires trust and confidence from below so he can rule effectively," in the words of author Jordan Vause. "There were no secrets" among men who "suddenly found themselves thrown together in a metal shell the size of a small apartment, in which they worked, ate common meals, literally slept in each other's bunks, grew rank and dirty together, and remained so for weeks at a time . . . each man knew everyone else intimately and soon found himself depending on everyone else for his life. If he made a mistake, others suffered for it . . . an enemy ship might escape, or the entire crew might die."

Indeed, it was this very intimacy that likely prompted Froemsdorf to suspect what he must not have known for certain: that several members of his crew questioned his leadership and feared his potential for recklessness. Before the *U-853* departed from Norway, twenty-year-old Machinist Mate 2nd Class Frederick Volk had written to his mother that he was worried about the mission because he had no faith in Froemsdorf. Theodore Woner, a *U-853* crewman who had missed the last cruise because of illness, later wrote that, "He [Froemsdorf] was a different personality [than Sommer] . . . at least some of the crew believed Froemsdorf was out to get a decoration." Even Sommer was concerned for the safety of his officers and crew under Froemsdorf's command. Sommer's wife would write later that her husband thought Froemsdorf was "very young and ambitious when he became commander. My husband asked him again and again not to act frivolously, for he knew the end of the war was near and . . . that all the fine fellows of his crew should survive."

Though he may have sensed his crew's misgivings, Froemsdorf knew nothing of these letters. For now, the correspondence he was most concerned with was the latest radio message sent by Karl Dönitz in Berlin: "Let us show our enemies that the destruction of Germany will cost them more in blood, treasure, and time than they can withstand," the dispatch read. "Let us exert all our powers to the utmost, for example, by sinking as many ships as possible for the Anglo-Saxons in total disregard of risk. Then their doubts as to whether this unconditional defeat of Germany is practicable and not too costly will increase."

Froemsdorf did not know whether he would have the opportunity to fulfill Dönitz's desire to sink Allied ships. Nor could he have known how he or his crew would react under combat stress.

As he finished reading Dönitz's secret communiqué, as the *U-853* moved slowly and cautiously toward the Gulf of Maine, there was one other thing Froemsdorf could not have known: Within hours, in a highly secure room inside U.S. Naval Headquarters on Constitution Avenue in Washington, D.C., a small, select group of American naval intelligence officers—the enemy—would be reading the same message.

5

Commander Kenneth Alward Knowles reviewed Dönitz's latest dispatch with great interest, along with the letter from the intelligence officer who had forwarded it to Knowles's U-boat tracking area, known as the Secret Room. "The general tone suggests that it may well be the prelude to the all-out U/boat offensive in the North Atlantic," noted the U.S. officer.

Knowles suffered from acute nearsightedness, but he seldom erred in his ability to see the big picture clearly. He was one of America's top intelligence officers, and the operation he commanded was among the most secret of the entire war. Indeed, in terms of sheer numbers, more people knew about the Manhattan Project to build the atomic bomb than knew about the Navy's U-boat Tracking Room and the sealed-off "Secret Room" within its perimeter in Washington, D.C. There, Knowles and a small handpicked team read and analyzed radio messages between Berlin and German U-boats that Navy cryptographers had intercepted and decoded. Intelligence derived from these messages was categorized under the top-secret and classified "Ultra" cover name, which technically referred to all high-grade signal intelligence (SIGINT) obtained from Axis radio communications, as well as the collective name for intercepts between the German Naval Command and the U-boats.

The Germans used a cipher machine called Enigma to put messages into secret form, and the British first broke the code after the capture of an Enigma machine from a U-boat in May of 1941. Between June and December of 1941, British cryptographers at Bletchley Park, England's code-breaking Government Communications Headquarters, were able to read German naval traffic (code-named "Hydra") within approximately forty-eight hours. But the Germans changed the Hydra code in February of 1942 to the more complex Triton code. This act "blinded" both British and American code breakers for most of the remainder of 1942, and this lack of intelligence—coupled with insufficient escort ships and planes—led to horrible Allied shipping losses for the year.

By the end of 1942, Allied code breakers had broken the Triton code, and the Ultra blackout ended. In the United States, these intelligence staffers were part of OP-20-G, the Navy's communication intelligence section: OP because it was a division of the office of the chief of naval operations; 20, the number of the communications division; and G for communications intelligence. OP-20-G began supplying Ultra information directly to the Commander in Chief, U.S. Fleet (COMINCH), headed up by Admiral Ernest J. King, and working closely with Bletchley Park.

On December 27, 1942, King created a special sub-tracking intelligence unit, designated F-21, and modeled after the British Operational Intelligence Center (OIC), headed up by Commander Roger Winn, whose operational intelligence methods focused not only on pinpointing *where* U-boats were located, but, through advanced analyses, predicting where they *might* attack. King directed Admiral Russell Willson, Chief of Staff of COMINCH, to select an officer who could study under Winn and learn about British intelligence in general. Willson's assistant, Admiral Francis "Frog" Low, immediately recommended a man he knew well, a reservist who had nearly six years of experience aboard destroyers and battleships, serving under both Willson and Low, before eye problems forced him to cashier out of the active Navy.

His name was Kenneth A. Knowles.

At first glance, Knowles seemed an unlikely candidate for the bold and daring decision-making that would accompany such a clandestine intelligence assignment. Nearly forty-three years old, married, and a father of two when Low recruited him, Knowles was both boyish- and bookish-looking, with horn-rimmed spectacles dominating his narrow face, a serious, studious man whose brother, Frank, once said was "born old."

The youngest of seven siblings whose ne'er-do-well father squandered an inherited family fortune by investing in a barren Nevada silver mine, Kenneth Knowles's approach to life was methodical and conservative, and he eschewed risk taking.

Yet, other personality traits made Knowles the perfect choice for managing the sub-tracking operation. He worked long hours, paid attention to detail, prided himself on his organizational skills, and was highly intelligent, graduating near the top of his 1927 class at the U.S. Naval Academy. "As a worker, he is par excellence," one Naval Academy classmate said of him. "If work makes a naval officer, then Ken is due to fly that two-starred flag some day, for he believes in getting results . . ."

Knowles was tough, too. Prior to entering the Academy, in the early 1920s, he had completed Marine Corps training at Parris Island, and was part of a company that marched from Parris Island to Gettysburg, Pennsylvania, to take part in a Civil War reenactment of Pickett's Charge. At the Academy he was a strong swimmer and a crack marksman, becoming captain of the naval rifle team. He had always been known as a serious officer who set high standards for achieving excellence. He was thorough, unassuming, shunned the spotlight, and possessed a keen, analytical mind. Admiral Low knew that Knowles's understated personality would be a plus in cooperating with the British, and his seriousness would ensure that the highly classified material that crossed his desk would remain secret.

Maybe most importantly, Kenneth Knowles loved the Navy. He battled a bout with depression after his eye problems forced him from active duty as a lieutenant in 1936, and then found a way to maintain close ties with the Navy by serving as an editor for Our Navy, the branch's official publication, for the next three years. He worked in the journal's offices on the tenth story of the Brooklyn National Bank, overlooking the Brooklyn Navy Yard. In his capacity as editor, he met frequently with ranking officers and covered many important events in the Navy Yard. He knew the Navy and its brass, and he had gained some notoriety as an intellectual and writer among active naval officers. He had remained close to Admiral Low—his two children knew the admiral as their "other Uncle Frank"—and when Low had asked him enthusiastically to run the sub-tracking room, Knowles had accepted in kind. Knowles was excited by the opportunity to serve under Low and Willson. He later remembered both of his former skippers as "SOBs, and as far as operations went, they were pretty strict on performance and so was I, so we fitted together pretty well."

✪ ✪ ✪

Knowles's unit formed a part of the thirty-man Combat Intelligence Section of COMINCH. The Combat Intelligence Section and its commander were designated F-2; Knowles and the Atlantic branch were F-21, and the Pacific branch was F-22. When, on May 20, 1943, Admiral King created the Tenth Fleet—the "fleet without a ship," an administrative body to direct the anti-submarine war—he designated Knowles's unit as the intelligence staff for the Tenth as well as the U.S. Fleet. Its principal function was to process and analyze intelligence from OP-20-G to track, monitor, predict the movements of, and defeat the U-boats.

F-21's U-boat Tracking Room was itself a confidential operation, but once Allied code breakers began experiencing even greater success at breaking German codes, Knowles decided that further compartmentalization was necessary, according to author and historian David Kohnen. He created a separate area within the F-21 tracking room known as F-211. Sealed off from the main tracking room, the space was widely referred to as the "Secret Room" among F-21 trackers. The Secret Room was kept locked, and could only be entered through the F-21 tracking room. Moreover, only the three men who worked in it—along with Knowles and a relief officer—had keys; except for a few high-ranking officers with special permission, "no other personnel have access to or participate in the activities of the room," according to F-211 regulations. In fact, very few people knew Knowles, his team, or Ultra even existed.

Validating Low's judgment, Knowles proved to be the perfect choice to command the U-boat tracking effort. He visited England to observe the Admiralty's OIC operation under the command of Roger Winn and his assistant in the OIC tracking room, Royal Navy Lieutenant Patrick Beesly. While in England, Knowles observed Winn and his tracking room staff gleaning operational intelligence from all sources—Huff-Duff intercepts, land-based radar sites, POW interrogation summaries, and radio transmissions that code breakers had decrypted from German Enigma machines. Knowles learned how the OIC collected information, and then distilled and sanitized it before staffers transmitted it over a teletype to operational intelligence headquarters in Liverpool. There, Admiralty strategists could consider Winn's analyses and guesstimates, and determine a proper course of action. By the time Knowles returned to the United States, "he was fully initiated into the small society of those who were familiar with the most secret aspects of Ultra special intelligence," biographer David Kohnen would write years later. "Moreover, Knowles was also experienced in all aspects of Admiralty OIC operations and he fully understood Winn's techniques in the art of tracking the enemy."

This knowledge helped Knowles quickly establish the foundation for a deadly efficient Secret Room in Washington, D.C., which was manned only by Knowles, executive officer Lieutenant John E. Parsons, USNR, and two other assistants. Knowles created the Secret Room to limit access to the raw cryptologic intelligence that the staff derived from all sources on a daily basis; the most significant information came from the text of deciphered enemy radio messages. Kohnen points out that these intercepts were sent directly to the Secret Room over a scrambled teletype by the OP-20-G code-breaking and translation specialists on Nebraska Avenue in Washington, D.C. In addition, the British Admiralty regularly sent "Ultra serials" that were delivered directly to the Secret Room in double-sealed pouches by commissioned U.S. naval officers.

By the summer of 1943, the most significant U-boat tracking work was performed in the security of the Secret Room, whose staff maintained three wall charts—one depicting the North Atlantic, one the South Atlantic, and a third, the Indian Ocean. They recorded individual U-boat positions with color-coded pins on the wall charts, and labeled the pins with the type and tonnage of the U-boat, and the names of known U-boat commanders.

Knowles and his team processed and analyzed the intelligence that helped American warships hunt down and destroy U-boats. Knowles and Admiral Low were usually in hourly contact, working together at keeping the American fleet updated on the latest enemy locations and activities. Knowles insisted on very strict procedures to accomplish this. The Ultra intercepts were *never* mentioned, and in fact, Knowles and his team were careful that they always had a "cover" story available as to how they learned about U-boat locations and movements, such as intercepted Huff-Duff signals or aircraft spotters. Under *no circumstances* could the information about Ultra leak, lest the Germans learn that the Allies had broken their Enigma codes.

In fact, the British OIC criticized the American Secret Room for using Ultra "offensively"—to coordinate hunter-killer attacks—which created tension in the friendship Knowles and Winn had developed. Winn was paranoid about *any* operation that might cause the Germans to realize that their codes and ciphers had been compromised. Knowles later wrote that the British concept of Ultra was more defensive, "a lifesaving operation" that was understandable, since "it was the only thing that we had to save Britain from complete destruction . . . so they were very cautious in utilizing Ultra. Whereas, over in my area, being younger at the game and also being somewhat aggressive, we were using Ultra more aggressively. There's quite a difference in philosophy here."

To ensure the circle of secrecy, Knowles himself met regularly with escort commanders before they departed for sea, providing them with detailed estimates of enemy trends in their planned operations area, but without giving these commanders direct knowledge of Ultra. Knowles's briefings soon became almost legendary for their prescience. One hunter-killer task group commander said in a postwar report: "There was a Commander Ken Knowles in Washington who ran this submarine estimate thing. He was a soothsayer. He could put himself in the position of a German skipper and just figure out what the guy was going to do, and where he would go. He was absolutely uncanny in his predictions . . . I treated the COMINCH daily estimate as Bible truth every day, and we based our operations on it completely."

Knowles himself either drafted or approved the daily U-boat situation estimate, with its forecast of where submarines were going, and then transmitted it to task forces at sea under the signature of the Commander in Chief, U.S. Fleet.

By meeting directly with convoy commanders, and sending encrypted dispatches directly to specific tactical units at sea, Knowles and his team were able to avoid communicating top-secret information to individual naval bases up and down the East Coast. Instead, in sharp contrast to the briefings they gave at-sea task force commanders, Knowles's team sent sanitized messages to base commanders. These most often took the form of highly general dispatches, such as "be alert" for enemy subs or "potential U-boat activity" in a large, general grid area, such as "from Nova Scotia to Cape Hatteras." As a result, as the war continued, operational base commanders came to view these messages as formalities, and—while perhaps not ignoring them altogether—often did not treat them as genuine warnings.

Still, for security reasons, Knowles would not budge on this point. "None of the operational commands were so informed [of specific intelligence gleaned from Ultra]," Knowles would write years later. "These restrictions were deemed necessary in the American Theater because of the wide separation of commands and the difficulty of maintaining security among them."

o ✪ o

F-21's and the F-211 Secret Room's clandestine battle against the U-boats was an extraordinary contribution during the last two years of the war. Acting on intelligence collected by F-21 and the Admiralty OIC, Allied convoys traversed the Atlantic safely while American hunter-killer formations brought the U-boat offensive to a grinding halt. Historian David Kohnen noted that between the summer of 1943 and March of 1945, Ultra intelligence provided by the Secret Room and British OIC was *directly responsible* for the liquidation of more than ninety Axis U-boats. Many years after the war, Knowles noted, "Throughout [the Battle of the Atlantic] were woven technical achievements of the highest order . . . But transcending all of these feats was 'Ultra intelligence,' the breaking of the German U-boat cipher. It gave first to the British and then to the Americans the edge of victory at sea; and from it flowed victory in Europe. Without it, the British could have been beaten to their knees. No wonder Churchill considered 'Ultra intelligence' his prime and sacred weapon—his Excalibur."

Rumors abounded in late 1944 and early 1945 that the last waves of German U-boats intended to smash New York and Washington with V-1 cruise missiles or V-2 ballistic rockets. Knowles thought that the belief took root with a secret OSS report in October of 1944 from Stockholm, in which sources indicated a U-boat would "depart for New York harbor to use V-1" for propaganda purposes. On November 6, OSS Stockholm followed this up with a report that said "four U-boats will be used in operation against New York." A similar message was dispatched from Stockholm on December 22, 1944.

The U.S. sub-tracking room would have been reassured when, on November 29, 1944, British intelligence wired the following message to OP-20-G: "We have of course received the rumours to which you refer that the Germans plan to use a U-boat (or U-boats) to fire robot bombs on the East Coast of the United States and—because, as you say, the project is worthy of considerable attention—we have been in close touch with the Admiralty in an effort to discover whether these rumours have any foundation. To date, [the Admiralty is] quite happy that the rumours are mere propaganda, and that they are not corroborated by any reliable high-grade evidence . . ."

Still, according to naval historians Clay Blair and Philip K. Lundeberg, following the secret British cable, two high-level American officials spoke publicly about German rocket attacks on New York City.

On December 10, 1944, New York Mayor Fiorello LaGuardia caused a near panic when he raised the possibility. Then, on January 8, 1945, Admiral Jonas Ingram, commander in chief of the U.S. Navy's Atlantic Fleet, also raised the specter of German rocket attacks, but said the U.S. Navy and Army Air Forces were fully prepared with a secret plan ("Bumblebee," later renamed "Teardrop") to "thwart any German U-boat missile attack on any shore of the U.S."

Then, Hitler's chief of war production, Albert Speer, further fanned the speculation when he announced in a Berlin radio broadcast that V-1 missiles and V-2 rockets "would fall on New York by February 1, 1945." This caused renewed panic in "the highest military levels in the United States," Blair wrote. The British Admiralty, though, remained calm, and on February 16, cabled this message to Admiral King:

A.   There was no evidence from photographic reconnaissance to confirm preparations by the Germans to mount such attacks.

B.   The V-2 ballistic missile could not be launched from a U-boat.

C.   The winged V-1 "buzz bomb" (i.e., cruise missile) *could* be stored in a topside hangar in knocked-down condition, assembled, and fired from launch skids on a Type 1X U-boat.

D.   The damage created by one V-1 (assuming it could hit a target) would be so negligible as to make the putative project not worthwhile.

E.   A missile attack from U-boats at this stage of the war was "highly unlikely."

Despite the British reassurances, the Americans proceeded with Operation Teardrop, Blair pointed out, mobilizing a massive number of American air and naval forces in late 1944 and 1945 to greet Dönitz's U-boats.

There were other rumors about the U-boats crossing the Atlantic in these latter stages of the war. Some claimed that these boats carried high-level Nazi officers seeking escape from Germany, or Nazi gold that the Reich was spiriting to South America, or even Japan. British intelligence had debunked the V-1 and V-2 story, and with his scholar's reliance on hard evidence, Knowles would have been skeptical of the other rumors as well.

Kenneth Knowles was a man who put his faith in facts; the fact was, while Dönitz's U-boats now making their way westward across the Atlantic were likely *not* planning to rain rockets upon New York City, they were intending to cause destruction in other ways.

It was up to Knowles and the Secret Room to track them and predict their next move so the American task force commanders could hunt them down.

6

Helmut Froemsdorf, Phyllis Westerlund, and Kenneth Knowles never knew each other, but their roles and fates became destined to converge three years earlier, when a bold German U-boat operation triggered an American response that would change the course of the war and alter history.

Beginning in the first half of 1942—when an America still staggering from Pearl Harbor suffered the deadliest foreign attacks in her Atlantic coastal waters since the War of 1812—and continuing into the spring of 1945, a stunning series of events coalesced into a wartime epoch breathtaking in its scope and its result. In its earliest phase, this sprawling drama drew its energy and urgency from the audacious confidence of German Grand Admiral Karl Dönitz, and the fearlessness of a seasoned group of his U-boat commanders, as they attacked merchant and military shipping along America's eastern seaboard with a ferocity that produced greater death and destruction than the Japanese attack on Pearl Harbor. Later, the hallmark of the era was defined in even more profound terms, spawned by America's astonishing unity during the Second World War: a national cohesiveness borne of strength of commitment and clarity of purpose that fueled the most prodigious industrial and manufacturing effort in human history. This achievement not only broke the back of the U-boat onslaught, it accomplished much more. It forged an unbreakable bond between America's men in uniform and her civilians on the home front, enabling her to reverse her early 1942 fortunes and win her greatest collective victory.

Had Helmut Froemsdorf been born a few years earlier, he likely would have participated in one of the most successful wartime operations against the United States in her entire history, one that struck fear into the merchant mariners who sailed along her East Coast and baffled the military experts who tried desperately to defend her. Froemsdorf's predecessors feasted on Allied shipping in the first six months of 1942, their U-boats prowling American waters like invincible steel sharks, lurking offshore, then searching for and destroying defenseless prey, with virtually no resistance. "For six or seven months the U-boats ravaged American waters almost uncontrolled," British Prime Minister Winston S. Churchill would write after the war, "and in fact almost brought us to the disaster of an indefinite prolongation of the war . . . the U-boat attack was our worst evil. It would have been wise for the Germans to stake all upon it."

The U.S. Navy had insufficient long-range aircraft in early 1942, and had lost two-thirds of its warships at Pearl Harbor. Most of its remaining resources and attention were focused first on defending against a feared Japanese invasion of Hawaii or even America's West Coast, and then, through the winter and spring of 1942, on unfolding U.S. naval disasters in the Pacific. Many of the precious resources remaining in the Atlantic were deployed to provide escort groups for troopships crossing the Atlantic. Converted liners like the *Queen Mary* and *Queen Elizabeth* could easily outrace U-boats and thus did not require escorts, but most of the American troops being sent to Europe and North Africa shipped out on smaller and slower vessels. Admiral King was holding other Atlantic resources in abeyance at Norfolk, Virginia, in the event they were needed to wage battle against the German surface navy, or be deployed rapidly to the Pacific.

All of these requirements left the Navy with little to defend its coastline from Kittery to Key West against the U-boats, save for, in the words of one historian, a "ragtag force of about twenty Coast Guard cutters, outmoded patrol craft, and gunboats left over from World War I, none of which could outrun a surfaced U-boat, and 108 aircraft, most of them unfit for anti-submarine warfare and manned by untrained and inexperienced crews." This ragtag force included the *PE-56* and a handful of other Eagle-class boats, which official naval historian Samuel Eliot Morison described as "square-built, slow, weak . . . the PEs were almost completely useless." President Franklin D. Roosevelt had prodded the Navy to build small craft such as subchasers before the U.S. had entered the war, but to no avail. "The navy couldn't see any vessel under a thousand tons," the president said. In a letter to Admiral King, Vice-Admiral Adolphus E. Andrews, commander of the Eastern Sea Frontier, wrote: "Should the enemy submarines operate off this coast, this command has no force available to take action against them, either offensively or defensively."

Admiral King did order fleet minelayers to mine the approaches to New York, Boston, and Portland harbors, as well as the approaches to Chesapeake Bay. "Otherwise," noted author Homer Hickam, "Admiral Andrews was on his own."

On December 9, 1941, two days after Pearl Harbor and two days before Adolf Hitler officially declared war on the United States, the Führer released Admiral Dönitz from all prior restrictions on naval warfare against America. Until this point, Hitler had sought to avoid attacks against merchant ships from the U.S., even when they were delivering supplies, food, oil, and munitions to the beleaguered British, who had been at war with Germany for more than two years. Later in the day on December 11, Dönitz recorded Hitler's decision in his war diary with satisfaction, and predicted, "there will hardly be any question of an efficient [defensive] patrol in the American coastal area, at least of a patrol used to [dealing with] U-boats. Attempts must be made to utilize as quickly as possible these advantages, which will disappear very shortly, and to achieve a 'spectacular success' on the American coast."

Dönitz prepared to send his U-boats westward to begin their attacks against the United States in a bold mission called Operation *Paukenschlag*, meaning "drumbeat" or "drumroll"; the German Grand Admiral chose the name to emphasize that his boats would strike a blow against the United States as suddenly and jarringly as a beat on a kettledrum. He believed that one hundred boats would be the operational ideal for *Paukenschlag*, according to author and historian Nathan Miller, but taking a realistic view, he asked the German Naval High Command for twelve of the long-range Type IX boats and a number of shorter-range Type VIIC to operate off Newfoundland. Much to Dönitz's chagrin, the High Command agreed to only six Type IXs—Germany would hold onto the others to both protect the coast of occupied Norway and remain at battle stations in the Mediterranean. One of the boats did not make the transatlantic voyage due to mechanical difficulties, meaning that Drumbeat would begin with just five U-boats. Disappointed but undeterred, Dönitz indicated his high hopes for *Paukenschlag* in his war diary: "The entrance of America into the war has provided the commanders with areas which are not hemmed in by defenses and which offer much better chances for success." Dozens of additional U-boats would follow the Drumbeat boats to America throughout the winter, spring, and summer of 1942, but any initial German success in U.S. and Canadian waters would depend on the skills of a handful of U-boat commanders.

The fifty-year-old German grand admiral had staked much of his prestige on this operation. A former World War I submarine commander, he believed, more than any other member of the *Kriegsmarine* command, in the destructive power of a coordinated U-boat offensive. He was a disciplined workaholic, a detailed planner, and a perfectionist who pushed himself and his subordinates to their limits and beyond. A strict disciplinarian, Dönitz, like all good leaders, also knew when to let up on his men. He considered his U-boatmen the elite of the German Navy, encouraged them to believe the same, and treated them as such. Dönitz met every boat that returned from a mission, attended the graduation parade for every training course, and set up rest camps at holiday resorts for U-boatmen who were on leave or not on patrol, and made sure the camps were stocked with fine food and wine. Historians Samuel W. Mitcham Jr. and Gene Mueller note that Dönitz "did everything he could to relieve the enormous stress involved in underwater combat service—and submariners loved him for it. Behind his back, they called him '*Vater* Karl,' '*Onkel* Karl,' or '*Der Loewe*' (the lion). Undoubtedly he had the respect and admiration of his branch . . ."

Hitler respected Dönitz, too, for his boldness and loyalty, but the Führer did not place as much faith in the effectiveness of the U-boats, or the potential success of *Paukenschlag*. For the sake of his reputation and his future, Dönitz knew the U-boat operation against America—a gamble, to be sure—had to work.

His plan had two major goals: to cripple England, and to force the Americans out of the war against Germany before they could even begin to fight. To accomplish this, Dönitz needed his U-boat commanders to sink merchant ships and oil tankers that delivered fuel, food, and supplies from South America, the islands, the U.S. Gulf Coast, and other places to America's eastern seaboard cities and to England; and to destroy as many American warships as possible to further decimate the

U.S. Navy. The physical and psychological effect on Germany's enemies would be incalculable.

Without sufficient food and supplies, the British would be brought to their knees. England's population was already suffering through the rationing of meat and cheese. Butter and sugar were scarce, eggs and fresh fruit only a memory for the British people, and fuel was reserved nearly exclusively for the war effort. Merchant ships from the Western Hemisphere supplied England with oil, gas, iron, tin, rubber, lumber, cotton, sugar, coffee, and Florida citrus, the latter of which historian Michael Gannon claims supplied British children with "practically their entire daily allowance of vitamin C." As for America, without heating oil from tankers that sailed along the East Coast, her population in the Northeast would freeze. For Americans, attacks so close to their home shores would also produce fear and confusion, and weaken their will to wage a European war.

Dönitz also knew this as 1941 drew to a close: The only way for Germany to lose the war would be America's ability to move millions of men and tens of millions of tons of weapons and supplies safely across the Atlantic so that they could be concentrated, when the time came, in the only place from which an assault on Europe could be mounted. That springboard was Britain. "To keep her [England] fit and fighting required a steady stream of supplies, of raw materials, of weapons, of oil, of food—not just in the future, but now as well," noted author Peter Kemp. "Britain had been, and still was being, attacked massively from the air, her cities shattered, and her factories put out of action, and she no longer had the industrial capacity, especially in shipbuilding and repair, to supply all her needs from her own resources. The Atlantic was every bit as important for her survival as it was to the outcome of the war as a whole. Without ships to bring in supplies needed to keep her in the battle, she would go down, and if that happened the map of Europe might as well be rolled up for the next century."

For Dönitz, Operation Drumbeat would be a matter of tonnage: He estimated that if his U-boats could sink 700,000 gross tons of Allied shipping per month, they would destroy vessels faster than Allied shipyards could replace them. Britain could not survive under such circumstances, and the United States could be forced to abandon the war effort.

On December 23, 1941, two days before Christmas and sixteen days after Pearl Harbor, the first of the *Paukenschlag* U-boats departed Germany's base in Lorient, France, bound for America's East Coast.

Dönitz instructed his captains to take up positions between Halifax and Cape Hatteras, where about 8.5 million tons of shipping were concentrated, and to remain unobserved until the prearranged launch date for the attack: January 13, 1942. Tankers would have the highest priority. With the ability of the *Paukenschlag* U-boats to travel virtually unimpeded on the surface in early 1942, they would reach America in plenty of time.

Dönitz wanted to take full advantage of the shock value of the unexpected appearance of U-boats in U.S. waters. A coordinated attack would give the Americans the mistaken impression that a vast number of U-boats had arrived to terrorize their coastline.

At the outset, Dönitz's operation succeeded brilliantly. The Drumbeat U-boat commanders, and those that followed in the succeeding months, gorged themselves on shipping targets along the East Coast of the United States and found America's coastal waters an undefended and fertile killing ground. The Germans mounted 184 war patrols to American waters from December of 1941 through August of 1942; these boats sank more than 600 ships for more than three million gross tons (including ships en route to and from the Americas). "[This] campaign was the single most important of the war in terms of sinkings achieved in a relatively brief time period for the effort expended—the high-water mark of the U-boat war," pointed out author and U-boat expert Clay Blair. "Only about six of the 184 patrols to American waters in this period resulted in no sinkings or damage to Allied shipping." In January alone during this "Second Happy Time" for the Germans, U-boats sank 71 ships for more than 400,000 tons. Dönitz's U-boats usually—though not always—lay submerged during the day, and surfaced at dusk to fire their deadly torpedoes at will at hapless and unprotected tankers and merchant ships; U-boat commanders referred to this period as the "Great American Turkey Shoot." By midyear 1942, more tonnage had been sunk by U-boats along the Atlantic coast than had been destroyed in the Pacific by the entire Japanese Navy from Pearl Harbor to Midway. "The Pacific Pearl Harbor lasted two hours and ten minutes on a Sunday morning. The Atlantic Pearl Harbor lasted six months," wrote author Michael Gannon. ". . . Overall, the numbers [of ships sunk in U.S. Navy–protected waters] represent one of the greatest maritime disasters in history and the American nation's worst-ever defeat at sea." Naval historian Samuel Eliot Morison pointed out: "The massacre enjoyed by U-boats along our Atlantic

Coast in 1942 was as much a national disaster as if saboteurs had destroyed half a dozen of our biggest war plants . . ."

From the beginning, when *Kapitänleutnant* Reinhard Hardegen of *U-123* jumped the gun on *Paukenschlag* by sinking the 9,000-ton *Cyclops* off Nova Scotia the day before the official start of the operation, the U-boat commanders boldly and successfully attacked. The next day, the *U-130* sank two freighters off Halifax, and on January 14, 1942, Hardegen sank a large Panamanian tanker, the *Norness*, within sight of the Nantucket lightship, which marked the dangerous shoals south and east of the island.

The U-boat war against America had begun with a vengeance.

Hardegen's experience epitomized the brazenness of the U-boats. After he sank the *Norness*, he moved down the coast searching for targets, and approached the outer reaches of New York Harbor in very shallow waters. He could see the lights atop the Ferris wheel at Coney Island, and was "close enough to see the glow of lights in lower Manhattan," according to Clay Blair. "Somewhat awestruck by this sight—and the realization that the men of the *U-123* were the first German warriors to see it—Hardegen invited others to the bridge . . ." Hardegen later wrote in his log: "We could make out many lights . . . probably a suburb of New York . . . distance to downtown about thirty miles. Depth approximately 33 feet. Cannot get any shallower or the topside bridge will not be submerged when diving." Later, near Long Island, *U-123* torpedoed the 6,800-ton British tanker *Coimbra*, bound for Halifax, which exploded in a giant fireball, killing thirty-six crewmen. "The effect was amazing," Hardegen wrote, "strong detonation, fire column reaching 200 meters and the whole sky was illuminated. . . . Quite a bonfire we leave behind for the Yankees as navigational help." On the south shore of Long Island, many residents saw the funeral pyre from their homes and alerted local authorities, with little response. As author Homer Hickam pointed out: "There were no other ships or airplanes visible, and the shore lights continued burning placidly as if nothing unusual were happening. Hardegen found himself no longer being very cautious. He stayed on the surface and kept moving south."

Hardegen captained the *U-123* down the East Coast, amazed to find that other coastal cities were also ablaze with lights, along with auto headlights, lighthouses, and lighted buoys. "It's unbelievable . . . I have a feeling the Americans are going to be very surprised," Hardegen wrote. It would be four months before a blackout would be imposed along the East Coast; officials from Atlantic City to Miami resisted, asserting that it would be bad for the tourist season. Morison called the delay in dimming the waterfront lights "one of the most reprehensible failures on our part . . ." U-boat captains noted that the brightness from the coastal cities illuminated the silhouettes of the slow-moving tankers and merchant ships, most of which traveled along their familiar routes with their own lights still shining. When he reached Cape Hatteras, Hardegen reported: "Our operation has been most successful: eight ships, including three tankers totaling 53,860 tons within twelve hours. It is a pity that there were not a couple of large mine-laying submarines with me the other night off New York, or ten or twelve here last night instead of one. I am sure all would have found ample targets. Altogether I saw about twenty steamships, some un-darkened; also a few small tramp-steamers, all hugging the coast. Buoys and beacons in the area had dimmed lights, which, however, were visible up to two or three miles."

The choked sea lanes off Hatteras proved especially fruitful for the U-boats; more than sixty ships were sunk off the North Carolina coast in the first few months of 1942. The U-boats' task was abetted by "clumsy handling of ships and unpracticed sea and air patrols," according to Dönitz. One commander, Jochen Mohr of the *U-124*, reported his success to Dönitz in a rhyme mocking the Americans:

> *The new moon—night is as black as ink,*
> *Off Hatteras the tankers sink,*
> *While sadly Roosevelt counts the score.*
> *Some fifty thousand tons.*
> —by Mohr

Panic raced up and down the Atlantic seaboard, as coastal residents witnessed explosions and daily watched in horror as debris, oil, and bodies washed up on their beaches. Wartime censorship prevented any widespread nationwide coverage of the astonishing attacks, but there were occasional newspaper stories, and news spread by word of mouth along the East Coast and trickled to other parts of the country, especially after servicemen began traveling the nation's rails and contacting home. Exact facts were elusive, but many people knew the German U-boats had arrived.

In late February, the *U-578* torpedoed the oil tanker *R. P. Resor* off the New Jersey Coast, her burning hulk clearly visible to crowds on shore (just two days later, the *U-578* would sink the USS *Jacob Jones II*, whose twelve survivors were rescued by the *Eagle 56*).

After Dönitz radioed to his U-boats that they could enjoy "unrestricted hunting from Hatteras to Key West," Hardegen guided the *U-123* down to Florida's St. Augustine Beach in April, where his crew members could see bathers on shore. There, he surfaced and torpedoed the SS *Gulfamerica*, an 8,000-gross-ton tanker steaming toward New York on her maiden voyage from Port Arthur, with ninety thousand barrels of fuel oil on board. Not satisfied that the tanker would sink, Hardegen ordered the deck-guns manned and prepared to shell her with artillery. Concerned that shells fired from the seaward side would overshoot and hurt innocent people or their beach homes, Hardegen maneuvered the *U-123* to the *Gulfamerica*'s shoreward—or port—side, where errant shells would pass harmlessly out to sea. "On shore, frivolity quickly turned to horror," author Michael Gannon reported, "as the shocked revelers beheld the funeral pyre at sea and the U-boat itself bombing the corpse. Their faces red from the glare, the witnesses stood in stupefaction, endeavoring to comprehend how a war they considered so officially remote from their daily lives could suddenly appear in front of them. By telephone they spread word of the experience to family and friends in nearby communities, including Jacksonville, Florida's most populous city at the time; soon the highways to the beach were clogged with the automobiles of the curious." For his part, Hardegen wrote: "All the vacationers had seen an impressive special performance at Roosevelt's expense. A burning tanker, artillery fire, the silhouette of a U-boat—how often had all of that been seen in America?"

And in June, thousands of horrified vacationers at Virginia Beach watched as a U-boat torpedoed two American freighters before their eyes. Later in the summer, Dönitz referred to this kind of event when he wrote: "Our submarines are operating close inshore along the coast of the United States of America, so that bathers and sometimes entire coastal cities are witnesses to that drama of war, whose visual climaxes are constituted by the red glorioles of blazing tankers."

Americans feared saboteurs, too, and it turns out, justifiably so. A March intelligence report from the U.S. embassy in Switzerland to President Roosevelt warned that German submarines were transporting groups of "two or three agents at a time" to the coast of northern and central America. The report proved prophetic, when, in June, one U-boat surfaced near Amagansett, Long Island, and another near Jacksonville, Florida, and each put ashore a party of saboteurs. The two four-man squads were equipped with explosives, detonators, maps of industrial sites, and thousands of dollars in cash.

Author Michael Dobbs points out that the saboteurs from the New York U-boat shopped at Macy's on the very day of a giant military parade through the streets of Manhattan. Mayor LaGuardia urged New York residents and office workers to display the Stars and Stripes as a symbol of the city's "grim determination to do the utmost in helping to defeat Hitler." More than two and a half million people—one third of the city's population—lined the streets to view what LaGuardia called "the greatest parade in New York's history." The parade included a contingent of 150 merchant mariners who had survived U-boat attacks in the Atlantic; one much-applauded banner read THE AXIS SUBS DON'T SCARE US—WE DELIVER THE GOODS. New Yorkers who cheered wildly as soldiers and sailors marched by had no notion that German saboteurs—who had arrived by U-boat the night before—walked in their midst. "While the saboteurs were shopping at Macy's, American bombers and fighter planes were roaring over Manhattan," Dobbs reported. Eventually, the FBI, with assistance from the Coast Guard, captured the two squads of Germans before they carried out any attacks; all eight were tried before a military tribunal and sentenced to death (two saboteurs testified against their comrades in exchange for lesser sentences).

There were less serious incidents, too, though most simply reinforced how close the U-boats were to the American shoreline. One day a school principal in Outer Banks, North Carolina, noticed that many of the boys who usually came to school barefooted were wearing new Florsheim shoes. He discovered that the shoes had washed up on shore—cargo from a merchant ship that had been sunk by a U-boat. The fishermen fathers of the boys had "quickly commandeered these shoes and the children wore them proudly," noted author J. David Brown.

Still, virtually every aspect of the U-boat attacks had sown shock and fear along the East Coast. "Burning hulks lit American beaches from Cape Cod to Hampton Roads, from the Outer Banks to the Florida Keys," historian David Kennedy wrote. "In New York harbor, merchant crews mutinied against sailing into the teeth of such danger. Coastal shipping slowed nearly to a standstill . . ."

Dönitz crowed about his U-boats' successes in his war diary: "Before the U-boat attack on America was begun, it was suspected that American anti-submarine activity would be weak and inexperienced; this conjecture has been fully confirmed . . . The crews [on anti-submarine vessels] are careless, inexperienced, and little persevering in a hunt. In several cases, escort vessels—coast guard ships and destroyers—having established the presence of a U-boat, made off instead of attacking her . . . On the whole . . . the boats' successes are so great, that their operation near the coast is further justified and will continue."

Meanwhile, under mounting criticism from President Roosevelt and the British, Admiral Ernest King had the task of developing the plan that would slow the U-boat juggernaut until the United States could gear up her war-production machinery.

The issue was convoys. The British wondered why the Americans had not developed a convoy system to protect merchant shipping, so that individual ships could not be picked off so easily. Why not transfer some American destroyers from the Pacific to the Atlantic to escort the convoys? German naval historian Jürgen Rohwer wrote after the war that the American delay of adopting East Coast convoys was "without doubt one of the greatest mistakes in the Allied conduct of the Battle of the Atlantic."

On March 12, 1942, Winston Churchill cabled President Roosevelt's troubleshooter, Harry Hopkins, demanding "drastic action" to expand the convoy network. While Roosevelt responded that the British bore responsibility for sending more anti-submarine vessels to the American coast, he also fired a shot across Admiral King's bow for not making the construction of smaller, faster escort ships a priority when he added: "My Navy has been definitely slack in preparing for this submarine war off our coast. As I need not tell you, most Naval officers have declined in the past to think in terms of any vessel of less than two thousand tons. You learned that lesson years ago. We still have to learn it." U.S. Army Chief of Staff General George C. Marshall wrote to King in June that the "losses by submarines off our Atlantic seaboard and in the Caribbean now threaten our entire war effort . . . I am fearful that another month or two of this will so cripple our means of transport that we will be unable to bring sufficient men and planes to bear against the enemy." And then in July of 1942, Roosevelt himself wired King about the delay in establishing convoys along the coast: "I think it has taken an unconscionable time to get things going . . . We must speed things up and we must use the available tools even though they are not just what we would like to have."

In some ways, FDR's and Marshall's criticisms were gratuitous swipes at King, who clearly recognized the U-boat threat and was equally frustrated at the Navy's inability to protect ships along the Eastern seaboard. Yet, King's abrasive personality and his fondness for alcohol and women made him a convenient, though hardly submissive, scapegoat. Tough, gruff, brilliant, stubborn, and a taskmaster with a temper, King did not suffer laziness or shoddy performance gladly. FDR, who admired toughness in his commanders, said of King: "He shaves with a blowtorch." One of King's daughters said her father was "the most even-tempered man in the Navy—he is always in a rage." King's weaknesses, wrote Professor William Love of the U.S. Naval Academy, "were other men's wives, alcohol, and intolerance." King made no secret of this; he once told an officer never to trust a man who didn't drink and enjoy the company of women.

King also detested the British, distrusting their motives and believing them to be arrogant. These feelings were mutual. A member of Churchill's staff would later say that King was "blunt and standoffish, almost to the point of rudeness . . . he was intolerant and suspicious of all things British, especially the Royal Navy." Even General Dwight D. Eisenhower would say of his fellow officer: "He is an arbitrary stubborn type, with not too much brains and a tendency toward bullying his juniors. One thing that might help win this war is to shoot King."

Ike's comments notwithstanding, King was recognized as a brilliant naval commander. He had been valedictorian of his high school class and stood fourth in his class at the U.S. Naval Academy. His breadth of naval experience—as a submariner, staff officer, aviator, aircraft carrier commander, fleet leader—and his encyclopedic knowledge of tactics, strategy, history, technology, and geopolitical realities made him one of FDR's strongest minds. His ability to handle unpopular, difficult, or dirty tasks made him an invaluable asset. King was rumored to have once said, "When they get in trouble they send for the sonsabitches." King acknowledged that he had never said it, but would have if he had thought of it. Historian Eric Larrabee described King as "a hard man in a hard time, well suited to lead a fighting fleet, but he was also a thoughtful man of breadth and decisiveness . . . if you measured up to his standards, he was loyal, considerate, generous, and he looked after his own people." Naval historian Morison called King a "sailor's sailor who neither had nor wanted any life outside the Navy. He believed that what was good for the Navy was good for the United States, the Americas, and indeed, the world." In addition to his knowledge and capacity for hard work, Morison describes King as a man of "complete integrity."

It was this complex man who was responsible for America's coastal defenses during the U-boat onslaught in the first half of 1942, and at the outset, he could do little. In Roosevelt's words, there was simply a "lack of naval butter to cover the bread." The U.S. Atlantic fleet was already hard-pressed to shoulder the modest share of the burden of escorting convoys across the North Atlantic, and, as historian David Kennedy asserts, "the sudden flaring of the Pacific war vacuumed up virtually all new naval construction." So anemic was the Navy's coastal defense, Kennedy points out, that the puny number of anti-submarine vessels at King's disposal was even supplemented for a time by the Coastal Picket Patrol, or "Hooligan's Navy," a motley armada organized by private yachtsmen, which included a "pistol- and grenade-toting Ernest Hemingway at the helm of his sport-fishing boat *Pilar*." Furthermore, the Germans were building U-boats at a much faster rate, and the British Ultra code breakers were blinded from deciphering encrypted messages to and from the U-boats after the Germans added a fourth wheel to their Enigma machines.

Facing the reality of the situation in the Atlantic—a woeful number of escort ships and a marauding U-boat force—King bluntly articulated his simple philosophy about convoys. He opposed weakly defended convoys, declaring that "inadequately escorted convoys were worse than none." Poorly defended convoys would, in King's view, merely provide a congregated mass of unprotected merchant targets for U-boats. King would order the occasional convoys when possible, but he also believed that a policy of "dispersal"—solitary merchant ships traveling at night— was preferable to an ill-defended convoy flotilla that would attract U-boats like hungry sharks to chum. King insisted that it made better sense to build escorts that could sink U-boats rather than to build merchant ships that U-boats could sink. "Escort is not just one way of handling the submarine menace; it is the only way that gives any promise of success." For the lack of escorts in early 1942, President Roosevelt blamed the Navy; King blamed the president. "Roosevelt said the Navy thought too big, King that the president thought too small," historian Larrabee asserts. "It was a debate over the size of escort ships in which the essential point, the compelling need for *any* warships appropriate to the task, did not find first place." Morison concluded that had Roosevelt's specific wishes and recommendations been followed earlier, "the Navy would have been better prepared to meet the U-boats."

Nonetheless, it was another Roosevelt declaration, one that produced little debate, which ultimately changed the tide of the Battle of the Atlantic and the war. It was a call to action to the American people, one the president first made in early 1942—a challenge and an exhortation that would ring across the country for the entire war.

From factories in the Northeast to farms on the Great Plains and in the South, from production plants in the Midwest to shipyards and aircraft plants on the West Coast, America mobilized in response to Roosevelt's call; the response from her people was enthusiastic, purposeful, and unprecedented.

It was a response that changed the nation and changed the world.

When President Franklin Roosevelt delivered his first Fireside Chat since Pearl Harbor to the American people at 10:00 P.M. on February 23, 1942, more than sixty million adults—80 percent of the total possible adult audience—were glued to their radios, many with world maps spread before them. Roosevelt had asked the American people to study a map as they listened to his remarks. "I'm going to speak about strange places that many of them never heard of—places that are now the battleground for civilization . . . I want to explain to the people something about geography—what our problem is and what the overall strategy of the war has to be . . . If they understand the problem and what we are driving at, I am sure that they can take any kind of bad news right on the chin." Responding enthusiastically to the president's request, American citizens by the thousands raced to their local stores to purchase maps. "The map business is booming," *The New York Times* reported.

Because George Washington's birthday (February 22) fell on a Sunday in 1942, it was celebrated on the Monday, which is the day FDR chose for his address. That allowed him to open his remarks with an analogy between Washington's bleak prospects throughout much of the Revolutionary War and America's current situation. "Selfish men, jealous men, fearful men proclaimed the situation hopeless," FDR said of Washington's predicament. But Washington "held to his course" and a new country was born. America was facing similar difficulties, suffering some early defeats—"from Hitler's U-boats in the Atlantic as well as from the Japanese in the Pacific . . . and we shall suffer more of them before the turn of the tide." The stakes were even larger today than in Washington's time. "This is a new kind of war," he told the radio audience. "It is different from all other wars of the past . . . It is warfare in terms of every continent, every island, every sea, every air-lane in the world." To win it, to carry the fight to the enemy in distant lands, "requires tremendous daring, tremendous resourcefulness, and above all, tremendous production of planes and tanks and guns and also of the ships to carry them," Roosevelt said. "And I speak again for the American people when I say that we can and will do that job."

FDR pointed out that the Axis powers were close to their maximum output of planes, guns, ships, and tanks. The United States was far from it, and with "uninterrupted production," the American people could create "not merely a slight superiority, but an overwhelming superiority." To accomplish this would mean the full conversion of every aspect of society and the economy to war needs. There could be no stoppage of work for a single day, and many conveniences and normal routines would have to be abandoned. "We can lose this war only if we slow up our effort or if we waste our ammunition sniping at each other," Roosevelt told his audience.

And the president asked for more from Americans. Not just for their labor and energy, but for their personal sacrifice, to put aside their own needs to foster a unified patriotic spirit for a cause greater than themselves. "This generation of Americans has come to realize, with a present and personal realization, that there is something larger and more important than the life of any individual or any individual group— something for which a man will sacrifice, and gladly sacrifice, not only his pleasures, not only his goods, not only his association with those he loves, but his life itself. In time of crisis when the future is in the balance, we come to understand, with full recognition and devotion, what this nation is, and what we owe to it."

The speech was a great success, "one of the greatest of Roosevelt's career," shouted *The New York Times*. For FDR, the proof would be in the response of Americans. He believed it was his job to unify the nation. "No one understood better than he the inner dynamics of American strength," wrote historian Eric Larrabee, "how to mobilize it, how to draw on it, how to gauge its limits. Once mobilized, it did not need to be driven; it needed only to be steered."

The February Fireside Chat was FDR's second important speech of 1942 on the need for America to quickly complete the gargantuan task of converting to a full wartime economy. The previous month he had warned Congress: "It will not be sufficient for us and the other United Nations to produce a slightly superior supply of munitions to that of Germany, Japan, Italy. The superiority of the United Nations in munitions and ships must be overwhelming . . . a crushing superiority of equipment in any theater of the world war." The president warned that civilian consumption had to yield for military production. "I was a bit appalled," he told reporters in January 1942, to learn "that so much of our production was still going into civilian use."

Historian David M. Kennedy described FDR's "breathtakingly ambitious" production goals: 60,000 aircraft in 1942 and 125,000 more in 1943; 120,000 tanks in the same period; 55,000 anti-aircraft guns; 16 million deadweight tons of merchant shipping. "The figures reached such astronomical proportions that human minds could not reach around them," the *U.S. News* reported. "Only by symbols could they be understood; a plane every four minutes in 1943; a tank every seven minutes; two seagoing ships a day." Donald Nelson, head of one of the principal mobilization agencies, was one of many people who were "startled and alarmed" when he heard Roosevelt's numbers. "He staggered us," Nelson recalled. "None of our production people thought that this volume was possible . . . We thought that the goals set by the president were out of the question."

But the American people did not. Driven by Roosevelt's repeated declarations in the rightness of their cause and his faith in their ability, they would *exceed* FDR's quotas over the next two years, in the greatest wartime production effort in history. Between 1942 and 1944, the American people would manufacture and deliver more ships, tanks, planes, jeeps, rifles, ammunition, artillery pieces, clothing, blankets, helmets, boots, and other materiel than any nation ever had. With astonishing efficiency, the nation would deploy food, medicine, weapons, clothing, and machines to millions of men in two separate theaters of combat along ocean- and land-supply lines that stretched thousands of miles—a feat no nation had ever accomplished.

It was this achievement that ultimately defeated the U-boats, broke the spirit of the Germans, and in the Pacific, caused the Japanese to fight with even greater desperation as the war continued and the Allies threatened their homeland.

America's conversion to a war economy had begun in 1941 but took on a new urgency in 1942. New plants were being built, and manufacturing facilities everywhere were retooling their operations to begin the production of weapons. Historian Doris Kearns Goodwin noted: "A merry-go-round factory was using its plant to fashion gun mounts. A corset factory was making grenade belts. A manufacturer of stoves was producing lifeboats. A famous New York toy concern was making compasses. A pinball-machine maker was turning out armor-piercing shells. Despite continuing shortages of raw materials, 1942 would witness the greatest expansion of production in the nation's history." The balance between the United States and her enemies changed almost overnight, historian Richard Overy pointed out. While every other major state took four or five years to develop a sizeable military economy, it took America a year. "In 1942, long before her enemies had believed it possible, America already outproduced the Axis states together," Overy said. And it was in the naval war that the difference was most notable—"for every one major vessel constructed in Japanese shipyards, America produced sixteen." By September of 1942, Goodwin observes, a "phenomenal" 4,000 tanks each month were rolling off America's assembly lines; Germany had been the previous leader in the production of tanks with 4,000 per *year*. In the summer of 1942, American weapons output surged past that of Britain; by 1944, it was six times greater.

America's economic conversion was perhaps most noticeable in the auto industry. In 1941, the industry produced 3.5 million cars; that figure dropped to an extraordinary *139* cars before the last day of civilian output on February 10, 1942. Small ceremonies were held in auto plants as the last chassis came down the line; machinery was ripped out and new tools installed to mass-produce war materiel and weapons. By 1945, the auto industry assembly lines supplied about 40 percent of the country's military equipment, according to Overy: almost all the vehicles and tanks, one-third of the machine guns, and 40 percent of the aviation supplies. The Ford Motor Company alone produced more army equipment during the war than Italy. The numbers were staggering: Ford produced 278,000 jeeps, 93,000 trucks, 8,665 bombers, 12,500 armored cars, 57,800 aero engines.

Overy points out that the numbers become even more remarkable when another major factor is considered: The production of weapons required a greater degree of precision and complexity than the production of autos. This meant that the production line required periodic updating and improvements, making long production cycles harder to sustain. "That the motor industry did adapt so successfully owed a good deal to

the character of the industry," he explained. "Annual model changes ac-
customed managers and workers to regular large-scale adjustments on
the factory floor; the large companies were used to a wide product range;
the workforce was compelled by the nature of the manufacturing process
to be flexible and adaptive . . . once the conversion was completed, the
industry began to overfill its [military equipment] orders."

And as the face of America's factories changed dramatically, so too
did the face of her workforce.

Soaring production needs and a shortage of men—sixteen million of
whom would eventually serve in the U.S. Armed Forces during World War
II—produced new opportunities for women. Phyllis Westerlund's work in
a Brockton detonator factory was representative of the contributions of
women across America. (Hundreds of women worked in Brockton's shoe
industry, which was consistently a national leader in the production of
boots and shoes for American GIs.) "Rosie the Riveter" became crucial to
America's war production machine; single women first, but later in the
war, married women with children—like Phyllis—constituted nearly half
of the female working population. At the peak of wartime employment,
historian Doris Kearns Goodwin reports that more than nineteen million
women were employed, totaling one-third of the civilian labor force.

Work shortages and production quotas also helped the plight of
blacks, many of whom migrated to northern factories from the south.
By 1942, more than half the defense employers had removed barriers
against black labor in war industries; Goodwin reports that in "hundreds
of cases, Negroes were working in firms which had formerly banned
them." In shipyards, black employment had risen from 6,000 to 14,000
in twelve months; in the aircraft industry, which had employed no black
workers in 1940, 5,000 blacks were employed by 1942. "The gains
were small but significant," Goodwin asserted. FDR said: "I look for an
acceleration of this improvement as the demand for labor in our war industries increases."

As they produced more, Americans also sacrificed more, heeding
FDR's clarion call for a unified war effort. In mid-1942, gas rationing
was added to the rationing of meat, butter, sugar, rubber, and other
products considered critical to the war effort. In large cities and small
towns across the country, Americans contributed to the country's need
for raw materials, money, and medical supplies by participating enthusiastically in paper drives, tin drives, bond drives, blood drives, clothing
drives, and scrap-metal drives.

American cohesiveness on Main Street and in its factories, shipyards, and aircraft production hangars resulted in a military economy that had pounded out "a fantastic statistical litany" by war's end, according to David Kennedy: 5,777 merchant ships, 1,556 naval vessels, 299,293 aircraft, 634,569 jeeps, 88,410 tanks, 11,000 chain saws, 2,383,311 trucks, 6.5 million rifles, 40 billion bullets—a "stupendous Niagara of numbers . . ."

Indeed, three weeks after D-Day in 1944, one million men had been put ashore in France, along with an overwhelming 171,532 vehicles and 566,000 tons of supplies. "As far as you could see in every direction the ocean was infested with ships," wrote war correspondent Ernie Pyle. Pointing out that American bodies and wrecked equipment were still strewn on the beaches, Pyle took consolation: "We had our toehold, and behind us there were such enormous replacements for this wreckage on the beach that you could hardly conceive of the sum total. Men and equipment were flowing from England in such a gigantic stream that it made the waste on the beachhead seem like nothing at all, really nothing at all." Looking out to sea at the immense armada of ships still waiting to unload, Pyle noticed a group of German prisoners: "They stood staring as if in a trance. They didn't say a word to each other. They didn't need to. The expression on their faces was something forever unforgettable. In it was the final, horrified acceptance of their doom."

Echoing Pyle, one German division commander at Normandy reported back on the visible effects of the American supply system: "I cannot understand these Americans. Each night we know that we have cut them to pieces, inflicted heavy casualties, mowed down their transport. But—in the morning, we are suddenly faced with fresh battalions, with complete replacements of men, machines, food, tools, and weapons. This happens day after day . . ."

Historian Bruce Catton, who said "the [production] figures are all so astronomical that they cease to mean very much," described America's output with a startling analogy: "Say that we performed the equivalent of building two Panama Canals every month with a fat surplus to boot; that's an understatement, it still doesn't begin to express it all, the total is simply beyond the compass of one's understanding. Here was displayed a strength greater even than cocky Americans, in the old days of unlimited self-confidence had supposed; strength to which nothing—literally nothing, in the physical sense—was any longer impossible."

○ ✿ ○

America's wartime production numbers sounded the death knell for Dönitz and the U-boats and proved the saving grace for King and the U.S. Navy. The huge increase in shipbuilding produced more than enough anti-submarine escorts to enable King to implement interlocking convoys up and down the East Coast later in 1942, making it maddeningly difficult for the U-boats to find unprotected targets. By 1943, the vast number of American ships and long-range aircraft—especially the B-24 "Liberators"—went on a deadly offensive against the U-boats.

In addition to American air and sea power, she had made enormous technological and intelligence advances that proved lethal to the U-boats: in radar, Huff-Duff directional equipment, weaponry, and of course, once the latest German Enigma codes were broken again in December of 1942, in the establishment of Kenneth Knowles's secret sub-tracking room to analyze Ultra intelligence.

During what the Germans called "Black May" of 1943, forty-one U-boats were destroyed, and the June and July kills brought the three-month totals to ninety-five. In his war diary of May 24, 1943, Dönitz—whom Hitler had promoted to commander in chief of the German Navy that January—wrote: "The U-boat losses of May 1943 have reached unbearable heights." Perhaps worse for Dönitz, his younger son, Peter, was lost in combat in May while serving as a watch officer on the *U-954*.

To regroup, Dönitz withdrew the majority of his boats from the North Atlantic. Germany would build more boats, including the snorkel type that would allow submersion for lengthy periods, but U-boats would never have the same impact on Allied shipping as they did in early 1942. In September of 1943, Winston Churchill announced to the House of Commons that in the previous four months, not a single merchant ship had been lost to the enemy in the North Atlantic, and that during the past fortnight not a single Allied ship had been sunk by a U-boat *anywhere in the world*. His remarks were greeted with loud and prolonged cheers.

Dönitz continued to send U-boats on missions, but fewer and fewer boats returned as they were hunted and destroyed by Allied ships and planes. Dönitz was personally shattered again when, on May 13, 1944, his elder son, Klaus, was killed on the eve of his twenty-fourth birthday when his torpedo boat was intercepted and destroyed by Allied warships off the English coast. After the D-Day invasion, U-boat operations moved from France to Norway, and Dönitz continued to feed his U-boat forces into battle "in a desperate and fanatical attempt to influence the course of events no matter what his casualties were," according to historians Samuel W. Mitcham Jr. and Gene Mueller. "His stubborn and unreasonable efforts were futile and were responsible for the needless deaths of hundreds of German sailors. Between June 6 and August 31 [1944] . . . 82 U-boats were lost."

The U-boat force would stay at sea, but it never again would be the scourge of the ocean.

By the end of the war, the U-boat losses were nearly incomprehensible. Of the 820 U-boats the German submarine branch committed to the Battle of the Atlantic from 1939 through 1945, 781—*95 percent*—were destroyed in action. Of the 39,000 U-boatmen who fought in this battle, 32,000 of them lost their lives, an 80 percent casualty rate, most in the last two years of the war.

By the time Dönitz dispatched his last group of U-boats in 1945, including Helmut Froemsdorf's *U-853*, he knew the Battle of the Atlantic and the war were long lost. The Atlantic had become a perilous place for U-boats; surfacing at all amid the relentless Allied air and sea patrols was virtually tantamount to self-destruction. Dönitz still inspired devotion, especially in the younger commanders like Froemsdorf, and in many ways, Dönitz likely viewed himself as more of a father figure to his crews after the death of his two sons; yet his decision to continue dispatching U-boats in 1945 was akin to a death sentence to his beloved U-boatmen.

His last desperate hope was that the boats could do enough damage to force Roosevelt and Eisenhower to negotiate some sort of favorable terms to end the war, rather than their insistence on Germany's unconditional surrender. But, even Dönitz must have realized that his hope was more like a prayer that would go unanswered.

7

The second long dispatch *Grossadmiral* Dönitz sent to the U-boat commanders who had departed from Norway appealed to their pride in Germany and the Führer:

"Above all, our honor demands that we fight to the end," Dönitz exhorted early in his message. "The same is required by our pride, which rebels against humbling ourselves before a people like the Russians, before Anglo-Saxon sanctimony, arrogance, and lack of culture . . . Thus, stern necessity, duty, honor, and pride bid us fight to the last if need be . . . Let us strengthen the determination of our soldiers to resist to the very last. Let us make our troops fanatical. Let us sow hatred for our enemies. Let us fill our soldiers with passion. Let us trust the leadership of Adolf Hitler without reservation."

For Kenneth Knowles and the Secret Room intelligence officers who read the intercepted message, it was another strongly worded passage that confirmed for them Dönitz's intention to launch a desperate final U-boat assault in the North Atlantic near American shores: "All in all, let us be proud of the fighting spirit of our Navy. Let us watch over it as our most precious possession. In whatever way the situation may yet develop, the Navy must stand like a belligerent block that cannot be diverted from its task. It will never bow under the hostile yoke."

8

Four thousand miles east of Kenneth Knowles's Secret Room and three thousand miles east of the U.S.-bound *U-853*, nineteen-year-old parachute infantryman James Lawton lay bleeding in a pile of rubble, convinced he was about to die. He was barely conscious after a shell from a German tank exploded against the building he was about to enter, but he was aware enough to know that something terrible had happened to his leg. Through the haze of semi-consciousness, he watched while a medic worked on him feverishly, shooting him full of morphine, wrapping a tourniquet near his hip, and treating his leg wound with sulfa packs to prevent infection. He heard the chatter of heavy gunfire all around him, but he couldn't move to find cover. He could barely move his head, for that matter; all he could do was grit his teeth in response to the pain that seemed to be devouring what was left of his shredded right leg.

Lawton and his unit, the 513th Parachute Infantry Regiment of the 17th Airborne Division, had jumped behind enemy lines on the morning of March 24, 1945, in what would be the final airborne invasion of Germany and the largest of the war, part of an enormous air armada to support the U.S. 9th and British 2nd armies as they crossed the Rhine, with the goal of capturing the Ruhr region, Germany's industrial heartland.

If they were successful, the German war machine would collapse, and the Allies would have a clear shot to Berlin. The airborne invasion, code-named "Operation Varsity," consisted of a massive assemblage of nearly 4,000 airplanes and gliders—troop carriers, transport planes, and fighters—from the U.S. 17th Airborne and the 6th British Airborne divisions. The 17th Airborne's parachute infantry's assignment was to secure an area northeast of Wesel by clearing out homes and buildings from which beleaguered *Wehrmacht* (German Army) soldiers hid to snipe at advancing Allied troops, establishing roadblocks, and making contact with advancing British forces northeast of town.

The C-46 that carried Lawton and forty-seven of his comrades had rocked and shuddered through bursting anti-aircraft flak for an hour before reaching the jump site, coming in low, under five hundred feet, then disgorging the paratroopers from two doors, part of a force of thousands of American and British paratroopers falling through the sky over Germany. Lawton hit the ground with the spray of machine-gun bullets raking the landscape all around him; after he found cover, he watched as plane after plane "exploded like firecrackers, one after another," the bellies of their fuel tanks pierced by automatic gunfire. He knew there would be heavy casualties across the 17th, and it was devastating to watch. "One plane would blow up and you knew those guys were gone," he would say later. "Then another. Same thing. Those guys were gone, too. You just believed it wouldn't happen to you."

For six days, Lawton had been part of small infantry teams that went house to house, "cleaning out" the *Wehrmacht* (most of whom surrendered after a few shots were fired through open windows), and rounding up prisoners. "You couldn't turn your back on anyone," he recalled later. The German Army was in dire straits, being squeezed by British and American forces in the west, and overrun by the Russians, who were advancing relentlessly upon Berlin, from the east. The 513th was responsible for making sure that advancing British soldiers did not become the targets of German sniper attacks.

Lawton had been awestruck, even a little saddened, by the utter totality of the destruction in the German towns that his regiment passed through. Most buildings were rubble, fires burned in cellars and on street corners, and many homes had been reduced to smoldering embers by the thousands of tons of Allied bombs that had rained from above. Lawton and his buddies had even slept near the fires to keep warm as they made their way to link up with oncoming British troops.

For nearly a week, Lawton had fulfilled his mission and avoided the persistent enemy fire that came from inside bombed-out buildings and from behind rocks. Then, without warning, the German tank had rumbled around a corner, come upon a group of Americans, and blasted away. Lawton had just reached the top of the stairs and grasped the doorknob when the shell screamed into the house, nearly pulverizing the structure and Lawton's upper right leg at the same time. Now, as he lay helpless with the medic kneeling beside him, Lawton silently recited the Lord's Prayer and the Hail Mary over and over again. It was Good Friday, and he doubted he would live until Easter. He had seen the amount of blood he had lost, and he knew his chances for survival were slim.

Suddenly, another tank shell exploded and Lawton saw the medic blown backward, picked up and tossed into the rubble like he was a rag doll. Lawton was alone now, unable to move, and he felt himself drifting away. He prayed harder for survival, but he added one caveat in his plea to God: "If you *are* going to take me, please do it quickly . . ."

As James Lawton prepared to die in Germany, President Franklin Delano Roosevelt arrived in Warm Springs, Georgia, desperate for rest to regain his own failing health. A month earlier, he had returned to the White House after an exhausting trip to Yalta to discuss postwar Europe with Churchill and Stalin. Following the grueling 14,000-mile round-trip, he addressed the House and Senate while seated. For the first time, he mentioned his polio infirmity in public, according to historian Michael Beschloss, telling Congress that sitting "made it a lot easier for me" not to carry "about ten pounds of steel around on the bottom of my legs."

FDR told lawmakers that Germany must never again be allowed to wage "aggressive war." This would not harm the German people, the president said; on the contrary, it would remove "a cancer from the German body which for generations has produced only misery and pain for the entire world." Vice President Harry Truman, seated on the podium behind Roosevelt, would observe years later that "it was the most poorly delivered speech he ever made." FDR's frailty made Truman feel "more than certain that the President wouldn't last" through his term. Poet Archibald MacLeish, recently appointed assistant secretary of state, wrote that he would never forget seeing Roosevelt after Yalta, "with the cold spring light on his face and death in his eyes."

Just before he left for Warm Springs, the president told a friend that he wanted to "sleep and sleep and sleep," and the day prior to his departure, a general who met with the president said he was "so shocked watching him" that he would have had a difficult time making a "sensible reply" to FDR's questions. The general observed that he had been "talking to a dying man." When Roosevelt's train pulled into the tiny station at Warm Springs at 2:00 P.M., the station agent recalled: "The president was the worst-looking man I ever saw who was still alive." Beschloss pointed out that, while in Warm Springs, an aide wrote in his diary: "He [FDR] is losing weight. Told me he has lost 25 pounds—no strength—no appetite—tires so easily." The aide told Roosevelt's doctor: "He is slipping away from us and no earthly powers can keep him here."

While God pondered FDR's fate, He wasn't yet ready for James Lawton. The man who doubted he would see Easter Sunday or his twentieth birthday woke up in an army tent hospital in Germany, where doctors told him his injuries were serious, but not life-threatening. From there, Lawton spent time in hospitals in Germany, France, England, and finally, the United States, eighteen months in all. The tank shell had smashed his femur to bits, ripped his sciatic nerve in half, and paralyzed his right leg. Osteomyelitis, an inflammation of the bone marrow, caused further complications, and atrophy shriveled the leg further. Before his eventual discharge in November of 1946, fifteen months after World War II ended, Lawton would have dozens of surgeries and skin grafts to repair the leg, mostly to no avail. He would have nothing but kind words to say about army doctors, nurses, and his overall hospital experience—he had even met Helen Keller when she visited his hospital ward in England—but he would never have full use of his right leg again.

His injuries didn't stop him. His battlefield experience earned him a Bronze Star and a Purple Heart, and James Lawton continued his achievements in civilian life. He would begin a political career when he returned to Brockton, Massachusetts, winning a seat on the City Council, and later, in the Massachusetts House of Representatives. He would earn his law degree, pass the bar, and work as a trial lawyer. Later he would become one of the youngest appointed probate judges in Massachusetts and enjoy a prestigious career on the bench for more than three decades.

His career would be important to him, but James Lawton's greatest blessing would be his family; his wife, Jeanne, and their five sons. James

Lawton was a strict disciplinarian, but he doted on his sons, teaching them how to hunt, fish, swim, play ball, work hard, and become men. Most of all, he taught them never to give up.

Imagine James Lawton's pride, then, when, more than fifty years after America's triumph in World War II, the youngest of those boys, Paul, whom James describes as a pit bull ("once he sinks his teeth into something, he doesn't let go until the matter is settled"), took on the United States Navy bureaucracy and won.

As a result, at the outset of the twenty-first century, James Lawton's son, Paul, would change history in an unprecedented way, and achieve long-overdue justice for a group of men who had been forgotten since his father's war.

9

April 13, 1945
Lieutenant (jg) John Scagnelli
Rockland, Maine

Lieutenant (jg) John Scagnelli, the *Eagle 56*'s engineering officer, tried hard to shake the unease that gripped him like a stubborn fever. It was a feeling that bordered on dread and left him wondering whether the world had spun out of control. The president was dead; what did that mean for the rest of them?

Saddened and shocked about FDR's death a day earlier from a cerebral hemorrhage, what worried Scagnelli the most was the leadership void it created. Scagnelli would celebrate his twenty-fifth birthday in a week; Roosevelt had been elected first in 1932, when Scagnelli was a twelve-year-old boy living in Manhattan's Little Italy during the Depression. Indeed, it was hard to imagine anyone else as president; like millions of other Americans, Scagnelli had simply assumed that Roosevelt would hold onto the job for as long as he wanted.

Scagnelli believed FDR had represented America's strength, and every serviceman he knew had great faith in the president's determination to lead the country to victory. Scagnelli didn't know much about Vice President Truman, and he wondered whether a relatively unknown man could command the respect of Churchill and Stalin, and strike fear into Hitler. Scagnelli thought FDR's death might convince the Germans that they could hold out a little longer. It might prolong the war and put them all in danger. Indeed, in the last couple of weeks, there had been general warnings to be on the lookout for U-boats from Halifax to Cape Hatteras. With FDR dead, would the Germans feel emboldened? Would Truman change the way we fought this war? What about U.S. Allies? Would the new president represent America's interest in postwar planning?

To do his small part to combat the geopolitical and psychological upheaval spawned by Roosevelt's death, Scagnelli would focus on those things he could control; most especially, that meant ensuring that the *Eagle 56* was shipshape from bow to stern, above- and belowdecks. As the vessel's engineering officer, Scagnelli was responsible for overseeing the operation of the engine- and boiler rooms, as well as the general functions of the ship. The members of the "Black Gang," the sailors who worked belowdecks, were under his command. It was a talented bunch who manned and maintained the *Eagle 56*, a group of men in whom he had great pride, some of the Navy's most meticulous and talented machinists; men like Harold Petersen, Johnny Breeze, Harold Glenn, and Fredrick "Mike" Michelsen, who used their heads and their hands to keep the *Eagle 56* running smoothly.

This was no small feat. Approximately 200 feet long, with a 33-foot beam, the *Eagle 56* was older than Scagnelli and hardly a state-of-the-art ship. In fact, she was a vestige of the last World War, when, in June of 1917, President Woodrow Wilson summoned Henry Ford to Washington and asked the mass production expert whether he could convert his auto production lines to shipbuilding. Wilson urged Ford to build anti-submarine vessels to combat the German U-boat menace in World War I. "What we want is one type of ship in large numbers," Wilson had said. No facilities were available at the Navy Yard to build the new craft, according to writer Frank Cianflone; thus, Wilson and then Secretary of the Navy Josephus Daniels asked Ford if he would undertake the task in his Detroit factories.

Ford agreed, and in January of 1918, the United States government issued a contract for Ford Motor Company to build one hundred PE (Patrol Escort) class boats by December 1 of the same year. It was actually a misnomer to call the USS *PE-56* the USS *Eagle 56*, though it was done often; the "Eagle" moniker for this entire PE class of vessel came from a December, 1917, *Washington Post* editorial calling for "an eagle to scour the seas and pounce upon every submarine that dares to leave German or Belgian shores." Ford set up production at his 1,700-

foot-long enclosed assembly line on the Rouge River in Dearborn, on the outskirts of Detroit.

The first of the cookie-cutter Eagle boats was launched on July 11, 1918, and six more boats were completed on schedule. But succeeding ships did not follow as rapidly. Ford's initial estimates that he could fulfill the Navy's expectations proved overly optimistic, due mainly to the inexperience of his labor force and supervisory personnel in shipbuilding. When World War I ended and the armistice was signed in November of 1918, only sixty Eagle boats were completed and the contract was suspended. Of these, seven were commissioned in 1918, and the remaining fifty-three were commissioned in 1919.

The *Eagle 56* (the Eagle-class boats were numbered one through sixty) was one of the latter group, commissioned on October 22, 1919, and launched on the Detroit River on November 13. Like many of the Eagle boats, she reached the North Atlantic by way of the Great Lakes' canals and the St. Lawrence River. On the way, according to *Seaweed's Ship Histories*, she was held up by ice in Quebec until May 8 of 1920, and finally reached the Portsmouth, New Hampshire, Navy Yard one week later. She was assigned to the District of Columbia Naval Reserve Force in November of 1921, and in 1926, was transferred to Baltimore, Maryland, where she continued duty as a Naval Reserve training ship. The *PE-56* was one of only eight of the original sixty Eagle boats to see service with the U.S. Navy during World War II.

Scagnelli knew of the *Eagle 56*'s World War II exploits: the rescue of the *Jacob Jones* survivors off New Jersey, the rescue of merchant mariners near Delaware Bay, the work in Key West, Florida, conducting anti-submarine warfare tactics and participating in the development of the Navy's top-secret "homing mine," or anti-submarine torpedo. Finally, in June of 1944, she departed Key West for the Boston, Massachusetts, Navy Yard, where she underwent repairs before reporting for operations at the U.S. Naval Frontier Base at Portland, Maine.

Since her arrival in Portland, she had towed the green cylindrical target float a few miles offshore to provide a target for the Navy and pilots stationed nearby. It was important work, but it was not considered tough or hazardous duty. In fact, many of the *Eagle*'s crew members, including Scagnelli, had seen action in the Pacific and off the coast of North Africa, and had been transferred to the *Eagle 56*, which was considered much less dangerous, and a "plum" location to finish the war.

The ship was armed with depth charges, but by 1945, the *PE-56* had her Y-gun removed to accommodate target-towing gear and her aft 4-inch deck-gun had been replaced by a single .50-caliber machine gun. In short, her days of taking part in any *real* combat were over.

Nonetheless, Scagnelli's responsibility was to keep the "tub" or the "old girl" operating at peak efficiency. The *Eagle 56*'s many paint jobs couldn't hide her age, but beneath her tired exterior, she functioned with precision, a source of immense pride to the Black Gang who toiled to maintain her machinery. The ship was dry-docked on April 5 in Rockland, less than two hours from its Portland home base. For better than a week, the Black Gang labored at overhauling the *Eagle*'s boilers and engines, wire-brushed and internally cleaned her drums and water tubes, and tested her boilers—which operated at 250 pounds of pressure per square inch at full steam—at a maximum pressure of 325 PSI without signs of any overall metal fatigue or weakness in her riveted joints. The *Eagle* was scheduled to emerge shipshape from dry dock in two days.

Scagnelli knew that Roosevelt's death had jolted his crew, too. The men went about their tasks methodically, but there was an uncertainty in the air, as though the world had lurched off-kilter. This feeling was reinforced by the abnormally warm weather; a heat wave had driven temperatures to 80 degrees along the mid-Maine coast, a figure that hadn't been reached in the middle of April since 1889. In Maine, April weather usually meant a raw, damp chill on the water, with cold winds buffeting the rocky coast. Adding to the unreality surrounding FDR's death was the sight of the shirtless *Eagle* crew members sweating as they worked on the ship.

Still, it was the work itself that restored some normalcy to this disquieting day. As they mourned the only commander in chief they had ever known, as they felt the hot April sun baking their backs, Lt. John Scagnelli and the Black Gang brought order to their lives by reverting to the familiar. That meant laboring for hours to prepare the *Eagle 56* for anything.

President Franklin Delano Roosevelt's death in Warm Springs, Georgia, on April 12, 1945, shocked America and her allies, etched deep lines of grief across the face of a nation, and plunged the country into mourning and uncertainty. "That first flash seemed incredible," one reporter recalled of the initial wire service report, "like something in a nightmare, for down under the horror was the comfortable feeling that you would wake to find it all a dream. The Romans must have felt this way when word came that Caesar Augustus was dead." Another journalist who had been having drinks at a hotel bar added: "Everybody left. I'm walking [on the street] and I can't stop crying. Everybody is crying." Even the normally staid *New York Times* was extravagant in its editorial praise: "Men will thank God on their knees a hundred years from now that Franklin D. Roosevelt was in the White House . . . It was his hand, more than that of any other single man, that built the great coalition of the United Nations . . . It was his leadership which inspired free men in every part of the world to fight with greater hope and courage. Gone, now, is this talent and skill . . ."

As word spread from city to town in the United States, people struggled to come to terms with Roosevelt's death. "For the millions who adored him and for those who despised him, an America without Roosevelt seemed inconceivable," Doris Kearns Goodwin observed. "He was in his thirteenth year as president when he died." Millions of Americans shared Scagnelli's experience; those who had just reached the legal voting age of twenty-one in time for his fourth election had been only nine years old when he took the oath of office for the first time. One school girl remembered her grief and fear after hearing of his death: "[I felt] that this was going to be the end of the world, because he was the only president I'd ever known. I was almost not aware that there could be another president. He had always been THE PRESIDENT, in capital letters." Dean Acheson, former assistant secretary of the treasury and of state, captured the feelings of ordinary Americans when he wrote to his son, serving in the Pacific: "Large crowds came and stood in front of the White House. There was nothing to see and I'm sure they did not expect to see anything. They merely stood in a lost sort of way. One felt as though the city had vanished, leaving its inhabitants to wander about bewildered, looking for a familiar landmark . . . Something which had filled all lives was gone."

In Washington, hushed thousands greeted the train that arrived from Warm Springs, Georgia, carrying Roosevelt's body, and thousands more attended his funeral in Hyde Park, New York. Newspapers published FDR's name on their war casualty lists. Yale University, from where he had received an honorary degree, included him on its roster of "war dead." In the days and weeks after her husband's death, Eleanor Roosevelt was greeted by porters, taxi drivers, doormen, elevator operators, passengers on trains, all of whom told her how personally bereaved they felt, "how much they had loved him, how much they missed him," Goodwin wrote. In a newspaper column, Eleanor told her readers: "It has warmed my heart to discover how many people would stop and speak to me as they left the train, often murmuring only: 'We loved your husband.' " Eleanor told of a man, visibly shaken, who approached her on the subway in New York: "He said, 'He was like a friend who came and talked to us every now and then.' These spontaneous outbursts of affection for my husband from casual people whom I have never seen before, are spoken so sincerely that I often wish my husband could hear them himself." Eleanor herself said simply: "I have lost my best friend." For decades after the president's death, millions of Americans could remember where they had been when they heard the news, whether at home or on some distant battlefield. Servicemen, especially, were shaken by the news, wondering what Roosevelt's death would mean to the enemy they faced.

Leaders in America and on the world stage were no less affected by the loss. Eisenhower and his commanders in Europe went to bed "depressed and sad," and Ike wrote: "In his capacity of a nation at war, he seemed to me to fulfill all that could possibly be expected of him." Winston Churchill described his emotions as equivalent to having "been struck a physical blow . . . my relations with this shining personality had played so large a part in the long terrible years we had worked together. Now they had come to an end, and I was overpowered by a sense of deep and irreparable loss." In a speech to the House of Commons on April 17, Churchill said: "I felt the utmost confidence in his upright, inspiring character and outlook, and a personal regard—affection, I must say—for him beyond my power to express today. His love of his own country, his respect for its constitution, his power of gauging the tides and currents of its public opinion, were always evident, but added to these were the beatings of that generous heart . . . it is, indeed, a loss, a bitter loss to humanity, that those heartbeats are stilled forever . . . for us, it remains only to say that in Franklin Roosevelt there died the greatest American friend we have ever known, and the greatest champion of freedom who has ever brought help and comfort from the new world to the old . . ." A tearful President Harry S. Truman asked reporters: "Please pray for me. I mean that!" He added: "There have been few men in all history the equal of the man into whose shoes I am stepping. I pray God I can measure up to the task."

In contrast, Nazi propaganda minister Josef Göbbels telephoned Hitler personally with the news of Roosevelt's death, according to historian David McCullough, "to proclaim it a turning point written in the stars."

In Portland, Maine, where the *Eagle 56* would return after its overhaul, the colors were lowered to half-mast at Portland Harbor defense posts, all liquor sales were banned in the city on Saturday, April 14, and theaters and department stores closed as well. On Sunday, Portland residents filled churches, both to pay their respects to President Roosevelt and to honor new President Harry S. Truman's "pray for me" request, which appeared in the newspapers. "Nothing could be more tragic than at this of all times when the German enemy must soon acknowledge utter defeat, Mr. Roosevelt should die," editorialized the *Portland Press Herald.*

Yet, one German who was not ready to acknowledge utter defeat—though Allied troops were closing in on Berlin—was Dönitz. On April 11, just one day before FDR's death, Dönitz sent a long message to his U-boats, including Froemsdorf's *U-853*, now bearing down on the Gulf of Maine. At the conclusion of the message, Dönitz called on his commanders to "clearly and plainly tread the path of soldierly duty . . . the honor of our flag on board is sacred to us. No one thinks of giving up his ship. Rather, go down in honor . . . The *Kriegsmarine* will fight to the end. Some day its bearing in the severest crisis of this war will be judged by posterity. The same goes for each individual . . ."

On April 15, the *Eagle 56* returned to Portland after ten days in dry dock. Her overhauling had been a success; the machinery that powered the *Eagle 56* had passed rigorous testing with flying colors.

Lt. (jg) John Scagnelli was pleased with the crew's job.

Now, he wanted to see how well President Truman did his.

Truman quickly allayed any fears Scagnelli had that the United States would veer from FDR's policies. On the afternoon of Monday, April 16, Truman delivered an emotional address to Congress, arriving in the Chamber to a standing ovation. His fifteen-minute speech, interrupted again and again by applause, called upon all Americans "to help me keep our nation united in defense of those ideals which have been so eloquently proclaimed by Franklin Roosevelt." Truman reiterated that he would prosecute the war without letup: "All of us are praying for a speedy victory. Every day peace is delayed costs a terrible toll. The armies of liberation are bringing to an end Hitler's ghastly threat to dominate the world. Tokyo rocks under the weight of our bombs . . . I want the entire world to know that this direction must and will remain—*unchanged and unhampered!*"

And then Truman uttered the words that reassured John Scagnelli and dashed any hope of Karl Dönitz's that the new president's resolve would not match Roosevelt's. "Our demand has been, and it *remains*—Unconditional Surrender," Truman declared to thunderous applause from Congress.

Dönitz's final U-boats—including Helmut Froemsdorf's *U-853*—approached the East Coast of the United States with the single goal of forcing Truman to change his mind.

Meanwhile, in Washington, D.C., intelligence experts in Kenneth Knowles's F-21 sub-tracking room and the adjacent F-211 Secret Room were analyzing Enigma intercepts and keeping tabs on the approaching U-boats. General notices were sent to base commanders up and down the East Coast to remain vigilant for possible U-boat traffic—but, as always, nothing more specific than that. Above all, no information could be released that would even hint to the Germans that their decrypted messages were being read by the British and Americans.

In fact, those documents—the precious top-secret Ultra intercepts—would remain classified for another forty years.

10

The heat wave that had passed through the mid-Maine coast ten days earlier was a distant memory, like some fast-talking traveling salesman who made many promises by daylight before sneaking out of town under cover of darkness. On this cold Monday morning, the temperature had not yet touched 40 degrees. Portland residents awoke to clear skies and blazing headlines in the *Press Herald*, the former a welcome relief after a windy, rainy Sunday, and the latter yet another indicator that the war in Europe was nearly over.

SOVIETS REACH HEART OF BERLIN—CITY BEING REDUCED TO RUBBLE, trumpeted the newspaper's front page. The Russians had rolled in from the East, encircled the city, and reduced the once-proud German capital to rubble with the pounding of their relentless artillery fire. Three days earlier, on April 20, with the Red Army on the doorstep and Allied planes bombing Berlin virtually nonstop, Nazi leaders had congregated at Hitler's headquarters, in the deep bunker far beneath the Reich Chancellery, to celebrate the Führer's fifty-sixth birthday. "[They] gathered for what they knew would be the last time," historian Ian Kershaw wrote. "In most cases [it was] to say their farewells. It was the start of the last rites for the Third Reich." Meanwhile, hundreds of thousands of German troops in the Ruhr region had already surrendered. With American and British troops on Berlin's doorstep in the West (PATTON WITHIN EIGHTEEN MILES OF BERLIN, the *Press Herald* had reported on April 17), the Third Reich's days were numbered. One German battalion commander wrote, "Who would have ever thought that it would be just a day's march from the Western Front to the Eastern Front! It says everything about our situation."

Portland residents were jubilant about Germany's imminent surrender and the end of the war in Europe, but the *Press Herald* also carried a gruesome reminder of the war's inhumanity that shocked the 750,000 residents of this industrial seaport city: AMERICAN CONGRESSMEN VIEW HORROR OF BUCHENWALD—RECEIVE EYEWITNESS PROOF OF GERMAN METHODS OF TORTURE, STARVATION, BESTIALITY. The Associated Press wrote, "They came at the personal invitation of General Eisenhower, who wanted them to see for themselves this village where decency was torn aside and men died like beasts in one of Germany's worst butcher shops." Eisenhower had toured a concentration camp two weeks earlier, and he wrote later that he had never before "experienced an equal sense of shock." He wrote to his wife, "I never dreamed that such cruelty, bestiality, and savagery could really exist in this world!" Now, the entire world was discovering the hell of the concentration camps. "As British tanks crashed through the gates of Belsen, the first large death mill to be liberated, skeletal women and men staggered to their feet as British soldiers cried through bullhorns, 'You are free! You are free! You are free!'" historian Michael Beschloss wrote years later. From another liberated camp, famous American broadcaster Edward R. Murrow described the horrors and told Americans over CBS Radio, "I pray you believe what I have said about Buchenwald."

The reports of the German death camps were the latest in a series of news items that could only have further fueled the desire of war-weary Portland residents, like residents of thousands of towns across America, to see an end to the fighting in Europe and the Pacific. Each week, the *Press Herald* listed the number of men on the casualty lists; the most recent toll contained a record eighty-eight names, including thirty-four killed, fifty-two wounded, and two captured as POWs. Ration guides were a regular newspaper feature, explaining in painstaking detail how and when Portlanders could purchase meat, sugar, shoes, gasoline, fuel oil, and processed foods. "Now Good: Red Stamps, T-5, 2-5, A-Z in Book 4, worth 10 points each," the *Press Herald* had pointed out in early April. Portland mothers who lost sons memorialized their boys and their sacrifice in the pages of the city's hometown paper: "Charles H. Coggswell, USMC, PVT, 23, died March 15 of wounds suffered on Iwo Jima, according to his mother, Mrs. Martha Coggswell of South Portland," the *Press Herald* noted in a small item.

Meanwhile, the horrendous casualty reports from the Battle of Okinawa in the Pacific began to find their way into the news pages. On April 19, reports listed 7,900 American casualties, including nearly 1,500 dead, on the small Japanese outer island. Americans were jolted to learn that one of those killed was famed war correspondent Ernie Pyle, who took a Japanese machine-gun bullet through the temple. "They are a rough, unshaven, competent bunch of Americans," Pyle had written of the Marines he was landing with just prior to the invasion. "I am landing with them. I feel I am in good hands." Privately, he told friends he had a premonition that he would die on Okinawa. "I'm not coming back from this one," he said. The *Press Herald* somberly informed readers that it would publish posthumously several columns that Pyle had already dispatched from the Pacific.

On the morning of Monday, April 23, it was unlikely that Ivar Westerlund would have had an opportunity to read the *Press Herald* at all. He had spent the previous day on furlough at home with Phyllis and the children in Brockton, Massachusetts, then barely caught the 4:30 A.M. bus for the three-hour ride to Portland. He told Phyllis that he had to catch that bus, because the *Eagle 56* was sailing sharply at 8:15 A.M. If Ivar missed it, he would officially be listed as AWOL, which would likely mean time in the brig, and possibly, a delay in his discharge once the war was finally over.

"Being caught AWOL," especially this close to war's end, would be "foolish" Ivar had told Phyllis. She got him to the bus in downtown Brockton with moments to spare, and he was on board the *Eagle 56* when she left port a few hours later.

Ivar Westerlund wasn't the only *Eagle 56* crew member who scrambled to catch his bus that morning.

At a little past 7:30 A.M., Esta Glenn stood on the top front step of her brownstone apartment building at 141 Spring Street in Portland and watched as her husband, Machinist Mate 1st Class Harold Glenn, darted toward the local city bus that would take him to the docks and the *Eagle 56*. Harold—or "Glenn," as Esta and his friends called him—

had had the weekend off and the two of them had taken their own bus trip out to Portland Head Light, one of Maine's most storied lighthouses, amid Sunday's rain and wind. Glenn had overslept and now scurried toward the bus to get to the *Eagle 56* before the ship's 8:15 departure time.

Sometimes Esta couldn't believe where she was, or how she had gotten here, three thousand miles from home *geographically*, but almost a different world in terms of climate and culture. She and Glenn had met at San Diego Gas & Electric Company. She was one of the company's two "feminine meter readers," lugging a seven-pound ledger on her daily rounds, a job she loved. Glenn worked as a mason, driving a company truck whose crew traveled from place to place around the city repaving streets that Gas & Electric had torn up to install or repair lines.

All of their friends thought Esta and "Glenn" made a beautiful couple. He was tall, about five feet, ten inches, with beautiful sky-blue eyes, a ruddy complexion, light brown hair, a dry sense of humor, and a love for life. Esta was a striking, slender, athletic, curly-haired brunette with mischievous eyes and a worldly toughness and easy confidence that served her well doing "men's work" in San Diego. Yet, their upbringings and backgrounds bore little resemblance. Esta was a native San Diegan, comfortable living and working in the fast-paced city. Glenn had grown up dirt-poor in Marissa, Illinois, a rural town in southwestern Illinois' St. Clair County, located across the Mississippi River from St. Louis. He had come to California in the 1930s to escape the poverty of farming in the throes of the Depression. "It was that old 'go west, young man, go west' bug that bit him," Esta would say to describe his uprooting.

After Harold had enlisted in the Navy in San Diego in June of 1942, he was assigned to the *Eagle 56* in Key West. They were married a little more than a year later, on August 6, 1943—Glenn was twenty-eight and she was twenty-six—and Esta joined him in Florida.

She befriended many of the other *Eagle* wives, including Alice Petersen, whose husband, Harold, was good friends with Glenn; Alice was only nineteen when she arrived in Key West, and Esta viewed her as a younger sister and a dear friend. Shipmates Harold Petersen and Harold Glenn often took liberty together. Esta thought it was because they were very much alike—neither "Harold" caroused much, and both of them were simple farm boys at heart. They even shared the same first name, and most of the guys referred to them by their last names. It was "Pete" and "Glenn," not "Harold" and "Harold" among the *PE-56* crew.

When the *Eagle 56* transferred to Portland, Esta and Glenn used their free time to bowl, hunt (she was a crack shot), fish, go to night-clubs, and even take trips when possible. They had traveled to Montreal, Quebec, and Boston when Glenn had leave, and they had big plans to travel much farther after the war. Glenn, especially, wanted to "see the world," infected with the same bug that had first driven him to California. The Navy had not offered that opportunity; Harold Glenn had been stationed stateside on the *Eagle 56* since his enlistment.

Now, as he darted down the stairs to his bus, Esta thought again that traveling wasn't *all* they were hoping to do after the Germans surrendered and Glenn was discharged; they also planned to have a family. Both of them agreed that it would be best to wait until the war was over. Navy life was no life for raising children. Back in San Diego, they would set up a home and start a family in a more stable environment. Esta looked forward to it. She longed to have children with the strong, gentle farm boy who had captured her heart.

As if he guessed what she was thinking about, Glenn, who was about to board the bus for the docks, asked the driver to wait a moment, whirled around, bounded back up the stairs, and pressed against Esta.

"What's the matter?" she asked, puzzled.

"I forgot to kiss you good-bye," her husband said, drawing her close and meeting her lips.

And then Harold Glenn ran down the stairs, boarded his bus, and was gone.

The seas were moderate, the clouds high and scattered, and the visibility unlimited when the *Eagle 56* eased out of Portland Harbor at 8:25 A.M., on its way to the Casco Bay towing-spar training area, located just a few miles off the coast. Skippered by Lieutenant Commander James G. Early, she carried sixty-two men, including John Scagnelli, Johnny Breeze, Harold Petersen, and Harold Glenn and Ivar Westerlund—who had arrived on time—and her mission today, as usual, was to tow a target buoy for naval aircraft bombing exercises.

As the *Eagle 56* sailed from Portland Harbor, she passed the famous Portland Head Light, which stood sentry-like protecting wayward ships from splintering on Maine's unforgiving rocky coast. Henry Wadsworth Longfellow often walked from downtown Portland to the lighthouse, where he would chat with the keepers, and where he was inspired to create his poem, "The Lighthouse," in which he wrote:

"Sail on!" it says, "sail on, ye stately ships!
And with your floating bridge the ocean span;
Be mine to guard this light from all eclipse,
Be yours to bring man nearer unto man!"

Early had no need for the assistance of the famous lighthouse beam on this clear, cold morning; as he piloted his ship into open water, rocks and shoals proved to be no problem. In fact, he likely had few worries about the *Eagle*'s routine mission. It is possible that Portland Naval Station Commander Ernest Freeman might have reminded Captain Early of the general U-boat warnings that had been issued by Washington, warnings that had been broadcast frequently during the war. But it is unlikely that, with Germany on the brink of defeat, either Freeman or Early would have been overly concerned.

In fact, *Eagle 56* crew member, Yeoman 1st Class Harold Ralph Rodman, twenty-one, who had recently returned from Europe and was assigned to *PE-56*, likely expressed the attitude of most of the crew when he wrote to his sixteen-year-old sister, Elaine, in New Jersey: "What could be safer than Portland Harbor?"

11

Lieutenant John Scagnelli stretched his six-foot, two-inch frame onto his bunk, preparing to take a short nap before he headed topside, as was his custom after noon chow, which he and most of the other morning-shift officers and crew members had just completed. "Noon" chow was always a little early, around 11:45 A.M. or so, and the *Eagle 56* had just completed her second bombing-run exercise.

Scagnelli would welcome today's nap more than usual. He had turned twenty-five just two days earlier, and the *Eagle*'s captain, James Early, had hosted a birthday party for him. By the time Scagnelli got home at around 4:00 A.M., he had a whopper of a hangover, and was thankful the *Eagle 56* was not sailing on April 22. After a quiet Sunday, Scagnelli awoke this morning clear-headed, though still a little tired.

Scagnelli was tall and strong, with dark hair and eyes, and broad shoulders made powerful from years of competitive swimming. His first competitions were informal, when, as a small boy growing up in New York, he and his friends would walk to Battery Park and dive into the water to retrieve pennies that tourists would toss from the cruise ships. The pennies looked as big as manhole covers to Scagnelli as they broke the surface and then tumbled in slow motion through the murky water, easy to spot and easy to catch. The boys dove again and again, collecting pennies until each had accumulated enough to afford a meatball sandwich from the Italian grocery store in their neighborhood. It was the beginning of the Depression and, though Scagnelli's father had a relatively secure job as a truck driver for the New York Department of Sanitation, even small change was hard to come by for an eleven-year-old kid. Diving for pennies was one way for John to fill his pockets.

Scagnelli began competitive swimming for real in high school, where he also played basketball and soccer; later, he captained the swim team and played football at New York University. He was ruggedly built and considered himself tough, but never bullied anyone; on the contrary, he remembered his Boy Scout days, when he had to walk from home, through a tough neighborhood, to reach his troop meetings. A nervous Scagnelli did everything he could to hide his Scout uniform, which would automatically label him a sissy and maybe earn him a beating. He rolled up his pant legs, removed his neckerchief, and squirreled his hat into his pocket. When he reached the meeting site, he straightened out his uniform and smoothed his hat to pass inspection. Scagnelli loved being a Scout and learned many things that helped him years later, but never forgot the fear he felt darting through the neighborhood, head down, praying no one would detect his uniform. Since that time, Scagnelli had made it a point never to pick on anyone smaller or weaker.

He entered NYU's physical education department, hoping to do something in the recreation field, and was one of the first in his neighborhood to attend college, thanks to his mother's persistent influence. "We'll find the money," she had said. But her dreams, and his, were interrupted by a surprise Japanese attack six thousand miles away on December 7, 1941, two months before his scheduled February 1942 graduation date. After Pearl Harbor he left school and enlisted, later took the Merchant Marine exam, and was accepted as a cadet in March of 1942. He trained for three months at the Chrysler Estate on Kings Point, Long Island. During an interview years later, he smiled when he remembered that his quarters were located in Mrs. Chrysler's former bedroom, and he had been completely mystified when he first saw the bidet. "What the hell do you do, wash your feet in there?" he had asked a buddy.

Eventually, Scagnelli was assigned to the USS *Mariposa*, a 672-foot-long troop transport that had been built for 4,200 passengers, but often carried more than 7,000 GIs, and he saw a good part of the world, sailing to Africa, India, and through the Strait of Gibraltar to French Algiers. The *Mariposa* came under heavy attack from German planes one night, and Scagnelli recalled the quick reaction of the Navy sailors on board to man the troopship's anti-aircraft guns. After he returned to the United States, he attended the Merchant Marine Academy again, and the Navy commissioned him as an ensign. He was assigned to sub-chasing school in Miami, where he learned how to detect and attack submarines. When he finished, the Navy assigned him to the *Eagle 56* in Key West.

By the time the *Eagle* sailed north to Portland, Scagnelli was a lieutenant junior grade (jg), but despite his officer status, had developed a close relationship with many men on the ship. "It was a happy ship," he would say one day. "We didn't stand on ceremony and we did a lot of things together. We had a basketball team and we played other teams in Portland, we spent time together around Portland. It was a good working ship."

Still, rank does pose restrictions on fraternization, so it was no surprise that Scagnelli was closest to the officers. He stood up as best man for Lieutenant Ambrose "Van" Vanderheiden when the soft-spoken, religious Wisconsin boy married his wife, Camilla, or "Cam," as Scagnelli knew her. Scagnelli was particularly close to Lieutenant Jack Laubach, the *Eagle*'s executive officer, whom Scagnelli respected, admired, and even envied a little. Laubach possessed many of the same qualities as Scagnelli—he was tall, strong, handsome, and athletic—and the two would spend hours talking about life and the future. They were both grateful for their stations in life, and often wondered how they could help others who were not as fortunate. Laubach, a commanding presence standing on the bridge puffing on his ever-present pipe, was a warm-hearted officer and friend. His men sought his advice, as did his own superior officers. Scagnelli admired Laubach for his resourcefulness, intelligence, and good judgment. Laubach was also married, had been for almost seven years, to his high school sweetheart, Ginny.

Scagnelli had mixed feelings about marriage. He was popular enough with women and had enjoyed dating different ladies in different ports, but he felt a pang of envy when Laubach talked about his love for Ginny and their future plans. People called Jack and Ginny Laubach the golden couple, and Scagnelli thought they looked perfect together each time he saw them; Jack, tall and blond, smiling down upon Ginny, with her dark hair and radiant face. Jack and Ginny had been best friends since childhood, and knew they would be together forever. Scagnelli sometimes wondered if he would ever find someone who was perfect for him. His whole future would have to wait until the war was over, and that seemed like it could be any day now. Berlin was under siege, and everyone was talking about Germany's imminent surrender.

Scagnelli felt his eyes growing heavy. Just before sleep closed in, a disquieting thought gnawed at him: The *Eagle 56* felt like it was at a dead stop. Even with the ship so close to shore, even as war's end approached, this violated naval regulations, and more importantly, rendered the *Eagle* an easy target for any German submarines still in the area.

A dead stop? Scagnelli convinced himself that he must be mistaken, but when he awakened, he would check with Commander Early just to set his mind at ease.

12

Deep below deck in the *Eagle 56*'s engine room, Machinist Mate 2nd Class Harold Petersen checked the instruments and gauges one final time before his relief, Fred Michelsen, arrived. Actually, "Mike" was a little late; normally the watch ended at 11:45, so perhaps chow had been delayed. Or maybe Mike, anxious about the upcoming birth of his first child, had been distracted for some reason. Whatever the cause of Michelsen's tardiness, Petersen didn't mind. Just three months shy of his twenty-third birthday, Harold Petersen was mature beyond his years and was seldom bothered by the small things. The *Eagle*'s officers put him in charge of the engine room first because of his thorough technical knowledge of how things work, but almost as importantly, for his level-headed temperament. That meant he would pay close attention to the condition of the evaporators, distillers, pumps, and throttle that powered the *Eagle 56*; it also meant he would remain calm in the midst of crisis.

Harold Petersen possessed a quiet confidence to go along with immense ability. He grew up in Henrietta, New York, a small farming community near Rochester, the "crossroad of Monroe County," with rolling, green hills, a landscape dotted with one-room schoolhouses and neat white churches. For as long as he could remember, Petersen could do just about anything he set his mind to, and most often, excel at it.

Strong and stocky, with big meaty hands, thick fingers, dark hair, and sharp blue eyes, he was both an excellent student and a star athlete at Henrietta High School. He could run a ten-second 100-yard dash, won a scholarship to the University of Rochester in football (though he did not attend college once war broke out), and was a tough shooting guard on the basketball team.

But Harold Petersen's first love—next to Alice, once his high school sweetheart and now his wife—was baseball. He played so well that the Pittsburgh Pirates had given him a tryout with their farm club in Allentown, Pennsylvania; he was a smart, tough catcher who worked well with pitchers and had a rifle for an arm. He drew raves from the second basemen and shortstops who handled his stinging and precise throws as he nailed runner after runner trying to steal. He received a follow-up letter from a Pittsburgh scout who said Petersen had one of the strongest arms he had ever seen, and that the Pirates were interested, very interested, in seeing more. The war had interrupted his plans, though, and now both Pete and the Pirates looked forward to his postwar baseball career. Petersen knew that he had the talent and the desire to reach the big leagues someday, and he longed for another opportunity.

Not that baseball was his *only* choice. Yes, he could throw and catch, but Harold Petersen could do just about anything else with his hands: carpentry, mechanical and electrical work, farming. And he was a modest man who, while he would thrive in the limelight, didn't need the limelight to thrive. The prospect of building houses or repairing engines to make a living was as pleasing and satisfying to him as donning shin pads and a chest protector and crouching behind home plate at Forbes Field. Baseball was certainly his dream, and if he could play it for a living, fine, but if not, Harold Petersen would still be a happy man. In fact, as long as he and Alice were together, he expected to be happy forever.

They had met when Pete was fourteen years old, an eighth-grader, and Alice Gilmore was in the sixth grade; Pete loved to say that their eyes locked one morning in the hall and their hearts had been joined ever since. It helped that Alice was also a top athlete. At school picnics and outings, Alice would win the girls' events, Pete the boys' contests; together, they'd win co-ed team competitions, with their particular specialty the three-legged sack race. He and Alice spent so much time together, and she was so liked by his class members, that by his senior year, when his classmates elected him president, the school allowed sophomore Alice Gilmore to accompany the Henrietta High Class of 1941 on their trip to Washington, D.C.

While he was in high school he learned from his dad how to build cabinets, refinish boats, and wield a torch to slice through steel. Clarence Henry Petersen was a talented, intelligent man, a former Navy man himself—an "adventurous Dane," Harold called him—who moved his wife, Ruth, and their five children around during the Depression as he built bridges for the WPA, and later settled in Henrietta, near Ruth's family. There, Clarence drove trucks hauling iron and tin to Buffalo, and built and repaired whatever anyone in Henrietta needed. Harold never remembered a repairman, carpenter, mason, or electrician visiting the Petersen house; his dad did all the work and Harold learned alongside his father.

Harold also never remembered his father complaining about work, even during the worst Depression days, an ethos Harold had adopted. In the summers throughout high school, Harold drove a horse and wagon hauling feed for a Henrietta farmer, and planted corn, peas, and potatoes by hand for fifty cents a day. He stayed with his grandmother, who lived a little closer to the farm. Harold never felt prouder than at the end of those summers when he returned home and handed the brown envelope, filled with his wages, to his mother.

After he graduated, Henrietta High hired him as an assistant coach to help out with all sports, which he did for the entire 1941–42 school year. On October 25, 1942, a few months after his twentieth birthday, he enlisted in the Navy. He left Henrietta and spent eight weeks in boot training, then another eight weeks at machinist school in Great Lakes, Illinois, before the Navy assigned him to the *Eagle 56* in Key West.

Later, Alice joined him in Key West and the two were married there in 1944. Pete liked Key West well enough, though every other doorway opened into a bar, and he didn't drink, smoke, or gamble. He never pretended he was better than anyone else, just didn't enjoy the activities that so many other guys loved. He would just smile when the other sailors called him "St. Pete," because he knew it was all in good fun. His performance aboard ship, his intelligence, and his toughness made him a respected member of the *Eagle 56* crew. What he liked most about Key West was the *Eagle*'s work: training officers in a new technology called SONAR (SOund NAvigation Ranger), and practicing anti-sub maneuvers and rescue techniques. It required timing, precision, and an ability to stay alert even during quiet times.

After the *Eagle* transferred to Portland, Alice worked with Esta Glenn at Cushman's Bakery, not far from the docks. Portland was an active little town, and Pete and Alice would go to dinner some nights, or take in a USO show. Meanwhile, Pete organized the *Eagle*'s basketball team, which competed well against the Army and Coast Guard teams. All in all, considering what American troops and sailors were going through in Europe and the Pacific, Harold "Pete" Petersen was grateful for his assignment aboard the *Eagle 56*.

President Roosevelt's death had left a lump in his throat. He was the best president that Pete knew—hell, the *only* one he knew—since FDR was elected when Pete was only ten. His first thought was that Truman wouldn't be able to fill Roosevelt's shoes, but then he reconsidered and decided to give the new president the benefit of the doubt. You don't get to that position unless you have some "smarts," Pete told his shipmates, and Truman's toughness reminded him a little of himself.

Now, with hot chow beckoning, Harold Petersen took one last long look around his engine room before Michelsen relieved him. Everything was functioning beautifully. The old tub might need a new paint job and a facelift above, but belowdecks, where the Black Gang labored, the *Eagle 56* purred as smoothly as a fine Swiss watch.

13

In the two years that Johnny Breeze had known Oscar Davis, Oscar had always been able to make him laugh. Today was no different, as Davis, looking to Breeze for help with a crossword puzzle, deadpanned, "Breezy, give me a four-letter word, starts with 's,' and describes what the food tastes like around here." Breeze cracked up, as he usually did when Oscar's dry humor interrupted the monotony of shipboard life. They were from different regions of the country, and different cultures, too: Breeze, from the urban, Pacific Northwest streets of Seattle, and Davis, from the dirt-poor farm town of Alto Pass in Southern Illinois. Still, the two had been close since Key West, and Breeze never failed to laugh when Oscar delivered one of his homespun country-boy quips like: "I haven't had this much fun since the hogs ate my little brother."

Johnny Breeze, "Breezy" to the *Eagle 56* crew, looked up to Oscar Davis, figuratively and literally. Since 1943, the two men had stood watches together in the *Eagle*'s boiler room (also known as the fire room) and the engine room, inseparable best buddies, or, as Breeze thought, as close as you could be working in the heat and noise of the fire room. Davis was only a year older than Breeze, but had become something of a protective father figure to him, especially since Breeze's own father had passed away suddenly at age fifty-four, just a year earlier. Davis was the toughest man Breeze had ever known; strong and tall—at five-foot-eleven, a full five inches taller than Breeze—fearless, an excellent athlete at Alto Pass Community High School. Davis excelled at basketball, baseball, and was a champion Ping-Pong player as well. With his dark, curly hair and hazel eyes, Davis had been popular with the ladies ever since high school. Breeze was neither a good athlete nor popular in high school, describing himself as a "skinny weakling," and had been married for a year to Dorothy Wells, a registered nurse whom he had met while he was on liberty at Old Orchard Beach in Maine. Breeze couldn't quite put his finger on what was missing from his marriage, but unlike Oscar, his dating days were over. In fact, Breeze wasn't sure what the future held, although he was sure of one thing: His goal was to become as talented a machinist as his father had been. Johnny could think of no better way to make a living or honor his dad's memory.

Born November 1, 1922, in North Seattle, Johnny Breeze was the first son in his family after three daughters, and as such, he was the pride and joy of his father, Percy Raymond Breeze (whom everyone simply called "Ray," since the old man hated the name Percy). Ray Breeze, an expert machinist, was the son of an even better machinist, a Welshman who immigrated to Canada, and eventually moved his family, including son Ray, to Seattle. When the First World War broke out, Ray Breeze returned to Canada and joined the Canadian Expeditionary Force, and served in England where he met his wife, Evelyn Ina Miles. They had two children in England—Johnny Breeze's oldest sisters, Eileen and Joyce—and then relocated to Seattle after the war.

Ray Breeze taught Johnny everything he knew about mathematics and machines, which was a great deal, and taught him other life lessons as well. He impressed upon Johnny the importance of reading, and was fond of saying that a man who *didn't* read was no better off than a man who *couldn't* read. He quoted from the Bible, and taught Johnny Breeze that the "Golden Rule" was the most important of God's laws; though Johnny was hardly religious, he tried to remember his dad's voice telling him to treat others the way he would like to be treated. Johnny's dad was also an outstanding chef (his mother couldn't cook at all), and he taught Johnny that it was perfectly appropriate for a man to feel at home in a kitchen, providing he took pride in his work there, too. Some of Johnny's fondest memories were the Thanksgiving and Christmas feasts that his father prepared.

During the Depression, Ray Breeze took odd jobs here and there, but never had steady employment. The family struggled. To help put food on the table, Johnny sold newspapers—*The Seattle Times*, *The Seattle Star*, and the *Seattle Post-Intelligencer*, on the corner of Third and Yesler, starting when he was nine years old. The *Times* and the *Star* sold for two cents each; when a man ordered both papers and handed Johnny a nickel, then asked for his change, Johnny always thought the man was a cheapskate. A penny meant something when a loaf of bread sold for a nickel, ten pounds of sugar for a dime, and gasoline for five cents a gallon. Every Saturday, Johnny's mother allowed him eleven cents from the money he earned to attend the Liberty Theater, which featured two cowboy movies. It was a long walk to the theater, but Johnny relished the extravagance of spending his money on a movie.

As the Depression neared an end, Ray Breeze went to work as a machinist for the University of Washington, and after school and on weekends Johnny would walk to the "U Dub" campus to work with his dad. Ray Breeze taught his son how to run an engine lathe, a belt-driven knee mill, and just about every other machine in the shop that was located on the top floor of Philosophy Hall. It was during these sessions that Ray Breeze talked to Johnny about the family's tradition of dedication to quality work, and the need to master advanced mathematics if Johnny wanted to become the best machinist he could possibly be. He insisted that Johnny take college prep courses. Johnny Breeze took his father's message to heart, and by the time he graduated from high school in June of 1941, he not only knew how virtually every mechanical tool and engine worked, he knew the theory behind *why* they worked.

Immediately after high school, Johnny labored for three months as a forest firefighter for the State of Washington Forestry Service, then landed a job at Boeing working on the B-17 heavy-bomber assembly line as a "C" mechanic in September of 1941, for sixty-two cents an hour. Three months later, the owner of a machine shop in downtown Seattle offered Johnny a job for $1.25 an hour. Johnny did such high-quality work that when he told the owner in October of 1942 that he was going to quit and join the Navy, the owner did his best to talk Johnny into getting a deferment, and even gave him two days off to think about it. When Johnny returned and told his boss he had enlisted, the machine shop owner was furious and never spoke to Johnny again. Good machinists were a rare commodity in Seattle during wartime.

Since he had not yet turned twenty-one when he decided to join the Navy—Johnny was just shy of his twentieth birthday—he had to talk his father into signing his enlistment papers. When Johnny had first asked his parents to allow him to enlist immediately after Pearl Harbor, his mother went into near hysterics; Johnny was never sure how much grief his father took the day Ray went home and told his wife he had signed the papers that allowed their son to join the Navy.

After boot training and sixteen weeks of machinist's school at the University of Kansas in Lawrence (a complete waste of time for Johnny, who knew more than the instructors), Johnny Breeze was assigned to the *Eagle 56* in Key West. He vividly remembered his first night aboard ship, when he was searching for his duffel bag on the PE boat's dark deck. Johnny had grabbed a flashlight labeled FOR EMERGENCY USE ONLY to illuminate the area, when a rugged, redheaded bosun's mate growled that Johnny was misusing the flashlight. Johnny, who by this time had packed on about thirty pounds of muscle after boot training, told the mate to mind his own business, and before he knew it, the mate had clocked him with a roundhouse right to the jaw, and then stepped back into a dark deckhouse. Johnny fell on his back, but shook the cobwebs away and got back up, charging into the deckhouse to retaliate, only to come flying back out when the bosun's mate hit him again. Luckily, a chief came by and ordered the redheaded mate below, but Johnny never forgot his introduction to the USS *Eagle*.

He took great pleasure, when, more than a year later, as he and Oscar were painting the *Eagle*'s hull, the same bosun stopped to watch their work, and proclaimed: "You morons are getting more paint on the dock than on the ship!" Oscar put down his brush, stood up to his full height, arms dangling at his sides like a big ape, and told the mate to go f—— himself, or else come forward and fight. "Red" backed down; Johnny could have hugged Oscar at that moment. "Too bad," Davis said, "I would have fought that son of a bitch!"

Johnny's affection for Oscar Davis probably intensified after Ray Breeze passed away. Johnny remembered getting the terse telegram when he was in Key West: DADDY DIED. PLEASE TRY TO GET LEAVE. MOM. He felt like he had been punched in the stomach. He hadn't known his father was sick, though from time to time he had heard that Ray Breeze suffered from angina. He learned later that when his father entered the hospital, he had forbidden his wife to call their son. "Don't bother Johnny," Ray Breeze had whispered from his hospital bed.

The painful telegram began a grueling six-day odyssey for Johnny, from Key West to Seattle, about as far as a person could travel and still remain within the borders of the United States. Johnny donned his dress whites, took a boat and a plane to Jacksonville, and then boarded a train for Chicago. He and a soldier shared a pint of the worst rotgut whiskey Johnny had ever tasted, and he stayed drunk for most of a full day. When he got to Chicago, Johnny slept overnight on a bench in the train terminal, before boarding another train for a three-day excursion to Seattle. By the time he arrived on the West Coast, Johnny's dress whites had been transformed into a sooty black cloak by the coal dust, grime, and dirt that had sifted through the cracks around the train's windows during the trip across the continent. He threw the uniform in the trash.

Ray Breeze had been dead for more than six days when Johnny's train chugged into Seattle. The funeral was over, but the family had delayed Ray's burial so Johnny could see his father one last time. His dad's skin was parchment pale, but Johnny thought he looked peaceful, his hair soft and gray. Johnny was conscious of how young his father was— Johnny's grandfather had outlived his own son—and how much he would miss the person who had influenced him the most.

After his father's death, Johnny redoubled his efforts to make Ray Breeze proud and become the best machinist he could be. The work on the *Eagle* was repetitive, but important, and Johnny dedicated himself to it. His responsibility in the fire room included manning the pump which fed the oil to the fire boxes on both port and starboard boilers, cutting in and cutting out the three burners in the port boiler, and communicating with the engine room.

It was hard, loud, hot work. The noise was so deafening that if the four-man crew wanted to communicate, a man had to put his mouth against the other man's ear and shout. Temperatures reached 150 degrees in the fire room, and the crew worked stripped to the waist, with rags tied around their heads to keep salty sweat from flowing into their eyes. The men had to boil the blue dye out of their dungarees in salt water again and again, to bleach their trousers nearly white, or else the heat from the fire room would cause the dye to run. Breeze had seen more than one sailor remove his dungarees and find that his legs were stained dark blue with dye that didn't wash off with just a single shower.

Today, Johnny Breeze and Oscar Davis worked the 8:00 A.M. to noon watch, and all had gone well. When they finished this crossword puzzle, Johnny looked forward to smoking his pipe for a few minutes before chow, then heading on deck to breathe in some fresh air, still cold and clean, even this close to the end of April. The day had grown overcast, reminding Johnny Breeze that winter lingered for a long time in Maine.

The air, though, was still warmer than the North Atlantic. Johnny had noticed this morning that the seawater that ran through the injection pump into the boiler's cooling system had registered only 38 degrees Fahrenheit, just six degrees above freezing.

14

What John Scagnelli, Harold Petersen, Johnny Breeze, Ivar Westerlund, Oscar Davis, Fred Michelsen, Harold Glenn, Harold Rodman, John Laubach, and James Early didn't know—nor did anyone else aboard the *Eagle 56* or at Portland base command—was that hundreds of miles to the south, the Secret Room team had been tracking a German U-boat prowling the Gulf of Maine for most of April. Yet, in the last few days, the sub had made no radio contact with Berlin, so it was difficult for Kenneth Knowles and his staff to pinpoint its movements. Knowles's last dispatch to Admiral Low, dated April 21, reported that two anti-submarine task forces were on the lookout for U-boats in the North Atlantic, and the Secret Room had also issued a general alert to operational base commanders to keep a sharp eye out for U-boats. This was particularly important since U-boats had sunk both a Canadian minesweeper and a freighter off the coast of Nova Scotia within the last ten days.

Knowles hoped that ships operating off the coast of Maine were paying close attention.

Lieutenant Commander J. A. Boyd, piloting the destroyer USS *Selfridge* in defense of Portland Harbor, was about seven miles away from the *Eagle 56*, when he noticed something highly irregular, and against all naval regulations: his navigational crew had tracked the PE-boat "at dead in the water," a dangerous condition to say the least. Even with Germany about to fall, the *Eagle 56* commander should have been more careful. With his ship at a complete stop, the PE captain left his vessel exposed to a possible U-boat attack, and all commanders had been warned of U-boats in the vicinity.

Actually, "exposed" was probably too mild a word—at a dead stop, the *Eagle 56* was a sitting duck.

April 23, 1945, 12:14 p.m
Helmut Froemsdorf
aboard the *U-853*
Gulf of Maine

For two difficult months at sea, it is likely that Helmut Froemsdorf had dreamed of this moment. His boat had been forced to remain submerged like a frightened rabbit for virtually the entire trip across the Atlantic, crawling beneath the surface to avoid detection and likely destruction from Allied ships and planes, which had killed more than one hundred U-boats and their crews in the first four months of 1945. The fifty-five men aboard the *U-853* would be growing restless and irritable, eating bland food, breathing stale air, living and working in cramped quarters alongside shipmates who had not changed clothing or showered in weeks due to a lack of space for personal effects and restrictions on the use of freshwater.

Now, the time for cowering and restlessness was over; precision and daring were the orders of the day. Helmut Froemsdorf, who had turned twenty-four years old less than a month earlier, would truly come of age on this raw April day in the Gulf of Maine. He was operating the *U-853* under power of her electric motors as she crept, submerged, toward the *Eagle 56*, the U-boat's sound masked by the noisy wake of the American destroyer, *Selfridge*, seven miles away. Froemsdorf would have celebrated his good fortune. The American subchaser was at a dead stop and made an easy target for the *U-853*'s torpedoes.

As he drew a bead on the *Eagle 56*, Froemsdorf may have recalled the glory days of his predecessors—of Sommer's bravery in the open Atlantic, of Hardegen's and Mohr's dramatic kills along the American East Coast during the Second Happy Time in 1942. He also may have thought about the last message he had received from Admiral Dönitz, on April 11, one that rose to the unwavering defense of Adolf Hitler, calling him the "single statesman of stature in Europe."

But perhaps it was the last portion of Dönitz's April 11 message that was uppermost in Froemsdorf's mind as he prepared to attack the *Eagle 56*, words that trumpeted the glory of the *Kriegsmarine* and its willingness to "fight to the end," words that heralded the bravery of its U-boat captains who would never "think of giving up [their] ship" and whose "bearing in the severest crisis of this war will be judged by posterity."

With the *U-853* less than six hundred yards from the *Eagle 56*, Froemsdorf ordered his torpedo crew to fire.

Part II

The Kills and the Court

15

The *U-853*'s torpedo detonated under the *Eagle 56*'s starboard side amidships, blowing the subchaser out of the water, breaking her keel, tearing her in half, and unleashing a geyser of water that shot one to two hundred feet skyward. The blast killed forty-nine men in all: five of the ship's six officers, including Commander James Early, plus forty-four members of her crew. John Scagnelli was the only *Eagle 56* officer to survive, and the only crewman to escape from the forward section of the ship. Johnny Breeze, Harold Petersen, Oscar Davis, and nine others from the stern half of the ship jumped into the freezing North Atlantic water and held on long enough to be rescued. Along with Scagnelli, they would become known as "The Lucky Thirteen."

Scagnelli's good friend, Jack Laubach, left his beloved Ginny a widow; Laubach and Early, the *Eagle*'s skipper, were last seen on the bridge. Ivar Westerlund, who arrived from Brockton, Massachusetts, in time to board the *Eagle* just before it left port, went down with the ship, leaving Phyllis a widow and their four children fatherless. Harold Glenn, who had kissed his wife, Esta, good-bye on the front steps of their apartment that morning, perished in the attack. Fredrick "Mike" Michelsen, who relieved Petersen on the engine room watch, also died in the explosion, leaving his pregnant wife, Pauline, behind.

Immediately after the blast the *PE-56*'s stern section began sinking quickly, although as many as two dozen men in the aft compartments were able to struggle topside, scramble up the pitching deck, and jump into the freezing water before the stern disappeared below the whitecaps about seven minutes after the torpedo struck. The severed bow portion of the ship also settled quickly amidships, pitched on her side, her tapered stern rising high in the air, perpendicular to the water, her exposed anchors and the large painted number "56" visible to the crew members who had abandoned ship. The bow section remained afloat for approximately fifteen minutes before it, too, sank beneath the choppy waves and went to the bottom.

All personnel on the bridge, including Early and the other officers, and virtually all the men belowdecks in the bow section—including those in the Chief Petty Officer (CPO) quarters, radio shack, wardrooms, officers' quarters, galley, and forward crew compartment—were killed and went down with the wreck. Only Engineering Officer Scagnelli escaped from the bow section. When Scagnelli was asked later if he could account for the loss of all the officers and crewmen on the bridge and in the chart house, he testified: "Their doors may have been closed and when the explosion occurred that may have slammed them tight. They have two doors, one on the starboard side and one on the aft port side. The port was dogged [locked]." Scagnelli was then asked whether he believed that most of the men in their living compartments were likely trapped in the ship's hull after the explosion. "Yes, sir," he said, "the explosion rendered a great many of them unconscious . . . As I came through [making his escape] I didn't hear any yelling or screaming or calling for help." Years later, naval historian Paul Lawton would write: "Many of the *PE-56* officers and crewmen were thrown against bulkheads and rendered unconscious by the explosion, becoming entrapped belowdecks, as their only means of escape became flooded, taking many men, still alive, down to the cold, dark, crushing depths of the North Atlantic, where they suffered agonizing deaths, entombed within the wreckage."

The tremendous explosion was witnessed by Cape Elizabeth's Casco Bay Magnetic Loop Receiving station, approximately five miles away, and by the Portland Harbor Entrance Control Post (HECP) at Fort Williams, about nine miles away. Reinforcing just how close the *Eagle* was to home, Portland residents reported hearing the roar of the blast, and some who lived in the city's highest hill sections saw the waterspout that erupted when the *Eagle* broke in half. The USS *Selfridge*, USS *Nantucket*, USS

Woolsey, and several other nearby vessels all witnessed the blast, sounded their General Quarters, and headed for the scene to begin rescue operations. *Selfridge* Commanding Officer J. A. Boyd (USN), whose ship was seven miles away, reported later that he witnessed "a white column of smoke and vapor about 100 feet high . . . [it] appeared larger than from a depth charge [that the *Eagle 56* carried], persisted for at least 20 seconds, and had the appearance of an external, rather than an internal underwater explosion . . . The explosion was heavy, the ship broke in two immediately . . ." Lieutenant Guy V. Emro (U.S. Coast Guard), commanding officer aboard the *Nantucket*, which was only two and a half miles away from the *PE-56* when she exploded, later recounted: "The immense amount of water in the air I judged to be about 250 to 300 feet high. . . . The explosion must have come from without [outside the ship's hull], due to the immense amount of water and parts of the ship lifted in the air. I have witnessed a boiler blow-out, but that explosion could be compared in no way to the power displayed in this one . . ."

As the rescue ships raced to the scene, their commanders and crews knew they were racing against time: God only knew how many *Eagle 56* crew members had survived the terrible explosion, but any sailor could figure out that they would not live long immersed in the icy water.

And there was another worry for these men to consider. It was true that they were just a few miles from the U.S. shoreline, most of them engaged in routine maneuvers on an overcast April day as the end of the war neared. Yet, they had to reconcile the reassurance of that reality against the foreboding unease they felt about the likely cause of the *PE-56* explosion—an enemy torpedo—and the obvious question *that* conclusion begged: Was the U-boat that fired the torpedo still lurking out there?

John Scagnelli could barely see. Darkness and blood obscured his vision as he stumbled, dazed, along the narrow corridor, groping his way and praying that the only ladder that led topside was still intact. The explosion had lifted Scagnelli off his bunk and flung him like a rag doll, headfirst into the bulkhead in his cabin, opening a deep gash in his scalp that now bled profusely. He had remained conscious after the collision with the bulkhead, which most likely saved his life. When he opened his stateroom door, the passageway had been pitch black, almost ghostly. Scagnelli heard no screams or shouts or running feet; the only sound was hissing steam escaping from broken pipes outside his stateroom. It was as though he were the only man on the ship. Scagnelli knew something terrible had happened—he first thought a mine or torpedo had rocked the *Eagle*—and he knew his only chance for survival was to get off of the ship. But where were the others?

His prayers, not the last he would utter on this day, were answered when he found the ladder and clambered topside, where he saw water spilling into the starboard passageway. The only way off the ship would be through the portside passageway, but to his horror, he saw that his exit was blocked by a metal food locker, six feet tall and nearly four feet wide, that had slid from its spot when the ship began to list, and wedged itself into the passageway. Scagnelli, standing six-foot-two himself, attempted to muscle the locker, but it wouldn't budge. Water poured in from the starboard side, and Scagnelli knew time was running out. He searched frantically for a way off the ship. Then he noticed the twenty-inch space between the top of the food locker and the ceiling of the passageway. He took a running jump and hooked his arms across the top of the food locker, hoisting his big frame off the floor, struggling to scrabble up the front of the smooth metal container, knowing time was short, feeling the ship listing more, hearing water rushing in faster. He flopped the upper half of his body across the top of the food locker, squeezed first his head and wide shoulders and then his torso and legs through the crawl space, and dropped on the other side of the locker into knee-high water on the open main deck. With a shock, he realized the explosion had broken the *Eagle 56* in half.

Immediately, he saw heads bobbing in the water a distance away, the first men he had seen since the explosion, *too* distant to have come from where he had been. They must have been in the *Eagle*'s aft, or stern, section—and where the hell *was* the stern? Scagnelli couldn't see it. He plunged into the freezing water and pushed off, swimming as hard as he could in the direction of his shipmates, trying to get as far from the ship as quickly as possible before it sank and its swirling downdraft sucked him under with it. Moments later, a safe distance away, he stopped swimming and started treading water. He looked back and saw the front of the bow section rise out of the waves and point heavenward, almost majestically, her white "56" in stark relief against her gray hull and the gray water and gray sky that filled Scagnelli's field of vision.

Then the *Eagle 56*'s broken bow section, from where he had barely escaped, seemed to shudder once . . . then once more . . . before plunging downward and disappearing beneath the surface, taking every man except a dazed Lt. John Scagnelli to the bottom with her.

✪ ✪ ✪

The *U-853*'s torpedo tore into the *Eagle 56* fourteen minutes after Fred Michelsen relieved Harold Petersen on the engine-room watch, its rocking blast killing Michelsen instantly. Petersen, who moments earlier had headed aft to splash cold water on his sweaty face, was about to reach into his footlocker when the explosion flung him headfirst into an upright locker and dislodged a bunk that slammed into Petersen's back.

He regained his composure and made his way to the next compartment, the mess hall, first to the starboard ladder, only to find the explosion had blown it from its hinges. The portside ladder was loose, but usable, and as Petersen approached it, he bumped into his friend, mess cook Robert Coleman.

"I can't swim, Pete," Coleman said.

"Bob, we have to get off this ship!" Petersen replied.

They had started up the ladder when Petersen heard loud moaning. He jumped off the ladder, searched frantically, and spotted an injured Fireman 1st Class Leonard "Leo" Surowiec lying amid some debris. Petersen hoisted him up, dragged his motionless body to the ladder, pulled him halfway toward topside, but Surowiec slipped from his hands. "I lost him," Petersen would say later, "and there was no time to go back down and get him."

Petersen reached the top deck and stood next to Coleman, the stern section of the ship sinking fast, the water ankle-deep.

"I can't swim, I just can't," Coleman shouted again.

"We have to go!" Petersen screamed, grabbing Coleman's arm. "Right now, or we're going under!"

They jumped into the freezing water together, and Coleman disappeared immediately. Petersen searched frantically, but knew he had to get away from the doomed *Eagle*, whose stern section sunk beneath the waves within seven minutes. "Bob never came up; I never saw him again," he would remember nearly sixty years later. "There was supposed to be a swimming test to get into the Navy. I never knew why he couldn't swim."

Petersen swam for his life, barely escaping the pull of the *Eagle*'s broken stern section. He headed for a floating fifty-gallon drum that was already supporting two other crew members. As he approached, he saw one man, his arms "nearly frozen stiff" from the bitterly cold water, lose his grip on the barrel and slip silently beneath the surface. Petersen wrapped his own arms around the barrel and saw bobbing heads around him—*Eagle* crew members treading water, trying desperately to hang on. He also spotted several floating pieces of wood shoring that had broken loose when the *Eagle* exploded. He left the barrel, collected as many pieces of wood as he could, and shoved them in the direction of his shipmates. Then he grabbed two more, for himself and Bill Thompson, who had been hanging onto the barrel.

"Take these, they're easier to hold onto," Petersen shouted.

"Pete," Thompson said, "I can't make it. I'm too tired. I'm too cold."

Growing numb himself, Petersen searched the horizon and saw a plume of black smoke—a rescue ship!—still in the distance but closing fast. He shook Thompson. "See that smoke?" he shouted. "See it? That's our rescue. Hang on—just hang on a few more minutes and it'll be here." Thompson nodded slightly, though Petersen saw that his lethargic shipmate's eyes had begun to glaze.

Petersen *willed* the rescue ship to move faster. Thompson was on the brink of giving up, with Petersen clutching him and hugging the shoring at the same time. For years after the sinking, Petersen would find it difficult to shake the guilt of failing to save the lives of two men—Surowiec and Coleman—within moments of the explosion; men he had touched, who were *in his grasp*.

Petersen vowed he wouldn't lose a third.

The explosion slammed Johnny Breeze to the deck and literally blew him out of one of his shoes. The pipe he had been filling with tobacco clattered across the floor. He and Oscar Davis, in the stern half of the ship, scrambled up, reached the escape ladder in the forward crew's quarters, and headed topside. Johnny Luttrell was ahead of them on the ladder, moving too slowly for Breeze, who cupped his hand on Luttrell's backside and hoisted him five rungs upward.

With Davis on his heels, Breeze stepped through the doorway of the after deckhouse onto the fantail of the ship, already tilted upward at a 20-degree angle and growing steeper, since this half of the *Eagle* was sinking from amidships. Breeze and Davis were in ankle-deep water, figuring out what to do next, when Davis grabbed his friend, pointed off the port quarter, and said, "Look, Breezy, there's a sub." Breeze looked quickly, saw the sub's black conning tower, but "didn't stop long enough to take a second look . . . we had to get off the ship and away from it before it went under and took us with it."

By now, the fantail was pitched at such a steep angle that Breeze and Davis were forced to crawl up the deck on their hands and knees, but quickly, as water was beginning to swirl onto the ship. Breeze reached as far as the depth-charge rack on the starboard side and was removing his remaining shoe when he looked over the side and saw a twelve-foot-long four-by-four length of shoring floating in the water. He forgot the sub, forgot *everything*, and concentrated on the piece of timber that he believed could save his life. Barefoot now, he jumped into the 38-degree water, Davis behind him, and latched onto the shoring. Immediately, Breeze spotted the lifeless body of his friend, Fireman 1st Class Norris Jones, floating toward him. "Jonesy" had been working in the fire (boiler) room at the time of the explosion, and, like every man in the scorching confines of the boiler room, had worked stripped to the waist. Breeze had to push Jones's body away from the shoring, and as he did, he saw that his friend had a terrible wound on his back, "a huge bump, a gnarled knot . . . the back was broken, you could tell. When the torpedo hit, he was probably thrown against something." Breeze would note emphatically later that Jones had no burns or scald marks on his upper torso, wounds which would surely have been visible had a boiler explosion shattered the *Eagle 56*.

Luttrell and Davis joined Breeze on the piece of shoring and they kicked frantically away from the sinking stern-half of the ship, which had all but disappeared beneath the waves. Breeze looked to his right and saw Lt. John Scagnelli swimming toward them. When the muscular Scagnelli grabbed onto the twelve-foot piece of shoring, his weight pulled all four men under briefly; the others popped up quickly, but Breeze couldn't get his head above the waves and he felt himself drowning, unable to breathe, but clinging to the wood for dear life. Mercifully, he felt Johnny Luttrell clamp his hand around the back of his neck and yank him to the surface. But would the shoring hold four men? Breeze wasn't sure it mattered anyway. He thought they were all going to perish from exposure. He saw heads bobbing in the water around him— later he said one man counted twenty-five in all—and saw men slip beneath the waves and never resurface.

Across from him on the four-by-four, Davis, for the second time in minutes, spotted a vessel. This time, it wasn't a German U-boat, but a rescue ship steaming toward them. "Look, Breeze, there's a ship," Davis said almost matter-of-factly.

Breeze didn't believe the ship would arrive in time. His body was numb from the cold; he couldn't feel *anything* unless he moved. He was a cocky twenty-two-year-old kid who liked to think he could do just about anything, but humble enough now to know he was in big trouble.

The *Eagle 56* was gone, both halves of her now deep beneath the surface, her bow section entombing as many as thirty sailors trapped inside. As many as two dozen escaped from the stern, but several of them had already died in the water, unable to cling any longer to the small chunks of debris that floated amid the choppy waves. The debris was the only evidence that the *Eagle* had ever been there. "The ship had two life rafts, located amidships . . . that were supposed to have automatically released and floated free in the event the ship went down," wrote Paul Lawton. "The life rafts did not deploy, however, and the few survivors, none of who [sic] were wearing warm clothing, foul-weather gear, or life jackets, struggled in the chilling waters to keep from drowning, clinging to any wreckage that remained afloat, including wood shoring timbers, oil drums, and milk cans which had floated free of the wreck."

As the rescue ships steamed toward Scagnelli, Petersen, Breeze, Davis, Luttrell, Thompson, and the rest, they were racing against time. The *Eagle 56* survivors immersed in freezing water were in danger of dying from hypothermia, the subnormal temperature within the central body. Skin and external tissue cools very quickly, and within ten to fifteen minutes, the temperature of the heart and brain begins to drop. When the body's core temperature—normal at 98.6 degrees Fahrenheit—drops below 97 degrees, shivering usually occurs and motor functions are reduced. At 92 to 95 degrees—moderate hypothermia—serious complications develop, including muscle rigidity that erases manual dexterity. Victims appear dazed, their speech slurred, shivering becomes violent and uncontrollable, amnesia can occur, and behavior becomes irrational. Hypothermia victims have been known to engage in "paradoxical undressing"—taking off clothing, unaware that they are cold. Lethargy, depression, and an "I don't care" attitude grip the victim. Severe hypothermia occurs when the body temperature drops to 92 degrees or below. Shivering occurs in waves, but then ceases because the heat output from burning glycogen in the muscles is not sufficient to counteract the continually dropping core temperature; the body shuts down on shivering to conserve glucose. The pupils dilate, the pulse rate decreases, and at 90 degrees, the body tries to move into hibernation, shutting down all peripheral blood flow and reducing breathing rate and heart rate. At about 85 degrees, the body enters a state of "metabolic icebox" in which the victim appears dead and is still alive. Death usually results when the body's temperature plunges to between 75 and 80 degrees; cardiac and respiratory failures occur as breathing becomes erratic and very shallow, cardiac arrhythmias develop, and any sudden shock may set off ventricular fibrillation, stopping the heart permanently.

Water temperature is only one factor in determining cold-water survival. Others include body size, fat, and activity within the water. Large people cool slower than small people. Fat people cool slower than thin people. By swimming or treading water, a person will cool about 35 percent faster than if remaining still. In water temperatures below 40 degrees, exhaustion and unconsciousness occur in fifteen to thirty minutes, and the expected survival time is as little as thirty minutes, and as long as ninety minutes at the outside.

As the *Selfridge*, the *Nantucket*, and the other rescue ships approached the scene, almost all of the freezing *Eagle 56* survivors were on the verge of moderate hypothermia. Every minute would count in the rescue, and the margin of error would be close to zero.

Clutching the same piece of shoring, John Scagnelli and Johnny Breeze, their bodies numb from the cold water, were engaging in the same activity, though neither would know it for years: each was praying. Scagnelli, who could no longer feel the scalp injury or anything else, struck a bargain with God: "Let me get out of this and I promise to devote my life to helping others." Breeze prayed, too, and for the first time in his life "actually believed someone could hear me . . . that someone was listening." After a few moments of begging God to spare him, Breeze realized he was being selfish. "It hit me that there were sixty-one other guys on the ship, and who the hell was I to just pray for me?" he recalled later. "I started to pray for them, and the good Lord saw fit to spare me."

Clinging to another piece of timber, an exhausted Harold "Pete" Petersen, who had spent his time in the water assisting his shipmates, felt the numbness consume his body "from bottom to top." Yet he refused to focus on his own plight. Instead, he continued to talk to Bill Thompson, imploring him not to give up, and by boosting Thompson he strengthened his own resolve. As the smoke plumes from the rescue ships grew closer, Petersen knew he couldn't hang on much longer, but he also knew that if *he* slipped under the water, Thompson would die, too.

16

By 12:35 P.M., when the USS *Selfridge* reached the scene of the explosion, the *Eagle* survivors had been neck-deep in the freezing water for twenty minutes, and most men were on the verge of succumbing. *Selfridge* crewman Edwin Walker recalled later: "I looked down into the cold, clear water and watched several [men] clinging to floating junk and such, but the water was so cold they soon turned loose and slowly sank. I always wish I had not been there and saw this . . . I hate to remember one sailor in a white T-shirt, husky, strong like a wrestler, holding onto a floating barrel or something like that, and he had his arms around it, and slowly he relaxed and slipped under the water. I watched him sink. He let out his breath and bubbles rose to the surface, but he held my attention until he was no longer visible. My thoughts were, 'There goes some mother's beloved son, and she will never know how he died.' I wish I knew who he was so that I could have told her."

The *Selfridge* lowered a whaleboat into the water and her crew members began the process of hauling aboard the *Eagle* survivors. *Selfridge* crew members were jittery about becoming sub victims themselves. "Our opinion [about the *Eagle* explosion] was sub," Walker said. "As we pulled survivors out of the water, we were a duck in the water, sitting as a perfect target for a submarine, and we anticipated a torpedo coming."

Their fears were not unfounded. At 12:48 P.M., moments after *Selfridge* crew members transferred a group of *Eagle* survivors from the whaleboat to the ship—including Scagnelli, Breeze, and Oscar Davis—the *Selfridge* made a SONAR sound contact indicating the presence of a potential enemy submarine at an estimated range of 1,125 yards to the northeast. When the SONAR man called out the contact, Captain Boyd immediately got under way and ordered a depth-charge attack. Many of the *Selfridge* crewmen watched in horror as the destroyer's screws began to turn, sucking several of the *PE-56*'s exhausted survivors, still in the water but so close to their rescue, to their deaths. Commodore Frank Walker was brokenhearted that the *Selfridge* left survivors in the water, "but the captain had no choice." The SONAR specialist on board offered the opinion that the sound contact was a good one. The *Selfridge* dropped depth charges set to explode at 50-, 100-, and 150-foot depths. All the charges detonated, but without positive results. Any German U-boat that had been prowling the area had eluded the *Selfridge*.

Before making a second pass over the target, the *Selfridge* was ordered by Portland Harbor Entrance Control Post (HECP) to break off the attack and pick up additional *Eagle 56* survivors and bodies.

Harold Petersen was still in the water, barely conscious, his frozen arms hugging a rope from the USS *Nantucket*, which had arrived at the scene moments after the *Selfridge*. He didn't believe he could last much longer; another three or four minutes and he would freeze to death. Petersen had helped Bill Thompson and other *Eagle* survivors aboard the *Selfridge*'s whaleboat, but there was no room in the boat for him. Petersen signaled that he could wait for the return trip, but then watched in despair as the *Selfridge* turned away. Were they leaving him? Perhaps worse, as the destroyer churned the water in front of him, Petersen feared that either her propellers would chew him up or he would be sucked under in her wake. Neither happened, though, and Petersen saw with relief that the *Nantucket*, which had slipped into the position vacated by the *Selfridge*, had tossed him a line. He had a momentary flash of panic once again, however, when his frozen fingers couldn't grasp the slick, stiff rope. Petersen flailed at the rescue line, slapped at it, but it seemed to wiggle away from him like a snake. Finally, he maneuvered the piece of shoring into a position that enabled him to lunge at the rope and catch it under his armpits in a death-grip. Now that he had it, Petersen would never let go.

He felt himself being dragged through the water, swallowing what seemed like a gallon of the salty Atlantic along the way, the *Nantucket* growing larger through his watery vision. When he reached the *Nantucket* and they hoisted him out of the water, Petersen felt a sense of warmth wash over him, a reassuring calm that he would never forget. The easy physical explanation was that the air temperature was warmer than the bitterly cold water; but for Petersen, there was almost a spiritual quality to the feeling that would be ingrained in his sensory memory even sixty years later.

They got him onto the ship, lowered him to the deck, and began cutting the stiff wet clothing from his body, tearing it away from his skin in near-frozen strips. A groggy Harold Petersen heard voices through his dream-like haze, men urging him to hang on, just before he passed out.

His entire body shivering violently and uncontrollably, John Scagnelli coughed and spat up the whiskey that the *Selfridge* medical team was trying to pour down his throat. He was surrounded by sailors and hands seemed to be all over him—bandaging his wounded scalp, holding his chin steady so he could drink the whiskey, piling blankets on top of his freezing body. His exhaustion was total; he remembered his weariness as he left the *Selfridge* whaleboat moments ago and began to climb the cargo net draped over the ship's side. The deck seemed miles above him, the net fraught with peril, his body unable to reach the top without assistance. The crew had finally dragged him onto the deck and rushed him below for treatment.

Grateful to be out of the water and aboard a rescue ship, Scagnelli now wished he could stop shaking.

As they carried him, naked but covered with blankets, on a stretcher through the *Selfridge*'s wardroom, Johnny Breeze heard Oscar Davis's voice and once again was reminded of his friend's ability to make him laugh, even in the most difficult of circumstances. For as long as Breeze knew him, Davis had a finicky shoulder joint that would cause his arm to dislodge completely from the shoulder socket. On several occasions, Breeze had watched in disbelief as Davis's shoulder became dislocated, and Davis would grab his arm just above the elbow, lift it parallel with his shoulder, and jam it back into the socket.

Now, Davis sat naked on the wardroom table, the ship's doctor examining him closely. Breeze heard the doctor say to Oscar, "There is something wrong with your arm, son," unaware that Davis's shoulder injury predated the *Eagle 56* explosion. Oscar Davis, who had just spent twenty minutes submerged in the 38-degree water, looked down at his crotch, noticed the "shrinkage factor," and said, "To hell with my arm, Doc—there's something wrong with my cock!"

Breeze smiled and closed his eyes, Oscar's laughter ringing in his ears, thankful that his friend was safe.

Aboard the *Nantucket*, Harold Petersen awakened to see an officer hovering above him, checking on his condition. The officer sported a black eye, pointed to it, and said to Petersen: "Here's the thanks I get for trying to help you out!" A puzzled Petersen had no idea what the man was talking about, and said so. "We were holding you down giving you morphine," the officer explained, "and then we went to give you some medicinal whiskey. You said, 'No thanks, I don't drink.' We tried to force it down your throat and you fought violently, and you took a swing at me—gave me this shiner."

Petersen smiled and wondered what his *Eagle* shipmates, especially the ones who called him St. Pete, would say when they heard this story.

The *Nantucket* steamed toward Portland with Harold Petersen as its only *Eagle 56* survivor. The *Selfridge* carried twelve survivors, and the only two bodies of crewmen that were recovered from the wreckage-strewn, oil-slicked water: Machinist Mate 1st Class George W. Neugen and Seaman 2nd Class Paul J. Knapp. The bodies of five officers and forty-two enlisted men went down to the bottom with the wreckage of the *PE-56*. As they returned to South Portland for transfer to the U.S. Naval Dispensary at Grand Trunk Pier, most of the thirteen *Eagle 56* survivors were given morphine, plasma, and warm blankets. *Selfridge* crewman Edwin Walker recounted: "After picking up survivors, our ships rushed to dock . . . where [they] were taken off to hospitals. I looked down into the faces of the survivors as they were carried off in stretchers; shocked, wounded, just hardly alive, frozen, miserable."

It would be weeks before the *Eagle 56* survivors, who had escaped death by perhaps mere minutes, learned that the loss of forty-nine of their fellow officers and crewmen was among the greatest U.S. naval tragedies within American coastal waters, and was the worst loss in New England waters during the war. But only three of the Lucky Thirteen would ever know that the *Eagle 56*'s story would become part of an unprecedented decision in naval history, and that its final chapter would not be written until a new century dawned.

17

Within hours of the *Eagle*'s sinking, the waters off Casco Bay and Cape Elizabeth were being swept by a fleet of naval vessels, including the *Selfridge*, which had returned to the scene, and destroyers USS *Craven*, USS *Woolsey*, and USS *Earle*, the destroyer escort USS *Evarts*, and the Coast Guard-manned patrol frigate, the USS *Brunswick*. They were assisted by the USS *Eberle*, USS *Muskegon*, USS *Rinehart*, USS *Uniontown*, and the USS *Wingfield*. They conducted anti-submarine warfare operations well into the late evening, joined by aircraft from the Brunswick Naval Air Station. The *Craven*'s war diary for the day reported starkly: "Eagle boat exploded and sank in the area today. Cause undetermined, may have been enemy submarine."

By this time, however, the *U-853* had already crept off into the relative safety of deeper waters, submerged on her electric motors and concealed by the area's rough-bottom topography, far from shore.

Phyllis Westerlund reread the telegram the messenger had delivered, convinced the Navy had made a mistake. The message said her husband Ivar was missing in action, but Phyllis knew that was impossible. He was with her last night! He had left her in the wee hours to catch his bus to Portland in time to board the *Eagle 56* before she sailed.

Ivar's brother, Ralph, was a career man stationed in the Pacific. Perhaps the telegram was intended for his family, Phyllis thought. Or maybe Ivar had missed the *Eagle 56*'s departure. Perhaps the bus had broken down? Maybe he was AWOL? Would being AWOL mean he was missing?

How could Ivar be missing?

How could the Navy have *lost* him?

He was with her last night.

April 24, 1945
Portland, Maine
Morning

Ginny Laubach, in shock, heard her brother's voice intermingled with the crackle of the telephone line over the miles between Portland and Baltimore. Years later she would tell John Barr's daughter, Peggy, that she remembered her brother's words clearly: "Hold on, Ginny, it might be a mistake," she heard him say. "Stay right there; I'm coming up."

She loved her brother for his comforting words, but she knew in her heart that it was not a mistake. Her Jack was gone. He had kissed her before the *Eagle 56* sailed, and told her, as he always had, not to worry, that he'd be coming back. She believed him every time because they had *always* been together; best friends since they were six years old, high school sweethearts, husband and wife for the past seven years, and future plans as big as the ocean itself.

But Jack was not coming back and she knew it. She knew, too, as she listened to her brother's voice breaking up over the phone line, her heart shattered, that for as long as she lived, she would never get over losing the love of her life.

The officer obviously had a first name, but Esta Glenn never knew it. She simply knew him as Captain Winel, the young Navy chaplain, the man about whom she would one day say was "the nicest person I ever knew." He had a soft voice, a kind face, and Esta trusted him immediately.

It was why, sitting with him now, she felt no self-consciousness about crying, no reluctance to hide her sobs or her tears; her world had fallen apart, she was 3,500 miles from home, and she felt completely alone. Captain Winel's presence offered her a little reassurance.

She knew he would have bad news. When her boss, Mr. Cushman, met her at the bakery early this morning, and told her they wanted to see her at the chaplain's office, she knew something terrible had happened. You didn't go to the chaplain's office to get good news. Cushman said he was unaware *why* she was being summoned, but she had suspected from the start that he was trying to spare her.

Captain Winel had spoken slowly and softly. There had been an explosion aboard the *Eagle 56*, and only thirteen men had survived.

Before he could proceed, Esta asked him point-blank: "And Glenn wasn't one of them?"

"No, I'm afraid not. I'm sorry," Captain Winel had replied.

Esta found it difficult to describe her exact emotions at that moment. A million images and thoughts raced through her mind in the most jumbled, convoluted way; her whole world seemed to fall apart instantly. She imagined she were in a dream. And then she had asked herself why. Why Glenn? Why her? Why now? And right after that, the coldness of being totally alone coursed through her like an electric charge. What would she do now? What *should* she do? The sobs wracked her then, the tears falling freely. Captain Winel simply waited silently.

After a few moments, the chaplain told Esta that the Navy would pay to send her home, and she could leave today.

"I'm not going home yet," she said to Captain Winel.

"Why not?"

"Maybe they'll recover the bodies," Esta replied. "I want to see Glenn again."

Captain Winel said Esta could stay in Portland as long as she liked, but in that same soft voice, also informed her of the reality she needed to accept: the body of Harold Glenn—her dear Glenn—and the rest of the poor men killed aboard the *Eagle 56* were lost at the bottom of the Atlantic Ocean.

18

The day after the *Eagle 56* exploded, the waters off the coast of Maine were teeming with ships conducting anti-submarine patrols, and they were assisted by patrol-bomber aircraft from the Brunswick Naval Air Station. USS *Muskegon*, USS *Earle*, USS *Eberle*, USS *Uniontown*, and the U.S. Coast Guard Cutter 92004 were hunting the U-boat off Monhegan Island, approximately fifty miles East-Northeast of Portland, when the Coast Guard cutter reported: "110 degrees magnetic, very likely submarine contact. Watch reports sub blew tanks."

The cutter's report seemed to confirm what the ship commanders and crews in the area had suspected when they watched the geyser of water spew from the exploding *Eagle*: a U-boat was patrolling the coast of Maine searching for American targets. Berlin was falling, the Third Reich was crumbling, but German U-boats continued their last desperate patrols in U.S. waters.

The search continued into the early afternoon, when, at just past 3:00 P.M., the USS *Muskegon*, part of the same patrol group, reported: "Sighted smoke on surface from no visible source . . . all hands to General Quarters . . . presumed to be enemy submarine using *schnorchel* (snorkel) . . . proceeding to investigate." Again, the patrol group could not locate the U-boat, but U.S. ships hunted into the evening and early hours of the morning of Wednesday, April 25, 1945, when at 3:50 A.M., the Coast Guard cutter reported: "Sub contact. Can hear electric motors and blow of tanks." The contact was lost, but nine hours later, according to historian Paul Lawton, at 12:50 P.M. on the 25th, the *Muskegon* reported that a sound contact at 72 fathoms (about 430 feet) at the mouth of Penobscot Bay was "classified as possible bottomed submarine" with "strong echoes." The *Muskegon* fired a full complement of Hedgehog depth charges with negative results. But, as she chased the contact further, she blew a gasket on a steam line to the galley and had to discontinue the search to make repairs. The *Earle* and *Eberle* maneuvered in the area and made several subsequent depth-charge attacks, and the *Muskegon* returned to the search after she completed repairs. The warships formed a scouting line at 2,500-yard intervals and swept the vicinity several times without regaining any good sonar contacts. In addition, a U.S. Navy blimp was dispatched to the area from the Naval Air Station in South Weymouth, Massachusetts, but her airborne magnetic anomaly detection (MAD) gear malfunctioned, and unable to acquire a contact, she returned to her base.

On Thursday, April 26, 1945, an air patrol squadron from Quonset Point, Rhode Island, Naval Air Station, flying anti-submarine patrol over the Gulf of Maine, picked up a blip on the radar screen at about 3:00 P.M. "The radar said there was a submarine sitting on top of the water about 40 miles away charging their batteries," said air crewman William Heckendorf. "We homed in on it and saw the oil slick on the water where it had been sitting. We dropped our sonar gear and picked up the sound of a submarine's engine. We pinpointed the sub and dropped two 500-pound depth charges. About five minutes later the ocean was full of debris and oil." Paul Lawton speculated: "It is possible that the U-boat attacked by the airboat was the one that torpedoed and sank the *Eagle 56*. It was a common ploy for U-boat commanders to discharge oil and fire debris out of their torpedo tubes to confuse attackers into believing they had destroyed the prey, thereby ending the attack."

If that was the case, Commander Froemsdorf's ploy was successful. The *U-853* was still at large and dangerous.

None of the patrol-group ships knew it, but Commander Kenneth Knowles and the F-21 U-boat Secret Room were also tracking the *U-853* through the Gulf of Maine. On April 24, it evaluated as "possible" the Coast Guard cutter's report of a U-boat contact near Monhegan Island. In an April 25, 1945, Secret Dispatch numbered 251515 to the

Commander of the Eastern Sea Frontier, Knowles drafted a message that, in part, stated: "one [U-boat] possibly 3600 6930 moving West to SW from radar contact 250153Z alternatively Gulf of Maine from PE incident." Three days later, on April 28, another secret COMINCH dispatch added: "one [U-boat] possibly . . . in Gulf of Maine from attack 271438Z (PE incident)."

At some point, probably after April 27, the *U-853* departed the Gulf of Maine and slowly headed south past Cape Cod and into Rhode Island Sound, according to Paul Lawton. For security reasons, however, the highly classified information from the Secret Room—about the presence of the *U-853* in the area of the *Eagle 56* sinking—would not be shared by the Office of Naval Intelligence with the Court of Inquiry investigating the loss of the *Eagle* and the death of forty-nine of her officers and crew members.

19

"Marissa operator, hang up! Hang up!" The sharp words were spoken by the Portland telephone operator to the operator in Marissa, Illinois, who was listening in on the small town's party line while Esta Glenn was trying to talk to Ira Glenn, Harold's father. Esta pictured the hard-of-hearing and stoic Ira on the other end of the line, holding the receiver of the old crank phone, straining to hear Esta's voice through the interference. Again, the Portland operator shouted: "Marissa operator, hang up!" And finally, Esta heard the loud click as the Marissa operator finally *did* hang up and the connection cleared, and Esta delivered the news to her father-in-law of his son's death. Ira, apparently in shock and perhaps still having difficulty hearing, simply said: "I'll get Mom." Seconds later, Harold's mother Nina was on the phone, and the wail she emitted after hearing of her son's death chilled Esta to the bone.

The Glenns' pain was magnified by the fact that Harold was the second son Ira and Nina Glenn had lost in this terrible war. In May of 1944, shortly before the D-Day invasion, another son, Harold's brother, Orville, a B-17 belly-gunner, was shot down over France. The crew's remains were never found, which meant that Ira and Nina Glenn had now lost two sons by violent means and would never know the comfort of seeing their bodies one last time.

Esta was grateful that she could finally contact her in-laws. For the first full day after the attack, she was ordered not to make any calls; the Navy wanted to contact the next of kin of each lost *PE-56* crew member before word began to spread informally. She also had a chance to visit the survivors in sick bay, though she technically wasn't supposed to be there since she wasn't related to any of the Lucky Thirteen. It didn't matter. She knew those fellows like brothers, especially Breeze and Pete Petersen, but Luttrell and Scagnelli, too. Alice Petersen, who had returned to Henrietta, New York, last weekend, returned to Portland immediately when she heard the news, and the two of them walked in to the sick bay together. "I wasn't supposed to go, but I needed to see them, to see Pete and the others, just to see them and make sure they were *really* there," she would say many years later.

They were there, all of them a little tired, a few of them banged up—Scagnelli's head still swathed in bandages, Petersen's back and hip injured—but otherwise in decent shape. They were so bored that Pete and Breeze had even taken the time to paint the head, its flaking walls in desperate need of a fresh coat, but there was no sign that they were leaving anytime soon. Outside contact was also restricted; Esta had been lucky to get in when she explained to the sympathetic guard that she was an "*Eagle* widow" and best friends with Alice Petersen. The fellows were talking amongst themselves about the cause of the sinking, and almost all of them said it was a torpedo; a bunch of the men had seen a submarine.

Visiting with the survivors comforted and pained her at the same time. They were safe and that was good, but Glenn's absence seemed *unnatural* in some way; Glenn belonged with those boys almost as much as he belonged with her. Plus, many of the other crew members whom she loved—"Mike" Michelsen and Jonesy, to name two—had gone down with the ship and were no longer a part of the *Eagle* family. In fact, she knew that the family would never again be the same, and she wondered how any of them would survive the loss. Ginny Laubach said she felt like dying each time she thought about the permanency of her separation from Jack. Esta had spent time over the last two days with a pregnant Pauline Michelsen, less than four months from giving birth, distraught about who would care for her and her child—Mike's child—now that her husband had died.

Before Esta concluded her phone calls with the Glenns in Marissa, Illinois, she had made arrangements for Harold's sister, Helen, to travel to Portland to be with her; she planned to stay in Maine for a few more days. Then she would return with Helen to Marissa and visit for a few weeks before returning home to San Diego.

They were short-term plans, but reassuring to her. Thinking about the next few days or weeks, concentrating on the mundane and the routine, this was the only way she could cope with her loss, the only way to get through the day without Glenn. When she let her thoughts get ahead of her, when she wondered what would *become* of her, an overwhelming loneliness gripped her like a hand squeezing her heart.

She and Glenn had shared such deep love, such big plans, had looked toward a glorious future ahead of them. The very last contact they had was a kiss on the front steps of their apartment building while the bus waited to take him to the docks. And now he was gone forever. This wasn't how it was supposed to happen—not at all.

Brockton, Massachusetts

In the late afternoon of April 25, Phyllis Westerlund sat motionless in her living room, wondering how she would find the money in September to buy school clothes for her older children. She was fully aware of how odd it was that she was thinking of such a subject, but she recognized that she was in shock at some level, some sort of dream-state that had fogged her mind since the Navy chaplain's visit earlier in the day.

The gentle man had confirmed what she had refused to let herself believe two days earlier: Ivar was dead. The *Eagle 56* had exploded and her husband had been killed. The chaplain urged her to take some solace from knowing that Ivar likely had been asleep in his bunk when the blast occurred, and had died "a beautiful death" by drowning without ever waking up. The chaplain's words did not register at first. She pleaded with him, *implored* him to understand how implausible his message was; she had dropped Ivar in downtown Brockton *that same day* and he had run up Main Street to chase the bus to Portland so he wouldn't be caught AWOL. Didn't the chaplain see how unbelievable it was for Ivar to be dead now? How impossible it seemed?

The chaplain had agreed with her, commenting on the mysteriousness of God's hand, blessed her, and walked out the front door moments later. Alone, she felt like she was losing her mind, could hardly believe the chaplain had even *been* in her house. She sat very still and cried for a while, then went and broke the news to her children. She told them that Daddy had gone to heaven because she couldn't think of anything else to say.

Then grief and fear seemed to engulf her. She was penniless with four children and had no idea what she was going to do. That's when she started to think about the school clothes—when you had no money, you couldn't buy clothes. The chaplain promised her that, as a war widow, she would receive some government money to help support the children, but it would take a few months to process the paperwork. September was a few months away. Would the money arrive in time? How much would it be? How would she survive in the meantime?

In the midst of these questions gnawing at her, she was struck by the aching irony that she and Ivar had always solved these kinds of problems together. Now, shocked, destitute, and unbearably lonely, she had no idea how she was going to manage on her own.

20

In a memorandum dated April 23, 1945—the day the *Eagle* went down—U.S. Navy Rear Admiral Felix Gygax, commandant of the First Naval District and Navy Yard in Boston, ordered Portland base commander Ernest J. Freeman to convene a Court of Inquiry (COI) "to inquire into all the circumstances connected with the loss of the USS *Eagle (PE-56)* off Portland Harbor."

Gygax's order stipulated that the COI should consist of Freeman as president, Lieutenant Commander William Coolidge and Lieutenant Commander Jackson Heire as members, and Lieutenant Commander Norman Kaufmann as judge advocate. "The court will make a thorough investigation into all the circumstances connected with the [*Eagle*] loss, the causes thereof, damages to property resulting therefrom, injuries to personnel incidental thereto, and the responsibility therefor," [sic] Gygax wrote. "The court will include in its findings a full statement of the facts . . . [and] will further give its opinion as to whether any offenses have been committed or serious blame incurred, and, in case its opinion be that offenses have been committed or serious blame incurred, will specifically recommend what further proceedings should be had."

Amid the formal legalistic language, Gygax's memo does not address—nor does any other surviving historical document—the apparent conflict inherent in appointing the Portland commander as president of the COI to investigate the shocking broad-daylight loss of an American warship, essentially on his watch, a scant few miles from the base for which he was responsible.

Gygax's order called for the COI to convene on April 24, or "as soon thereafter as practicable," which turned out to be Thursday, April 26. The COI was not conducted in the traditional manner, where witnesses were examined in a courtroom before the standard tribunal, but in an informal way while the *Eagle 56* survivors were still in the Grand Trunk Naval Dispensary. Scagnelli recalled being "confined to bed and still in my hospital clothes" when the COI questioned him, while Mary Alice Heyd, twenty-one-year-old Navy WAVE and legal yeoman and stenographer, took shorthand notes of his testimony. The Lucky Thirteen had been kept isolated in sick bay since their rescue, and several said suggestions had been made by unidentified Portland naval brass that "there was no submarine" and "you did not see a submarine" before being questioned by the COI.

"They had already prejudged that it was going to be a boiler explosion," Scagnelli said. "Some of our guys were saying, 'Impossible—we saw the goddamn sub.'" Johnny Breeze's buddy, Oscar Davis, maintained for years afterward that he had been pressured into recanting his account of seeing the U-boat. And a half-century after she had recorded the COI proceedings, Mary Alice (Heyd) Hultgren recounted how she was convinced by the survivors' testimony that they had been the victims of a U-boat torpedo attack.

If there was pressure applied to the *Eagle* survivors before the official COI, it was unsuccessful. Six of the Lucky Thirteen, including Davis, would testify that they had seen a submarine (Breeze was not asked), and the rest—including Scagnelli and Petersen—said they were convinced the explosion was caused by an external force. Still, the line of questioning from the three-member COI focused quickly and continually on the possibility and plausibility of a boiler explosion, despite Scagnelli's early testimony that "all engines and boilers were in good condition and recently had been overhauled . . ."

Also conspicuously absent from the COI proceedings were the deck officers and SONARmen of the USS *Selfridge*. "They stacked the deck with that Court of Inquiry," Scagnelli would say later. "It was an embarrassment to the Navy, allowing an enemy warship to get in so close, to almost penetrate the inner harbor of Maine. People would have asked, 'Where were your surveillance ships?' Secondly, I think they didn't want people to know U-boats were still operating so close to our shores—hell, people believed the war with Germany was almost over, and it turns out it was! Here's the other thing: Supposedly one of the members of that Court of Inquiry was an engineering officer. How much experience did he have on board ships? Did he understand the workings of boilers? Did he know that it would take *ten boilers*—all exploding at the same time— to even begin to do the damage that was done to our ship?"

The Court of Inquiry convened at 10:40 A.M. on April 26, and Scagnelli was the first witness sworn in by Judge Advocate Norman Kaufmann. After establishing Scagnelli's duties and responsibilities aboard ship, as well as his ordeal trying to escape the doomed vessel after the explosion, court officials quickly homed in on the "boiler-explosion" theory with their questions:

> Q. Could you tell from the sound of the explosion whether it appeared to be an explosion of something inside or outside the ship?
> A. I felt as if it was a force from outside the ship . . . It was very similar to a depth-charge explosion.
> Q. You have seen depth charges explode?
> A. Yes, we have dropped numerous depth charges on numerous occasions.
> Q. Have you ever seen a steam boiler or engine explode?
> A. No, I have not.
> Q. What safety appliances are on the boiler to prevent explosions?
> A. Duplex safety valves.
> Q. What type of boilers?
> A. Water tube express type—3 drum.
> Q. How many in operation?
> A. Two.

And then later, questioning focused on the qualifications of the Black Gang that worked for Scagnelli:

Q. Could you tell us what personnel was in the boiler room
during the morning and comment as to your opinion of
qualifications and efficiency?

A. In the engine room we had a machinist mate first class, Fredrick
Michelsen, Earle Young, machinist mate second class, Ralph
Woods, machinist mate second class. In the fire room [boiler
room] John Gonzales, water tender second class, Norris Jones,
fireman first class, and Maurice Manning, water tender third class.
All of those men are competent men. They had been trained and
drilled in their jobs and also in casualty water if there was any
accident that happened. Below, I believe they would have taken
steps to correct the casualty.

And a short time later:

Q. Have you had any flarebacks on these boilers from time to
time?

A. No, sir.

Q. Do you feel that flareback may result in damage of the boilers?

A. Yes, if it is strong enough, [it] instantaneously will cause the boiler
brickwork to fall out and cause injury to the personnel.

Q. Could the flareback sever the two water drums or water tubes
from the drum to the top header?

A. I don't believe so.

Q. In most cases a flareback would never cause an explosion of
this type?

A. No sir.

Court questioners, who did not pursue with Scagnelli the possibility
of a German U-boat having been in the area, used their time before a
lunch break and immediately after to continue their relentless focus on
the *Eagle*'s boilers, despite Scagnelli's precise answers and clear skepticism at the line of questioning:

Q. What would happen if the water level [in the boiler] was low and
the water tender noticed it was low and introduced cold water?

A. If you already had water in the steam and you eject cold water you
would get a violent action of water and it might be an additional

strain on the steam drub, but it wouldn't cause the explosion, because you already have water in the drum.

Q. Don't you feel that is a thing that may result in serious damage?

A. Yes, if it was due to cold water. [But] since we do have a cold water feeder on the ship and the water is carefully checked to see that it is heated to the proper temperature before being admitted into the boiler, I feel that there would be no chance of any serious accident.

Q. From your experience with steam vessels, do you think that the explosion could have occurred from a boiler explosion?

A. On that small ship and [with] the extent of the damage, I don't think it could have.

Scagnelli was warned not to share his testimony with any other *Eagle 56* survivors, and was dismissed by the court. He left believing he had dispelled the COI of any notion that the *Eagle* had been destroyed by a faulty boiler.

The court questioned two other crew members on Day 1: Bill Thompson, whom Harold Petersen had implored to hang on while they floated in the water, and Oscar Davis, who had been working a crossword puzzle with Johnny Breeze when the *Eagle* exploded.

Thompson was asked if he had "anything to do with the amount of water in the boiler," and replied: "Yes. I always kept the water half full in the boiler." Beyond that, the court asked him a few routine questions about his job on board ship, and his escape from the stern section, but did not pursue a potential cause of the explosion.

With Davis, however, the story was different:

Q. From where did you jump off the ship?

A. I went to the top of the aft deckhouse. Then it was sinking and [the water was] over the aft deckhouse. The water was past my knees when I left the ship.

Q. Did you see any other ship in the water near you?

A. When I got to the top of the deckhouse, I went up and two life rings were there and I tried to get one to take it over the side. Someone said, 'There's a submarine.' I looked over the starboard side and there was a sub.

Q. Did you notice at the same time you noticed the submarine the other half of the *Eagle*?

A. No, sir. I would swear it couldn't be the other part of the bow of the ship. When I was in the water I went straight over the port side and I could see the 56 right straight on. The 56 was on the port side.

Q. You did not observe the submarine at the same time you observed the bow of the ship?

A. No, sir. We just took one look at the sub.

Q. Where was the submarine?

A. Just aft of the starboard beam about midway.

Q. Was there anything about the explosion in this case that would make you believe it was caused by a boiler or engine blowing up?

A. I think it sounded like a depth charge. That was [what] I thought it was when I first heard the explosion.

April 27, 1945
Court of Inquiry—Day 2

The drama of Davis's testimony that ended Day 1 did not immediately carry over to the second day of the court's deliberations. Harold Petersen and Johnny Breeze led off the second day with relatively uneventful accounts. Petersen emphasized that everything in the engine room was "operating normally" when he left the watch, and later described seeing many dead fish when he jumped into the water, indicating the concussive presence of an underwater explosion—perhaps caused by the detonation of a mine, depth-charge, or torpedo. Petersen also testified that he heard one fellow say, "There's a submarine." When Petersen glanced quickly he saw only the bow of the *Eagle*, then heard his shipmate reply: "Over further." Petersen added: "But I didn't wait to look as the ship was going down pretty fast, so I jumped." For his part, Breeze testified when asked that the blast that rocked the *Eagle* was "much more forceful" than a depth-charge explosion.

It wasn't until the court questioned *Eagle 56* Seaman 1st Class Daniel E. Jaronik that it elicited important new testimony that would prove even more revealing than Oscar Davis's account—though the Court of Inquiry would not realize it. Jaronik pointed out that shipmate Lawrence Edwards had pointed to a submarine off the *Eagle*'s fantail.

Q. The object that you saw, could that have been the bow of the ship [*Eagle 56*]?

A. No, sir.

Q. How did you determine it was not the bow of the ship?

A. I looked at it for a couple of seconds. Edwards said it was a submarine and I looked . . . It was all black and I could see red and yellow markings on it.

Q. Were there any red or yellow markings on the USS *Eagle*?

A. No, sir.

Q. Was there yellow paint on the deck of the USS *Eagle*?

A. No, sir.

Jaronik's testimony must have puzzled the Court of Inquiry. At the time of the *Eagle 56* sinking, the Navy knew that Germany's long-range Type IXC/40 snorkel-fitted U-boats were, in fact, painted all black. Yet, no American—not the COI, not the Office of Naval Intelligence (ONI), not even Ken Knowles or his Secret Room colleagues—had any way of knowing that one particular U-boat, the *U-853*, bore a red-and-yellow conning tower insignia of a trotting horse and shield, a symbol of her crew's pride and defiance.

Daniel Jaronik had seen something that no American knew to be true about the *U-853*. It would be another two weeks before Jaronik's testimony would be borne out by other sources. Unfortunately, the Court of Inquiry would issue its ruling in just five more days.

21

Six days after the *Eagle* had exploded and sunk—and one day after Kenneth Knowles had transmitted another Secret Dispatch warning of a U-boat leaving the Gulf of Maine—a U.S. Navy Hellcat fighter plane on a training flight from Charlestown, Rhode Island, sighted a submarine briefly surfaced approximately ten miles east of Wellfleet, Cape Cod. A number of U.S. Navy and Coast Guard warships pursued the sub, apparently the *U-853*, now heading south after departing the Gulf of Maine.

The chase was unsuccessful. Once again, Froemsdorf and the "Tightrope Dancer" had eluded their pursuers.

Portland, Maine

After three consecutive days of questioning witnesses, the Court of Inquiry members investigating the sinking of the *Eagle 56* had much to contemplate during their Sunday, April 29, recess—whether they chose to is a matter lost to history.

There were the words of crew member Lawrence Edwards, who said he saw an object five- or six hundred yards away from the *Eagle* that he was "almost sure" was a submarine. "It seemed like a submarine surfaced," he said. "It was in the swell and it was sort of lifted." Edwards also dispelled the notion that a depth charge could have discharged accidentally. "They [depth charges] were all right that morning, with the safety valves set," he said. "It was almost impossible for them to go off." Then the court asked Edwards: "Could this object you saw have been the other half of the ship?" Edwards replied: "I don't think so. I saw the bow of the ship and it was sticking up at that time. The bow was painted blue."

Even more precise was the testimony of Radioman 3rd Class John Wisniewski, who said: "I saw the submarine on the starboard bow [at] roughly speaking about 500 yards [away]." Wisniewski clearly told the court that he saw the sub and the *Eagle*'s bow simultaneously. "Yes, sir. [When he saw the sub] I didn't think it [the bow] was more than 100 feet away, sir." Further, Wisniewski said he had witnessed a boiler explosion in the past, and that the *Eagle*'s explosion in no way resembled such a blast. "When I saw the boiler explode I saw a lot of steam and it is a different sound." Wisniewski said.

Machinist Mate 3rd Class Cletus Frane didn't see a sub, but offered his unwavering opinion on the nature of the explosion: "I don't think a boiler would spread [sic] the ship in two." When the court asked the follow-up question, "No explosion in the boiler or engine compartment would have given you that?" Frane responded: "No sir." *Eagle* crewman Joseph Priestas also discounted a boiler as the cause of the explosion, saying, "I don't think it had enough pressure to cause that much damage."

And most recently, it was the Saturday testimony of the USS *Nantucket* commander, Coast Guard Lieutenant Guy V. Emro, who witnessed the explosion, claiming it was notable for "the immense amount of water in the air [which] I judged to be about 250 or 300 feet high." Emro was then asked several follow-up questions on the potential cause of the explosion:

Q. Did the explosion appear to come from within or without the ship?

A. The explosion must have come from without due to the immense amount of water and parts of the ship lifted into the air.

Q. Have you ever observed a depth charge exploded?

A. I have observed depth charges and also army mines discharge. No explosion I have ever seen equaled the force and the amount of water and debris lifted by this explosion.

Q. Have you ever witnessed a boiler or engine room explosion?

A. I have witnessed a boiler blow-out—the water tube type of boiler . . . but that explosion could be compared in no way to the power displayed in this one.

Emro's strong testimony was noteworthy for several reasons: first, unlike the *Eagle* survivors, he was not scrambling to escape a doomed ship and could thus provide a more detached description of events; second, he dismissed either a mine or a depth charge as the cause of the explosion, saying that this explosion was more thunderous than any he had ever seen; and third, like Wisniewski, he too had seen a boiler explode, and Emro was even more emphatic about the fact that the blast that broke the *Eagle* in half was *far more powerful*.

Emro was two and a half miles away from the *Eagle* when she exploded, and thus, of course, never saw a submarine. He also never declared his opinion that a torpedo had shattered the *Eagle*, but his testimony eliminated virtually anything else. Had the Court of Inquiry members asked him to *speculate* on a potential cause of the explosion, which they did not do, it is hard to imagine that Emro would have cited anything other than a torpedo from a German U-boat.

22

With the Third Reich in its death throes, Berlin resembled the entrance to Hell during the final days of April 1945. As Adolf Hitler descended deeper into paranoia and madness inside his bunker thirty-three feet beneath the floor of the Reich Chancellery, where he was ensconced with his girlfriend Eva Braun and many members of his inner circle, death and violence raged across the city. Conquering Russian tanks rumbled through the crumbling city, and Russian shells made the bunker ceiling "tremble," according to historian Michael Beschloss. Hitler's SS and Brownshirt execution squads tore through Berlin with increased urgency and bloodlust; these roving squads "entered houses where white flags had appeared and shot down any men they found." Hitler had spread the word that "traitors" should not be spared, even at this late date, and he spat that term most vociferously in the direction of German citizens intending on surrendering to Russian forces.

Meanwhile, Russian shells and Allied bombs had killed thousands more, and Russian troops—in gruesome payback for the Nazis' invasion of the Motherland, the destruction of her cities, and the mass starvation of her citizens—executed civilians, and raped and violated German women in many quarters of Berlin. "The smell of decomposing corpses spread from the piles of rubble which had been buildings, and the smell of charred flesh from the blackened skeletons of burnt-out houses," wrote author Antony Beevor. German historian Joachim Fest credited Harry Hopkins, adviser to Roosevelt and Truman, with an accurate comparison "when he drew on an image from the dawn of history" to describe the scene, "comparing the sea of ruins that was Berlin to the destruction of Carthage."

Inside the bunker, Hitler's loyal secretary Martin Bormann wrote in his diary on April 29, "The second day which has started with a hurricane of fire." Hitler had received word that Italian partisans had shot Benito Mussolini one day earlier and dumped his body in Piazza Loreto in Milano. "After several women had squatted over the dead *Duce* and lifted their skirts to urinate in his face, the mob hanged him by his heels," historian David Kennedy recounted. On April 29, German forces in Italy surrendered. Then, Hitler received word from Reuters news agency that *Reichsführer*-SS Heinrich Himmler had attempted to negotiate a separate surrender with the Allies, even to the point of implementing an unconditional surrender. "The news hit Hitler like a thunderbolt," Fest wrote. "Himmler's betrayal signified the collapse of a world. After all, Himmler had constantly talked of loyalty and had invoked it as the highest principle . . ." One woman in the bunker recounted: "Hitler raved like a madman. He turned a dark red and his face became almost unrecognizable."

It was likely at this point Hitler finally realized that all was lost and decided to bring things to an end. At midnight, with Bormann and Josef Göbbels as witnesses, a civil magistrate married Hitler and Eva Braun after they declared they were both of "pure Aryan descent and free of any hereditary diseases," Fest pointed out. After the marriage, he dictated his last will and testament, deciding to "choose death . . . of one's own free will" rather than to "fall into the hands of the enemy who needed a new spectacle, staged by Jews, for the amusement of their inflamed crowds."

Adolf Hitler named Fleet Commander Karl Dönitz to succeed him as head of state and supreme commander of the armed forces. Dönitz had remained loyal and above suspicion even as other Hitler supporters had evoked the Führer's mistrust. "Referring to a navy code of honor that ruled out any thought of surrender, he assigned Dönitz the task of carrying on the war even to his death, to the ultimate doom," Fest wrote.

The next afternoon, April 30, 1945, the newly married couple, Adolf and Eva Braun Hitler, committed suicide, Adolf by gunshot and Eva by poison. Their bodies were doused with gasoline and burned in the Reich Chancellery garden; Hitler, fearing his body would be exhibited like a trophy in Moscow, had issued instructions for its cremation. It was an ignoble end for the man who had visualized a glorious thousand-year reign for Germany and the Third Reich. "Hitler had visualized his burial atop the roof of the bell tower that was to dominate the banks of the Danube in Linz [Austria], his hometown," Fest wrote. "Instead he was buried behind the devastated Reich Chancellery in a wasteland of rubble, tamped into earth that had been plowed up by incessant bombardment, among chunks of blasted concrete and heaps of garbage."

Bormann sent a signal to Dönitz at his headquarters on the Baltic coast near Kiel, informing him of his appointment as Hitler's successor. "Written authority is on its way. You will immediately take all such measures as the situation requires," Bormann wrote.

Karl Dönitz, the father who had lost two sons in this war, the undisputed architect of the elite U-boat service, the leader whose bold, daring attacks on America in 1942 inspired his men to unflinching loyalty, the strategist who still hoped to alter the Allies' demands for "unconditional surrender" with a last desperate U-boat assault along the U.S. coast, had become, officially, Germany's last Führer.

April 30, 1945
The Secret Room
Washington, D.C.

With Berlin in shambles and the end of the war with Germany approaching, the ever security-conscious Kenneth Knowles believed the Tenth Fleet had to look to the future and make immediate provisions to bury Ultra intelligence secrets as deeply as possible.

In an April 30 memo entitled "Security of COMINCH (F-21) and Admiralty (OIC) Serials," sent to the Tenth Fleet's communications officer, with copies to the deputy commander in chief and the chief of staff for the anti-submarine division, Knowles outlined his concerns:

> Beginning in 1942 and continuing to the present time, there have
> been a series of dispatches enciphered in a special key between
> COMINCH (F-21) and Admiralty (OIC). In general, these dispatches
> refer to U/Boat Tracking and contain Ultra intelligence. They are
> classified, however, as "Secret" and bear the designation "No Distri-
> bution" so they would not be filed with other Top Secret dispatches

which are seen by a relatively large number of officers in COMINCH headquarters.

As these dispatches are now in the secret files . . . the information contained therein would be available to various officers and civilian historians who may examine these files following the defeat of Germany.

In order to protect sources of information, it is strongly recommended that these F-21 and OIC serials either be destroyed or their classification raised to "Ultra Top Secret" and turned over to O-20 for final custody. A complete file of these dispatches held by F-21 will be turned over to the Flag Secretary for final disposition upon the dissolution of this section.

Knowles would get his wish, and as a result, Ultra intelligence would remain Ultra Top Secret and classified for the next forty to fifty years. Even the presence of the U.S. and OIC Sub-Tracking operations was known only to a handful of officers and staff members, and the effectiveness of their work in the Battle of the Atlantic would remain largely overlooked until the mid-1980s. In a Top Secret postwar report dated January 1, 1946, written by Admiral Francis F. Low, who recruited Kenneth Knowles, Low stressed the crucial importance of Allied operational intelligence: "I do not believe that there is any other way around the fact that the single most important point which must be covered is the maintenance of a high degree of effective operational intelligence for use in combat. Combat intelligence multiplies our effective forces by factors which are impossible to achieve by simply building more units and training more men . . . The Battle of the Atlantic was, in large measure, a battle of wits in which intelligence played the major role. Unfortunately, this fact is fully understood only by a relatively small group of officers because of the highly classified nature of the subject."

As a result of this secrecy, the Court of Inquiry reviewing the sinking of the *Eagle 56* in 1945 never knew, of course, that Kenneth Knowles's group was actively tracking Dönitz's final U-boat patrols to America, including a specific U-boat, the *U-853*, through the Gulf of Maine. This vital nugget of information would have been impossible for the court to ignore—or at least consider—in its final report.

But because of Knowles's insistence that his team's records be reclassified to "Ultra Top Secret," the truth about the *Eagle 56* would remain buried in files for more than a half-century.

Karl Dönitz, Germany's new leader, was far from Berlin on his first days in office. He had relocated his headquarters—and the capital of the Reich—to the Naval Cadet School near Flensburg, at the far north of the Schleswig-Holstein peninsula, on the border of Denmark. At 9:30 P.M. on the night of May 1, he addressed the German nation in a radio broadcast and stated that Hitler had fallen "fighting at the head of his troops," and announced his succession. "The German people are bowed in reverence," Dönitz said. "He [Hitler] early recognized the danger of Bolshevism and dedicated his life to this struggle. At the end of this battle and of his undeviating straight life's path stands the heroic death in the capital city of the German people."

Very few people in Germany's once proud capital city of Berlin heard Dönitz's broadcast because of the lack of electric current. The city stood literally on the verge of collapse. "Flames in bombarded buildings cast strange shadows and a red glow on the otherwise dark streets," author Antony Beevor wrote. "The soot and dust in the air made it almost unbreathable. From time to time, there was the thunder of masonry collapsing. And to add to the terrifying effect, searchlight beams moved around above, searching a night sky in which the Luftwaffe had ceased to exist. Meanwhile, the last vestiges of the Third Reich in the city were coming to an end."

On the evening of May 1, General Helmuth Weidling, the commandant of the city of Berlin, ordered his troops to stop fighting the Russians to end the senseless bloodshed. In a message to his troops, he wrote: "The Führer committed suicide on April 30, 1945, thereby abandoning all those who swore loyalty to him . . . I am ordering an immediate halt to all resistance. Every hour you continue to fight prolongs the terrible suffering of Berlin's civilian population and of our wounded. By mutual agreement with the High Command of the Soviet Army, I order you to stop fighting immediately."

Inside Hitler's bunker, propaganda minister Josef Göbbels and his wife, Magda, had poisoned their six children earlier that evening. Magda and Hitler's personal doctor had opened the mouths of the sleeping children—who had been given morphine earlier—put an ampoule of hydrogen cyanide poison between their teeth, and forced their jaws together. "Only her oldest daughter, Helga [age 12], who in the last few days had been anxiously asking what would become of them all, appeared to have resisted," Fest wrote. "The bruises on the body . . . seemed to indicate that the poison was not administered without the use of force." Once the deed was done, Joseph and Magda then took poison and shot themselves. Their bodies were then doused in gasoline and set afire, igniting "the last funeral pyre of the Third Reich," in Beevor's words.

Nevertheless, on May 2, Dönitz—far removed from the catastrophic conditions in Berlin—dispatched a message to all military forces, including his U-boat commanders, that demanded their loyalty and continued resistance. The communiqué, which was intercepted by Kenneth Knowles's team in the United States sub-tracking room in Washington, D.C., read in part:

> My comrades! The Führer has fallen. True to his great purpose of saving the culture of Europe from Bolshevism, he dedicated his life and met a hero's death. In him, we have lost one of the greatest heroes of German history. In awe and grief, we lower the flag for him. The Führer designated me as his successor and Chief of State and Supreme Commander of the Armed Forces . . . I must continue the battle against the English and the Americans as long as they obstruct me in the prosecution of the battle against Bolshevism . . . I demand discipline and obedience . . . Only through the unconditional execution of my orders will chaos and ruin be avoided. [Any German military man] is a coward and a traitor who now shirks his duty and thereby brings death and slavery to German women and children . . . German soldiers, do your duty. The life of our people is at stake.

Yet, despite the bravado in his May 2 message, in the final hours of the Third Reich, Dönitz feverishly sought to accomplish two goals from his northern outpost headquarters: end the war against the Western Allies as soon as possible, while simultaneously saving as many German people as possible from the Soviets. "He sent every available naval and merchant vessel to the Baltic ports still in German hands, with orders to bring out every refugee he could," wrote authors Samuel Mitcham Jr. and Gene Mueller. "The troop units still fighting were ordered to cover the evacuation of the refugees and then escape to the west themselves. It has been estimated that two million civilians escaped Soviet captivity in the eight days that Dönitz prolonged hostilities."

Thus, in the first two days of May 1945, a bizarre contrast was playing out on land and under the sea. In Berlin and across Germany,

Hitler's fighting men were laying down their arms and German civilians were literally running for their lives to escape the dreaded Russians. Yet, thousands of miles away, German U-boats—including the *U-853*—were still prowling the East Coast of the United States, desperately looking for the final kills that could salvage a measure of pride and, perhaps, concessions for Germany in her final hours.

23

On the same day that Führer Dönitz issued his message to the German military, and eight days after the *Eagle 56* exploded, the Court of Inquiry in Portland ruled that a boiler explosion, "the cause of which could not be determined," sunk the *Eagle* and killed forty-nine of her crewmen. The court also found "that all equipment on the USS *Eagle 56* for combating magnetic mines was in operation at the time of the accident," that there was "no culpability on the part of any person in the Naval Service contributing in any way to the accident," and that each of the dead crew members died "in [the] line of duty and not due to his own misconduct . . . [but] not the result of enemy action." The Court issued its opinion after six days of testimony.

Judge Advocate Norman Kaufmann wrote the following opinion on behalf of the court:

> The only plausible conclusion that this court can logically reach is
> that the explosion in this case was in the boiler. All the characteristics
> of a boiler explosion were present. The shape of the column as testi-
> fied to by the eyewitnesses indicated an explosion emanating from a
> confined opening of a definite shape. The height of the column

would not have been as great had the blast come from a depth charge, a mine, or torpedo, a large part of the force in such cases being exerted downward and the hull of the ship breaking the force of the upward movement. The color and quick dissipation of the column showed a composition of steam and water.

There was no fire, smoke, flame, or flying debris such as would have been present had the ship been torpedoed. Had it been blown up by mine or depth charge the water would have been discolored and there would have been more dead fish on the surface. The presence of a submarine would have been detected. The most rational evaluation of the contact obtained by the *Selfridge* was that of a rock pinnacle and this is borne out by the lack of any positive evidence on the surface achieved by the pattern of eleven depth charges. No evidence has ever been discovered of enemy mine-laying operations in these waters despite continuous and comprehensive sweeping over a long period.

That was it—a short, two-paragraph argument that barely touched on the facts and testimony in the case. The Court of Inquiry simply *ignored* testimony from the survivors who saw a submarine or who swore the explosion could not have come from an internal source. It simply ignored extensive testimony from Scagnelli and the Black Gang members that the *Eagle*'s boilers had been completely overhauled just two weeks earlier, and that the boiler pressure could not have come close to reaching a danger point, particularly with the *Eagle* at a dead stop. And, the COI dismissed the *Selfridge* sound contact as emanating from a rocky pinnacle, despite the fact that the captain believed the contact was probable enough to *actually turn his ship away* from the task of rescuing the *Eagle* crew members immersed in freezing water to pursue the U-boat, thereby sucking those poor sailors to their deaths.

The COI's line of questioning, from the beginning, indicated that members had prejudged the cause of the *Eagle 56* explosion. While the Court of Inquiry was not privy to the specific Ultra U-boat intelligence developed by Kenneth Knowles's sub-tracking room in Washington, D.C., it appears likely that the Portland base commander, Captain Ernest Freeman, had apparently failed to heed the general warning to keep his commanders on the lookout for German U-boats. With the overwhelming evidence that the Court of Inquiry gathered *against* a catastrophic boiler explosion, it is difficult to plausibly argue anything other than this: In his effort to avoid a disastrous black mark on his military record, perhaps even a court-martial, for losing a ship just a few miles from shore with Germany's surrender imminent, Freeman apparently influenced the COI's questioning, and its final ruling, in an effort to keep that record unblemished.

"The cause of the *Eagle 56* sinking was not technically a cover-up if the term 'cover-up' means it extended to the highest levels of the Navy," Paul Lawton would say years later. "That did not happen. What *did* happen, according to the weight of the evidence, is that a definite cover-your-butt situation occurred at the Portland operational level. Freeman rushed the Court of Inquiry and hoped its ruling would get lost in the end-of-the-war shuffle and celebration. And for nearly sixty years, it did."

Even Rear Admiral Felix Gygax, commander of the First Naval District and Boston Naval Yard who appointed the Court of Inquiry, would be highly skeptical of its findings when he reviewed them one month later. Questioning a COI's decision in an official memorandum—in this case, the cover sheet to the COI transcript—is an unusual occurrence; certainly an uncustomary straying from unwritten military protocol. Yet, as the "convening authority," Gygax expressed his skepticism in no uncertain terms:

The Convening Authority has determined by separate investigation that so far as is known there were no friendly mines, torpedoes, depth charges, or other explosive mechanisms that were unaccounted for and that could have caused the explosion that resulted in the loss of the USS *Eagle (PE-56)*.

With respect to that part of the opinion of the court of inquiry giving the cause of the accident as that of a boiler explosion, the Convening Authority considers that the *evidence does not support this unqualified conclusion and believes that there is at least equal evidence to support the conclusion that the explosion was that of a device outside the ship, the exact nature of which is undetermined. It might have been an enemy mine or an enemy torpedo.* [author emphasis]

It would seem that the boiler explosion, if it occurred, and in any case, the disrupted steam connections, could have been incident to, and could have augmented the effect of, *a water column produced by an explosion outside the vessel.* [author emphasis]

Subject to the foregoing remarks, the proceedings, findings, opinion, and recommendation of the court of inquiry in the attached case are approved.

By stating only that there was "at least equal evidence" to support an external explosion—but not a *preponderance* of evidence to do so— Gygax stopped short of overturning the Court of Inquiry's decision. By virtue of his memo, the Navy officially concluded that the *Eagle 56* was sunk by undetermined causes, but "not by enemy action."

Gygax's cover letter, so clearly skeptical of the COI's conclusions, was dated June 1, 1945, but remained classified for forty years afterward, and buried for more than half a century.

24

Reserved and undemonstrative by nature, Commander Kenneth Knowles was not one to issue congratulatory messages on any sort of regular basis. For nearly two and a half years, he and his team had performed the most serious work, requiring all of them to labor for long hours under demanding and mentally exhausting conditions, often engaged in life-or-death situations. A workaholic himself, it was rare for Knowles to return home before 11:00 P.M., and it was often after midnight when he walked through the door and his wife would wake their two children so they could see their father for the first time that day. He often received calls at home in the wee hours; his CHestnut 3618 phone number was well known to the watch officers seeking his wisdom or a decision. Knowles's intelligence, intensity, and dedication were his hallmarks, well known across the Tenth Fleet, and he expected—and had received—nothing less from the men who worked with and for him.

Now, with the Battle of the Atlantic virtually over and the end of the European war imminent, Knowles believed his team's loyalty and devotion during the past thirty months *deserved* official commendation. In a memo to the Assistant for Combat Intelligence, he requested Navy Unit citations for his three-man Secret Room team: Lieutenant John E. Parsons (USNR), Lieutenant (junior grade) John V. Boland (USNR), and

Yeoman 1st Class Samuel P. Livecci—the only "regular navy" enlisted sailor who served in the F-21 organization during the war. Knowles also requested a citation for Ensign Rene B. Chevalier (USN), who was assigned to the Secret Room staff until April of 1944. "[They] have been associated entirely with U/Boat intelligence, and in my opinion each has made outstanding contributions to the successful prosecution of the war in the Atlantic Theater," Knowles wrote.

For Boland, Chevalier, and Livecci, Knowles recommended a Letter of Commendation with a citation ribbon for their "meritorious conduct in a position of considerable trust and responsibility in the Atlantic Section of Combat Intelligence . . ." Knowles singled out Parsons for his most effusive praise, recommending him for a prestigious Legion of Merit citation, "for exceptionally meritorious conduct in the performance of outstanding services in the Atlantic Section of Combat Intelligence. . . . through his outstanding ability and sound judgment, Lieut. Comdr. Parsons contributed in a marked degree to the successful prosecution of the naval war in the Atlantic . . . He was instrumental in analyzing enemy intelligence and contributed materially to the success of offensive operations against the German U/Boats."

In addition, Knowles recommended to Admiral King that the United States Navy accord "suitable recognition" to Knowles's British counterpart, Commander Roger Winn of the Admiralty OIC. "At the height of the U/Boat offensive in the Western Atlantic in May 1942, Captain Winn visited Washington and was instrumental in setting up the U/Boat Tracking Room in this Headquarters along the lines of the Admiralty Tracking Room, and in introducing tracking methods which have proved of inestimable value. Since then Captain Winn has been untiring in his efforts to provide this Tracking Room with enemy intelligence obtained from British sources and in furthering the exchange of views between the respective Tracking Rooms. Throughout the war, Captain Winn has given unstintingly of his energies and of his unquestioned ability to the successful prosecution of the Battle of the Atlantic."

Knowles acknowledged in his citation recommendations that he would submit a complete report to Admiral King "on the activities and methods used by this section . . . upon the defeat of Germany [when] the Atlantic Section, Combat Intelligence of this headquarters will be dissolved." In the meantime, fiercely loyal and exhaustingly thorough, Knowles wanted to ensure that the individual achievements of his team members would not be overlooked in the flurry of celebrations and avalanche of paperwork that would inevitably result from the end of the war.

May 5, 1945
Germany

Across the Atlantic Ocean, from his headquarters near the Danish border, Admiral Karl Dönitz issued a message to his U-boat commanders vastly different in tone than Knowles's. Whereas the American Secret Room commander celebrated victory, Dönitz acknowledged heartbreaking defeat to his beloved U-boat commanders.

On May 3, still trying to surrender as many forces as possible to the British and Americans rather than the feared Russians, Dönitz had sent a special emissary to British commander Bernard Montgomery proposing that the three German armies facing the Red Army in the north surrender to Anglo-American forces. "The German aim was to avoid, at all costs, surrendering to the Russians, and to stall for time in order for as many Germans as possible to escape to the west to avoid certain Red Army retribution, which had already been unleashed in an orgy of mass killings, rapes, and plunderings," military historian Carlo D'Este wrote. Montgomery asked Eisenhower, who formally rejected the proposal, stating that any German surrender must be "unconditional and simultaneous" in all theaters. However, as Eisenhower later recalled, as a "tactical" matter, he authorized Montgomery to accept the military surrender "of all forces in his allotted zone of operations . . . including those in Holland and Denmark." The agreement took effect at 8:00 A.M. on May 5, and as part of the terms, Dönitz agreed to direct all U-boat skippers to cease fire and prepare to surrender.

He radioed to them on the morning of May 5:

My U-boat men!

Six years of U-boat warfare lie behind us. You have fought like lions. A crushing material superiority has compressed us into a very narrow area. A continuation of the struggle is impossible from the bases that remain. U-boat men, unbroken and unashamed, you are laying down your arms after a heroic battle without an equal. In reverent memory, we think respectfully of our fallen comrades, who have sealed with death their loyalty to the Führer and the Fatherland. Comrades, maintain in the future your U-boat spirit with which you have fought at sea bravely and undeviatingly through the long years for the welfare of the Fatherland. Long live Germany! Your Grand Admiral.

It was Dönitz's final message to his undersea warriors, many of whom were still unswervingly loyal to him to the end. Not everyone believed it. Heinz Schaeffer, commander of the *U-977*, was incredulous when he picked up Dönitz's signal in the English Channel. "He did not believe that Dönitz was responsible for it; it was the work of an impostor, or the *Grossadmiral* had been forced to do it," wrote Jordan Vause, who quoted Schaeffer as saying, "I couldn't conceive it possible that our leaders had sunk so far as to send out official orders to surrender."

But Herbert Werner, commander of the *U-953*, received Dönitz's message with a sense of welcoming relief, which he described many years later:

"The Admiral who had led the U-boats to glory and to disaster mourned for the faithful who lay on the bottom and gave thanks to those few survivors of the monstrous battle. This was the message that put an end to the suffering. It admitted defeat for the first time. The murdering had finally come to an end. Henceforth, we would be able to live without fear that we had to die tomorrow. An unknown tranquility took possession of me as I realized that I had survived. My death in an iron coffin, a verdict of long standing, was finally suspended. The truth was so beautiful that it seemed to be a dream."

For Dönitz, who had begun the war with glorious dreams of U-boat dominance and remarkable early successes, but had since seen horrible deaths claim thousands of his beloved U-boatmen and two of his sons, this last message summed up both his irrepressible pride and the wrenching pain and bitterness that consumed him at war's end.

Because Ultra records remained classified until after Dönitz's death, the grand admiral was at least spared the humiliation of knowing—though he may have suspected—that U.S. Navy cryptographers in Washington, D.C., as they had been doing since 1942, intercepted even his final radio message to the U-boats, decoded it, and sent it along to Kenneth Knowles in the sub-tracking Secret Room. Knowles quickly prepared and distributed a memo to F-20 watch officers explaining the procedure that U.S. and British warships should follow in anticipation of the widespread surrender of German U-boats.

25

U-boat commanders Herbert Werner and Heinz Schaeffer may have responded in markedly different ways to Führer Dönitz's surrender message, but it is at least clear that they received the dispatch. Did *U-853* commander Helmut Froemsdorf, submerged off the coast of Rhode Island, ever hear Dönitz's signal instructing U-boat commanders to cease hostilities?

It is possible that Froemsdorf's radio equipment was damaged by one of the depth-charge or Hedgehog attacks conducted by the *Selfridge*, *Muskegon*, *Evarts*, or *Eberle*, in their pursuit of the *U-853* as she departed the Gulf of Maine. Yet, it is just as likely that Froemsdorf foolishly disregarded Dönitz's order, balked at surrendering, and decided to go down fighting.

The real answer will never be known.

What *is* known to history is that on Saturday, May 5, 1945, at just past 5:30 P.M., *after* Dönitz's order to surrender, the *U-853* spotted and locked in on another easy target: the aging 5,400-ton collier *Black Point*, moments after she had passed the Point Judith, Rhode Island, Coast Guard Station lighthouse on her way to Boston to deliver a load of soft coal. *Black Point* captain Charles Prior had just picked up 7,700 tons of coal in Newport News, Virginia, and was steaming northeast, unescorted, for the Edison power plant at the L Street wharf in South Boston, by way of the intracoastal waterways of Long Island Sound,

Rhode Island Sound, and eventually, the Cape Cod Canal. "That day in 1945 was foggy along the eastern seaboard and merchant ships were not equipped with radar," noted *The Boston Globe*. "Twice during his steam up Long Island Sound, Prior lost sight of his own bow and had to anchor." In addition, Prior was not in convoy, nor had he been for several weeks now that the U-boat threat was considered minimal.

By late afternoon, however, the seas had calmed, the fog had lifted, the sun had emerged, and Prior was standing on the *Black Point*'s bridge. The *Globe* reported: "The only other traffic in sight, far off to starboard, were two small freighters, a tugboat pulling lazily at three barges, and the Yugoslavian freighter *Karmen*." Captain Prior was about to light a cigarette when a huge explosion rocked the ship. As glass shattered and doors splintered around him, Prior's first thought was, "Jesus, we've hit a mine." The explosion blew away forty feet of the ship's stern and she began to sink fast. Naval historian Paul Lawton wrote: "Merchant crewman Joseph Raymond Tharl later recalled that he had been belowdecks, eating his regular Saturday dinner of franks and beans in the galley amidships [when the explosion occurred]. He raced to the radio room and started transmitting an SOS distress signal, as Captain Prior struggled to pry the stunned third mate Homer Small's hands from the ship's helm. Captain Prior then rushed to secure the ship's records and gave the order to abandon ship. In the excitement and confusion following the explosion, several sailors were crushed and injured or killed as lifeboats swung wildly from their davits . . ."

By 5:55 P.M., both the 40-foot stern section and the 230-foot bow section had sunk beneath the waves. Eleven crewmen and one armed guard went down with the ship.

The freighter *Karmen* rescued the thirty-four survivors, including Captain Prior, and quickly broadcast an alarm after her crew members witnessed an inexplicable sight that left no doubt that the explosion aboard the *Black Point* was not caused by any mine, but an enemy torpedo. For some reason, once again, the *U-853* had mysteriously surfaced, this time for a few minutes. Officers and crewmen aboard the *Karmen* saw several *U-853* crewmen off her aft deck, and some later said that the U-boatmen were trying to deploy a yellow inflatable raft or retrieve something from the water; however, within moments, the *U-853*'s crew "scrambled back down the hatches," according to Lawton, and the U-boat quickly dove from view as the *Karmen* broadcast her SOS radio distress signal.

✪ ✪ ✪

Four Boston-bound American warships, heading to port for repairs and provisions, heard the alarm broadcast by the *Karmen*: the *Ericsson*, the *Moberly*, the *Amick*, and the *Atherton* all began to chase the *U-853*. Other U.S. warships, including USS *Action*, USS *Barney*, USS *Breckenridge*, USS *Blakely*, USS *Newport*, the USS *Restless*, and the USS *Semmes* soon arrived on the scene and established a barrier patrol around the search area to prevent the U-boat from escaping her hunters. Further south, destroyers USS *Baldwin*, USS *Frankford*, and USS *Nelson* received a dispatch from the Commander Eastern Sea Frontier to join the hunt for the *U-853*.

As the net of surface ships drew tighter around the German U-boat, the relatively shallow waters and flat-bottom topography of Rhode Island Sound also worked against her, failing to offer the protective cover she enjoyed off the craggy coast of Maine, where it was much more difficult for SONAR to detect submarines. There was one spot, about nine miles south of the sinking of the *Black Point*, that the American hunters believed the U-boat might choose to hide. In this area, known as East Ground, a steeply rising shoal could allow a submarine to lie alongside and escape a destroyer's detection. In addition, according to Navy Ensign D. M. Tollaksen, son of the *Moberly*'s commanding officer, "there was a possibility of a wreck in the area, which would further confuse the search . . . once the above course of action was deemed most likely for the German submarine skipper to follow, the search plan was set up to sweep across this area and back."

The search plan worked. At approximately 8:15 P.M. on May 5, the USS *Atherton*, skippered by Lieutenant Commander Lewis Iselin, picked up a sound contact on the *U-853* as the U-boat crept slowly south on her electric motors, close to the bottom, attempting to escape detection. At just before 8:30 P.M., the *Moberly* dropped thirteen magnetic depth charges on the sound contact, one of which detonated. The USS *Ericsson* arrived on the scene to join the *Atherton* and *Moberly* in their search and follow-up attacks on the SONAR contact. The *Atherton* made two subsequent Hedgehog attacks before marking the area with a lighted buoy, and breaking off the attack to conduct repairs and reload her Hedgehog spigot launchers. The three warships regained sound contact quickly, this time presuming it was the U-boat lying dead in the water at a depth of one hundred feet with her propellers silent. At a quarter to midnight on May 5, Atherton fired a pattern of Hedgehogs, and "evidence of a hit began to well up to the surface, indicating the *U-853* had been damaged, if not destroyed," Paul Lawton wrote.

Moberly sonarman second class Richard I. Duburg, recalled: "After the attack our searchlights in the dark revealed air bubbles and oil welling to the surface with bits of wood, cork, and dead fish, a rubber inflatable raft, life jackets tied in knots, wooden flagstaff, a pillow with an embroidered duck on the corner, the Captain's cap, and a whiskey wood crate . . ." The *Atherton* picked up the contact again after this attack and held it for about twenty minutes while circling the area. "There was no noticeable movement of the submarine," Tollaksen wrote.

The *Atherton* attacked again in an attempt to split the sub's pressure hull, dropping a pattern of depth charges set to explode at 75 feet in water that was between 100 and 128 feet deep. After the attack, at 1:00 A.M. on May 6, the *Moberly* and the *Atherton* turned on their searchlights and saw additional debris and dead fish. At 2:41 A.M., the *Atherton*, which had circled the area every twenty to thirty minutes to keep track of the position of the contact and hunt for more wreckage that might have come to the surface, reported that there were three pools of oil coming from the submarine which were spaced about thirty feet apart. The *Moberly* reported that an oil slick and much debris extended half a mile from the position of the last attacks. The *Ericsson* and the *Atherton* began searching for evidence of the submarine's destruction, and found "a large number of German escape lungs and life jackets, several life rafts, abandon-ship kits, and an officer's cap which was later judged to belong to the submarine's skipper," Tollaksen recounted.

Between 5:30 and 6:00 A.M. on May 6, two U.S. Navy blimps, *K-16* and *K-58* from Lakehurst, New Jersey, arrived on the scene to search the area of the debris field and diesel oil slick, photograph the area, and mark the position of the stricken submarine with smoke and dye markers. The *K-16* soon made a strong sound contact on the *U-853*, marked the position, and reported that the target was stationary. At that point, the destroyers made additional Hedgehog and depth-charge attacks to crack the hull of the submarine and bring up more debris to the surface. "From time to time, the attacks would be discontinued and boats lowered to pick up more wreckage," Tollaksen described. "*Ericsson* recovered a chart desk, a life raft, a rubber hood for foul-weather gear, and some bits of cork."

Blimp *K-16* dropped a sonobuoy on an oil slick, and SONAR operators in both blimps heard sound which they described as a "rhythmic hammering on a metal surface which was interrupted periodically." About ten minutes later, they heard "a long, shrill shriek and then the hammering noise was lost in the engine noise of the attacking surface ships."

Could the hammering have been the last desperate poundings of any surviving *U-853* crew members, begging the attacks to stop? Some U-boat commanders have described the concussive force and deafening blasts of depth-charge and Hedgehog attacks as the equivalent of being inside a 55-gallon metal drum while several people are bashing the sides of the drum with sledgehammers. According to Paul Lawton, the trapped *U-853*, lying dead on the bottom, underwent a sixteen-hour-long deluge of twenty successive Hedgehog and depth-charge attacks, during which more than fifteen tons of explosives were dropped on the crippled U-boat, including two hundred depth charges. Her crew members would have endured unimaginably horrific pain and trauma from the terrible pounding that she absorbed as she lay helpless. "I don't think there's a hull that took a bigger beating during the war," reported *Atherton* commander Lewis Iselin years later. Writers Henry Keatts and George Farr noted: "The monstrous detonations of Hedgehogs and depth charges would have pounded against the U-boat with sledgehammer blows. The crew was probably thrown about inside like toys until concussions finally blew the pressure hull open and the sea rushed in."

At 10:45 A.M., Task Force Commander F. C. B. McCune, aboard the *Ericsson*, declared the U-boat "sunk and on the bottom," but still the bombardments did not cease. The vessel *Semmes* was given permission to enter the area to test her new experimental SONAR gear on the bottomed submarine. Marker buoys were dropped and the vessels made practice Hedgehog runs. Finally, at 12:24, the *Ericsson* marked the position of the dead submarine with a buoy line and the attacks were discontinued. Years later, *The Boston Globe* would quote a former U-boat crew member as speculating that "it is entirely possible . . . that several Germans [in the *U-853*] in the airtight forward compartments would have survived all the practice runs and were still alive when the bombing stopped at 12:24 P.M. By then, the men may have gone insane. Their deaths would have come from suffocation, as the world above prepared to celebrate peace."

McCune later expressed surprise that the U-boat made no attempt to surface or fire her torpedoes, an indication that she was probably critically damaged early in the attacks. Otherwise, Froemsdorf likely would have blown his ballast tanks and surfaced to give his crew at least a fighting chance to escape before the *U-853* was destroyed. Instead, he apparently had little choice but to play possum on the bottom, hoping the attacking ships would be convinced of a kill and leave, allowing the U-boat to inch away and perhaps live another day.

His last desperate strategy failed utterly.

On the afternoon of May 6, 1945, diver Edwin J. R. Bockelman from the Navy salvage and rescue vessel *Penguin* descended 130 feet to the bottomed U-boat to confirm the kill and examine the wreckage. He landed on the U-boat's conning tower, reported massive damage to her hull, and found her hatch crammed with the bodies of several German naval officers and crewmen wearing escape equipment. Despite the danger from many unexploded depth charges surrounding the wreck, Bockelman recovered the body of one dead crewman—twenty-two-year-old seaman Herbert Hoffmann—from the conning tower, which he brought to the surface as evidence of the kill.

Before he returned to the surface, Bockelman identified the boat by its number, *U-853*, painted on her conning tower. Although there is no historical document that confirms it, Bockelman likely spotted something else painted on the conning tower: the red trotting horse and yellow shield insignia of the *U-853*, the "red and yellow markings" that *Eagle 56* crew member Daniel Jaronik had seen as he abandoned ship and later testified about during the Court of Inquiry.

All fifty-five officers and crewmen aboard the *U-853* were lost; Froemsdorf's final, meaningless attack on the *Black Point* led to a horrible death for himself and his crew.

In all, the *U-853*'s attacks killed sixty-one men aboard the *Eagle 56* and the *Black Point*, bringing the total dead from these incidents to 116 Americans and Germans in the final two weeks of World War II. The *U-853*, the final German U-boat sunk in the Battle of the Atlantic, had been responsible for the final German kills of an American warship and merchant ship.

As to the question of whether Froemsdorf's radio equipment did or did not pick up Dönitz's final "cease-fire" message, the German U-boat archives would report years later that, while there was no radio message

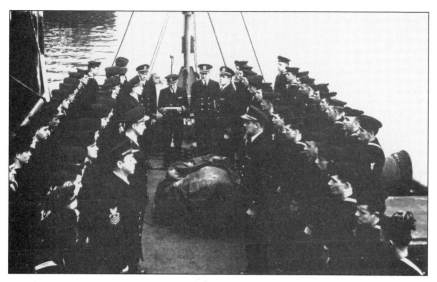

During a change-of-command ceremony on January 23, 1945, outgoing *Eagle 56* skipper Lt. Cmdr. John L. Barr, Jr. reads the order that designates Lt. James G. Early as the new commander of the subchaser. Barr relinquished command of the *Eagle* to see action against the Japanese in the Pacific, a decision that haunted him after his old ship was torpedoed on April 23, 1945. (*Official U.S. Navy Photograph*)

The USS *Eagle 56*'s "Black Gang" in Key West the summer before the ship departed for Portland, Maine. Lt. John Scagnelli is on the far left with dress shirt and tie. Harold Petersen is second from left, kneeling, in front row. Next to him is Oscar Davis. Johnny Breeze is standing directly behind Davis (second from left in second row). Joseph Priestas, the fourth living survivor, is directly to Breeze's left. (*Photo courtesy of John Scagnelli*)

The *Eagle 56* in drydock in Boston in 1944 before she sailed up to Portland, Maine. (*Photo courtesy of John Scagnelli*)

John Scagnelli aboard the *Eagle 56* in 1944. (*Photo courtesy of John Scagnelli*)

John Scagnelli as a cadet at the U.S. Merchant Marine Academy in 1942. (*Photo courtesy of John Scagnelli*)

The only known official photo to exist of Helmut Froemsdorf, commander of the *U-853* when she sunk the *Eagle 56* and when she was "killed" by American warships just hours before World War II ended in Europe. (*Photo courtesy of the U-boot Archiv*)

The crew of the *U-853* is assembled on deck in this photo taken in June of 1943. At the time, her commander was *Kapitanleutnant* Helmut Sommer, bottom row, fifth from right with a white dress belt. To his left, also with a white dress belt and a hanging ceremonial dagger, is Helmut Froemsdorf. (*Photo courtesy of the U-boot Archiv*)

Esta and Harold Glenn at their wedding reception in Marissa, Illinois, on August 6, 1943. (*Photo courtesy of Esta Glenn Smith*)

Ivar and Phyllis Westerlund, sometime in 1944. (*Photo courtesy of the Westerlund family*)

Alice and Harold Petersen, January 1, 1944, in Rochester, New York. (*Photo courtesy of Harold Petersen*)

Johnny Breeze, *Eagle 56* survivor, in his dress whites, Key West, Florida, 1944. (*Photo courtesy of Johnny Breeze*)

Commander Kenneth A. Knowles, whose subtracking "Secret Room" played a major role in helping the allies win the Battle of the Atlantic. (*Photo courtesy of Dr. Kenneth A. Knowles, Jr.*)

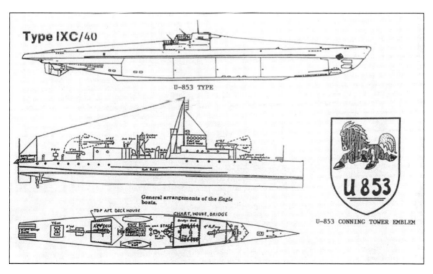

Profiles of the Type IXC/40 German U-boat *U-853*, with her conning tower emblem depicting a red trotting horse on a yellow shield; and a Ford Motor Company Eagle Class subchaser similar to the USS *Eagle 56 (PE-56)*. (*Courtesy of Henry Ford Museum; Sharkhunters International; and the Submarine Force Library and Museum*)

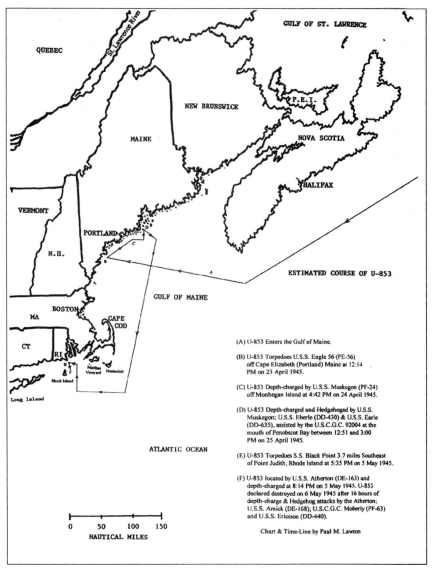

The estimated course of the *U-853* upon entering American waters, tracking her attack on the USS *Eagle 56 (PE-56);* the U.S. Navy's subsequent depth-charge and Hedgehog attacks on the *U-853;* her sinking of the SS *Black Point;* and the ultimate destruction of the *U-853* by the U.S. Navy. (*Courtesy of Paul Lawton*)

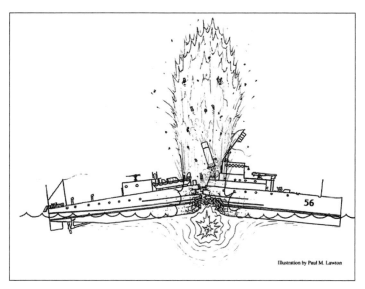

Paul Lawton's illustration of the external underwater explosion that tore apart and sank the *Eagle 56* less than 5 miles southeast of Cape Elizabeth, Maine, at approximately 12:14 PM on Monday, 23 April 1945.

Survivors from the sinking of the *Eagle 56* being rescued and assisted aboard the U.S. Navy destroyer, USS *Selfridge (DD-357)* from the chilling 38–degree waters of the North Atlantic off the Coast of Cape Elizabeth, Maine, at approximately 12:30 PM on 23 April 1945. (*Courtesy of Paul Lawton and Clifford Chambers*)

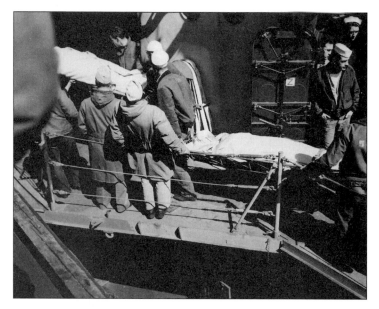

The USS *Selfridge* crew delivered injured *Eagle 56* survivors to Grand Trunk Pier in South Portland, Maine, in the early afternoon of April 23, 1945. Survivor on the stretcher shown could possibly be John Scagnelli, whose head was swathed in bandages because of a scalp injury. (*Photo courtesy of John Scagnelli*)

A starboard view of the U.S. Navy destroyer USS *Selfridge* (DD-357), which participated in the rescue of *Eagle 56* survivors. (*Photo courtesy of Paul Lawton and Clifford Chambers*)

The U.S. Coast Guard lightship "Light-Vessel" (LV-112) USS *Nantucket*, taken while on-station on the Nantucket Shoals sometime before World War II. Crew members from this ship rescued Harold Petersen from the freezing water on April 23, 1945. *(Courtesy of the National Archives)*

The USS *Moberly*, one of several ships in the hunt for the *U-853* after she sunk the *Eagle 56*. *(Photo courtesy of the National Archives)*

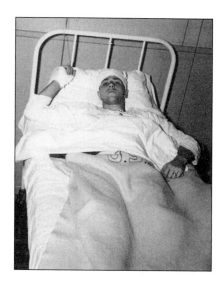

Lt. (jg) John Scagnelli in his hospital bed following the *U-853*'s attack on the *Eagle 56*. Scagnelli received serious lacerations to his scalp and injured his wrist, in addition to the hypothermia he and the other survivors suffered. (*Photo courtesy of John Scagnelli*)

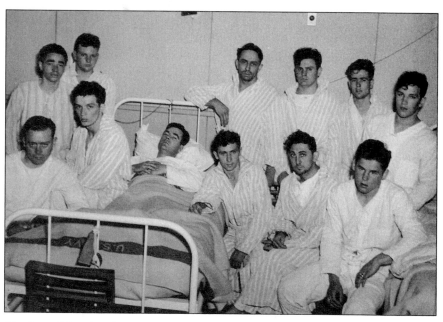

Twelve of the "Lucky Thirteen" *Eagle 56* survivors are shown in the dispensary shortly after their rescue (John Scagnelli is in a separate bed). Harold Petersen is on the far right, second row. Johnny Breeze is sitting on the bed. Joseph Priestas, the fourth survivor who emerged just as this book was going to press, is directly across from Breeze with his right arm on the bed. Oscar Davis is in the back row, two people left of Petersen. (*Photo courtesy of John Scagnelli*)

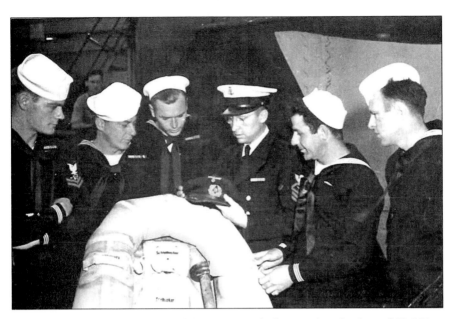

Unidentified crew members of the USS *Moberly* examine the hat of *U-853* commander Helmut Froemsdorf, which floated to the surface after massive depth charge bombardments against the stricken U-boat. The entire fifty-five-man *U-853* crew was killed. (*Photo courtesy of the National Archives*)

This story from the *Brockton Enterprise* on May 9, 1945, shows Phyllis Westerlund with her four young children shortly after learning that her husband and their father, Ivar Westerlund, had been killed in the *Eagle 56* sinking.

Paul Lawton (center) and Johnny Breeze show *Portland Press Herald* headline on the *Eagle 56* disaster to Alice (Heyd) Hultgren, who was the Court of Inquiry WAVE stenographer in 1945. The article appeared a couple of weeks after the sinking, once the war had ended in Europe. Breeze and Hultgren provided Lawton with sworn affidavits on the *Eagle* case in 1998, which began the long effort to rewrite Naval history. (*Photo courtesy of Paul Lawton*)

This Associated Press photo of living survivor Harold Petersen was published in newspapers across the country after the Navy reversed the 1945 Court of Inquiry ruling—which initially held that the *Eagle 56* sunk due to a boiler explosion—and attributed the sinking to a torpedo attack from the *U-853*. (*Photo courtesy of Harold Petersen*)

From left, Paul, Fred, and Bob Westerlund, sons of *PE-56* casualty, Seaman 2nd Class Ivar A. Westerlund, display brass memorial plaque and wreath, about to be cast into the North Atlantic in the area of wreck of the USS *Eagle 56* in July 2000. The plaque reads: "In memory of the 49 U.S. Navy officers and crewmen lost aboard the U.S.S. *Eagle 56 (PE-56)* during World War II, on April 23, 1945." (*Photo courtesy of Paul Lawton*)

Members of the USS *Eagle 56 (PE-56)* search team who have hunted (as yet unsuccessfully) for the ship's wreckage are shown here (from left): Tom Mackie of Trimble Navigation, Inc.; Gary Kozak of Klein Associates, Inc. (sidescan SONAR expert); Fred Westerlund; *Salvage One* Captain Jay Lesynsky; Paul Westerlund; Bob Westerlund; Team Leader Paul Lawton; Chris Hugo; and Scott Uhlman. (*Photo courtesy of Paul Lawton*)

During the Purple Heart ceremony aboard the USS *Salem* in Quincy, Massachusetts, on June 8, 2002, Paul Lawton (left) paid tribute to *Eagle 56* survivors (from left) John Scagnelli, Harold Petersen, and Johnny Breeze. (*Photo courtesy of Paul Lawton*)

Judge James R. Lawton (retired), a World War II Purple Heart recipient himself, lent his assistance to his son Paul's efforts to rewrite Naval history. The elder Lawton's war record and service inspired Paul's interest in military history and protocol.(*Photo courtesy of Paul Lawton*)

John Scagnelli, the lone surviving officer of the *Eagle 56* sinking, proudly displays the Purple Heart medal he received fifty-seven years after the tragedy. (*Photo by the author*)

A portrait of Joseph Priestas, who was the fourth living survivor from the *Eagle 56*. He emerged just as this book was going to press. (*Photo courtesy of Paul Priestas*)

from the *U-853* after the *Eagle 56* was destroyed, there was a brief message from the U-boat to Berlin that did get through after she sunk the *Black Point*. This indicates, but does not *prove*, that Froemsdorf received the cease-fire message and foolishly chose to disregard it; it does confirm that his radio was working for at least a brief period afterward.

Whether the cocky U-boat commander was unaware of the cease-fire and the war's end, or risked the lives of his brave crew in a fool's mission—knowing that he would never be able to outrun American pursuit or be allowed to surrender after sinking the *Black Point*—is a mystery whose answer is forever lost with Froemsdorf at the bottom of the Atlantic Ocean.

An answer to another mystery was also lost when the *U-853* and her crew were destroyed: why she surfaced after torpedoing the *Eagle 56* and the *Black Point*. Paul Lawton and other historians have speculated that she was required to surface after failing to maintain proper "trim control" after launching her torpedoes. "In order for a U-boat to maintain proper 'trim' (the control of a submerged submarine's depth and equilibrium), the crew had to regularly track the boat's displacement (weight) throughout her patrol," Lawton explained, "including daily measurements of fuel, food, and freshwater consumption, garbage, human waste, and the discharge or ordnance (torpedoes, mines, artillery, and anti-aircraft munitions) . . . rapid and extreme changes in the boat's buoyancy and trim . . . such as that resulting from a submerged torpedo launch, required excellent training, experience, and discipline, in order to keep the boat from broaching the surface, potentially exposing herself in a vulnerable position, and compromising some of the tactical advantage obtained from a submerged attack . . . anything short of perfect execution could cause the boat to sink below periscope depth, or rise uncontrollably [above] the surface . . . this phenomenon was not uncommon with inexperienced U-boat officers and crewmen, particularly those lacking sufficient experience in the firing of live, or practice, torpedoes . . ."

Lawton and others have also cited alternate explanations for the *U-853* breaking the surface after her attacks, including the "intentional, though highly dangerous acts of defiant bravado by the young Commander Froemsdorf" to view the results of his kills, or "his desire to get a better view of the destruction he inflicted for the purpose of battle damage assessment."

One final perplexing question may never be answered: Why were *U-853* crew members attempting to launch an inflatable life raft after sinking the *Black Point*? Did Froemsdorf order the launch, and if so, for what reason? Or, did some *U-853* crew members, fearful that Froemsdorf's torpedoing of the collier would lead to their deaths, decide to defy their commander and attempt, albeit unsuccessfully, to abandon their U-boat and take their chances on being plucked from the ocean by an American ship?

26

A mere eleven hours after Commander McCune pronounced the *U-853* "sunk and on the bottom," and six hours after Edwin Bockelman dove to the wreck to confirm the kill, German Chief of Staff General Alfred Jodl and Admiral Hans-Georg von Friedeburg, the latter Karl Dönitz's friend and personal representative, signed unconditional surrender papers in Reims, France. While it was early morning on May 7 in France, it was still 9:41 P.M. on May 6 over the grave of the *U 853*. Both the U-boat's and the Third Reich's reigns of terror had ended in total defeat.

Terms of the German surrender agreement called for all hostilities to cease at midnight on May 8, 1945, officially Victory in Europe (V-E) Day. Allied Supreme Commander General Dwight D. Eisenhower showed his disdain for the enemy by declining to be present at the surrender ceremony. Ike, who had proclaimed, "I won't shake hands with a Nazi!" after the Axis forces surrendered in Tunisia in 1943, harbored even deeper hatred for the evil that Jodl and von Friedeburg represented, according to biographer Carlo D'Este, especially after Eisenhower had viewed the concentration camps and other evidence of Nazi atrocities. After Jodl had signed the papers, he said with much difficulty: "With this signature, the German people and armed forces are, for better or worse, delivered into the victor's hands." Then, he was brought to Eisenhower's office, where Ike asked him through an interpreter if he thoroughly understood all provisions of the document he had signed. Jodl answered in the affirmative, and Eisenhower responded: "You will, officially and personally, be held responsible if the terms of this surrender are violated, including its provisions for German commanders to appear in Berlin at the moment set by the Russian high command to accomplish formal surrender to that government. That is all."

Jodl made a slight bow, saluted and left. He would be tried and convicted of war crimes at Nuremberg and hanged in 1947.

After the Germans departed, Eisenhower seemed to relax, as a horde of photographers was admitted to his office to record the scene. "Although he was exhausted," D'Este recounted, "Dwight Eisenhower's famous grin reappeared at a historic moment, as he signaled a V for victory by holding aloft the two gold pens with which German surrender documents had been signed. Eisenhower telephoned [General Omar] Bradley with the news; in turn Bradley rousted Patton from sleep and said: 'Ike just called me, George. The Germans have surrendered.' "

Before he fell into bed exhausted at 5:00 A.M., Eisenhower had one other task: to draft a message to the Combined Chiefs informing them that the Germans had surrendered. Ike received recommendations from his staff on possible wording for the momentous dispatch, most containing flowery and resounding phrases to immortalize the moment, but he rejected them all. "Eisenhower understood that it was not his place to announce the end of the war in Europe," D'Este pointed out. "That was a function reserved for the heads of state, who would make the formal announcement."

And so Eisenhower, who often authored lengthy messages, crafted the briefest cable of his tenure as supreme commander to the Combined Chiefs of Staff, that was, in D'Este's words, "utterly devoid of self-congratulation [and] as unpretentious as the man itself." It read simply: THE MISSION OF THIS ALLIED FORCE WAS FULFILLED AT 0241, LOCAL TIME, MAY 7TH, 1945.// SIGNED//EISENHOWER.

Churchill had wanted to make the announcement of the German surrender at once, but Stalin insisted they wait until the official surrender document was signed in Berlin so that his top military officers could be present; President Truman agreed that the announcement would be made by all three Allies at the same time the following morning, May 8, V-E Day.

Truman, who turned sixty-one on V-E Day and had been president for a little more than three weeks, broke the news to reporters at 8:30 A.M., and at 9:00 A.M., he spoke to the largest radio audience yet recorded, according to historian David McCullough: "This is a solemn but glorious hour. I only wish that Franklin D. Roosevelt had lived to witness this day . . . We must work to finish the war. Our victory is but half-won . . ." He told the nation that "our rejoicing" over victory in Europe was "sobered" by the "terrible price we have paid to rid the world of Hitler and his evil band." In a separate statement, he called on Japan to surrender, warning that "the striking power and intensity of our blows will steadily increase."

Cities across the world—including New York, Chicago, Los Angeles, London, Paris, and Moscow—erupted in wild celebration, but not Washington, where it was raining, and thousands of government workers, having listened to Truman's broadcast, remained at their desks. "I call upon every American to stick to his post until the last battle is won," Truman had stated.

Elsewhere, there was dancing in the streets, rockets and guns firing into the air, sirens howling, light beams from every window—the release from the blackout that had covered Europe for the previous five years. "In Moscow, crowds swarmed into Red Square, brushing aside police reinforcements," historian Stephen Ambrose recounted. "A thousand guns fired thirty rounds each to signalize complete and total victory." George Kennan, U.S. chargé d'affaires, made a speech from the U.S. embassy balcony, where the Red banner hung beside the Stars and Stripes. The crowd roared: "Long Live Truman! Long Live Roosevelt's memory! Long live the great Americans!"

Spontaneously, all of London turned out into the streets to celebrate. Churchill appeared on the balcony of the Ministry of Health, above the vast crowd that thronged Whitehall and declared: "This is your victory." The crowd roared back to the Prime Minister: "No—it is yours." Historian Robert Rhodes James called it, "an unforgettable moment of love and gratitude." Churchill told the crowd: "In all our long history, we have never seen a greater day than this . . . it is a victory of the great British nation as a whole." Warning that the Japanese were still a menace to Britain and her Allies, he said that the British people now had to turn themselves to "fulfill our duty to our own countrymen, and to our gallant allies of the United States, who were so foully and treacherously attacked by Japan. We will go hand in hand with them. Even if it is a hard struggle, we will not be the ones who will fail." Churchill remembered his friend, Franklin Roosevelt, and the "valiant and magnanimous deeds of the USA under his magnificent leadership." He predicted that those remarkable deeds "would forever stir the hearts of Britons in all quarters of the world in which they dwell."

Later, Churchill would call the unconditional surrender of Germany "the signal for the greatest outburst of joy in the history of mankind," writing that while all the Allied nations felt "inexpressible relief," in England, the end of the war in Europe bordered on a spiritual experience. "For us in Britain and the British Empire, who had alone been in the struggle from the first day to the last and staked our existence on the result, there was a meaning beyond what even our most powerful and most valiant Allies could feel," Churchill wrote. "Weary and worn, impoverished but undaunted and now triumphant, we had a moment that was sublime. We gave thanks to God for the noblest of all His blessings, the sense that we had done our duty."

In Brockton, Massachusetts, V-E ceremonies were "tinged with solemnity and attended by a hushed and subdued crowd" of about two thousand people, reported the *Brockton Enterprise*. Brockton's mayor told the crowd that it was not a night for frivolity and fun-making, but a night for people to pray for the servicemen who weren't coming back. "This war is not yet over," he said. "We still have an enemy in the Pacific to defeat. We must keep at our war jobs, continue to buy bonds, and give blood and pray that the final peace will come soon."

For those who had lost loved ones in the war against Germany, like Phyllis Westerlund, V-E Day seemed hollow and unreal. On May 8, the *Enterprise* featured a large photo of Phyllis and her four children under the headline WESTERLUND KIDDIES MISS DAD ON VICTORY DAY. The caption noted that V-E Day was "small consolation" for Phyllis. An accompanying story described how Mrs. Ivar Westerlund would "carry on" despite the loss of her husband, but also added: "Still stunned by the news of the burden she must now bear alone, [Phyllis] says in a lonesome voice, 'Oh, why wasn't it over before?' "

Years later, Phyllis said her memory of V-E Day itself was hazy; her only clear recollection of that time was the feeling that Ivar's death was like a bad dream, "something that happened to other people, but not to you."

27

With censorship rules relaxed along the East Coast now that Germany had surrendered, and next of kin notified, the news of the *Eagle 56* and the *Black Point* sinkings finally hit the press the day after V-E Day, more than two weeks after the *Eagle* had exploded and four days after the *Black Point* went down. Some featured the *Eagle* story as a stand-alone account; others combined the two sinkings with the sinking of another oil steamer, *Atlantic States,* in which one man died, and ran headlines that said RECENT ATTACKS BY U-BOATS KILL 62 OFF ATLANTIC COAST.

The *Eagle 56*'s "Lucky Thirteen" had been interviewed in the dispensary, in the midst of their Court of Inquiry testimony, which they were forbidden to discuss. The Associated Press disseminated the story to several papers on May 9, 1945, and *The New York Times* ran its own original piece on the same day: 49 LOST OFF MAINE IN NAVY SHIP BLAST read the *Times* headline to its story, which ran inside the paper, and 49 DIE IN SHIP BLAST 3 MILES OFF MAINE shouted the larger *Boston Daily Record* headline above the AP story on page two. NAVY SEEKS CAUSE OF BLAST THAT KILLED 49 read another headline to the AP report; many newspapers ran smaller versions of the story. All three of these reports left the cause of the explosion in question.

Several papers carried hospital photos of the Lucky Thirteen or the solo photo of an exhausted and somber Scagnelli, his scalp and forehead covered in bandages. "It was the Navy's greatest loss of life in New

England waters in this war," *The New York Times* reported somberly in its lead paragraph. "Publication of the tragedy was permitted tonight by the Navy Department after next of kin had been notified," the AP dispatch read.

Both the AP and the *Times* accounts mentioned that some survivors reported seeing a submarine. "The Navy reported that [a] destroyer dropped depth charges, believing contact had been made with a submarine, but later it was thought a piece of the hull might have been encountered," the *Times* reported carefully, then adding: "Survivors said the explosion, which they described as a vertical one, was so devastating that everything inside the ship fell apart." The AP added: "So rapid was the sinking that the men ran from their quarters to the deck and merely walked into the water as the ship already had settled to bring the ice-cold water chest-high. Several performed heroic acts, but many were unable to stand the cold, rough water and slipped beneath the heavy ground swells within a foot of their shipmates. Others didn't have a chance, for they were badly injured."

The press interviewed Scagnelli extensively, "newsmen crowding around his bed . . . his head and right hand swathed in bandages," and reported in detail on the lone surviving officer's escape from the forward section of the ship. Scagnelli praised Harold Petersen "for his efforts to aid others in the water," and he "stressed that all engines and boilers were in good condition and recently had been overhauled." Johnny Breeze reported that he owed his life to Seaman John Luttrell, "who held me when I thought I was going down."

What was ironic about the press accounts was that the stories were written and filed well before they were *published*. Some papers had updated their May 9 accounts to reflect reality; but others still reported on May 9: "A Navy court of inquiry today was investigating a mysterious explosion which shattered a Navy Eagle boat and took the lives of 49 men three miles offshore April 23."

These stories appeared one week *after* the Court of Inquiry had ruled already that the *Eagle* was destroyed by a catastrophic boiler explosion.

May 17, 1945
U-boat Tracking Room
Washington, D.C.

Nine days after V-E Day, the Secret Room prepared an "Anti-Submarine Bulletin" reporting that thirty-five U-boats had surrendered to the Allies, "in accordance with surrender orders broadcast initially on 8 May." The *U-805*, a 740-tonner, was the first to "report her position in plain language" on May 9, and proceed to port. Since then, six more U-boats surrendered in the western Atlantic, arriving in Philadelphia, Portsmouth, New Hampshire, Shelbourne, Nova Scotia, and Bull's Bay, Newfoundland. One other U-boat, the *U-234*, a 1,600-tonner bound for Japan, was expected to arrive in Portsmouth on May 19. The *U-234* was carrying two Japanese officers and a valuable set of plans, according to the bulletin, when she was met by a U.S. escort. "In accordance with the national custom [of Japan], the Japs committed *hari-kari* [suicide] before the U-boat was met," the Secret Room bulletin reported matter-of-factly.

In the Eastern Atlantic, another twenty-eight U-boats had surrendered, the majority of which arrived in British ports. One of these, the *U-532*, was returning from the Far East with a cargo of tin, rubber, and quinine. Other boats surrendered off Portugal and reported to Gibraltar, while "a large number of U-boats have been captured in enemy ports, but the situation has not been clarified at this writing," the bulletin stated.

Despite its attack on the *Eagle 56*, one other U-boat would have had the same opportunity to surrender, had she not sunk the *Black Point* in a foolish assault two days before war's end. Now, the *U-853* lay broken and still at the bottom of the Atlantic, her entire fifty-five-man crew dead inside, an already rusting memorial to her commander's vainglory and his meaningless sacrifice of some of Germany's bravest young sailors.

May 23, 1945
Flensburg, Germany

Since the German surrender, the Allies had occupied this city in Schleswig-Holstein, near the German border, while Karl Dönitz's skeleton government still went through the fiction of functioning. "Every morning its members held cabinet meetings and solemnly discussed and voted on plans that they had no powers to implement," noted authors Ann and John Tusa. "The Allied authorities simply could not work out the correct protocol for taking the surrender of a government that had ceased to exist in consequence of its unconditional surrender. So for the moment they were leaving it some trappings while acting elsewhere as if it did not exist."

Finally, though, the Allies put the vanquished government out of its misery when U.S. Major General Lowell W. Rooks of the Allied

Control Commission summoned Dönitz to the liner *Patria* and arrested him. American economist John Kenneth Galbraith recalled standing on the upper deck of the Hamburg-American vessel and watching Dönitz as he "came smartly along the quay, saluted the ship and flag, and marched up the gangplank" to surrender the final tattered remnant of the Third Reich.

28

Esta Glenn watched through tearful eyes as the wreath rode the gentle Pacific swells, gliding atop a wave's foamy crest one moment, dipping into a deep-blue trough the next. She leaned on the destroyer's rail, felt the ocean spray in her face and hair, the salt mixing with her tears on this saddest of Memorial Days.

The Navy had invited her and other area war widows to drop wreaths into the Pacific as part of solemn ceremonies to honor the memories of their husbands who had been killed in action. Esta did so with pride; she could think of no better way to honor Harold than to memorialize him at sea. Her Midwest farm boy had developed strong sea legs during his *Eagle 56* service, and she knew in her heart that he would approve of her decision to accept the Navy's invitation. She believed Glenn was watching her now, looking down on the destroyer with his razor-blue eyes, sporting his cocky smile. She was a continent away from where her beloved had slipped beneath the waves forever, but she felt close to him here on the water. As the wreath swirled and skimmed along each crest, she never wanted to lose sight of it, fearing, if she did, that she would lose Glenn once and for all, too, a pain she did not think she could endure. She even thought fleetingly about stepping over the rail and diving into the rolling Pacific, peacefully dropping beneath the surface, sure that she would be reunited with Glenn moments after she stopped breathing. But then she thought this would be unfair to the Navy men who had arranged and invited her to this Memorial Day ceremony. So she was content to watch the wreath and think about him.

After she left Portland with Glenn's sister, she had spent three weeks in Marissa, Illinois, with Glenn's family, where they had grieved together. It was her first visit since her wedding reception. She would never forget the oppressive *stillness* of the Glenn farm, more claustrophobic and stifling than she had remembered despite its expansive acreage, the smell of manure and damp hay as foreign to her as the salty Pacific air had been to Harold when he first arrived in California. She understood fully why Harold had pulled up stakes and ventured to the West Coast, and also why he had suggested that they settle in California after the war.

Marissa was made even worse during her recent visit by the pall of loneliness and death that hung in the air, as thick and heavy as a blanket of humidity. After what she considered a respectful stay of three weeks, she bade her in-laws farewell—were they considered her *former* in-laws now that Glenn was gone and their connection severed?—and fled Marissa to return home. Alone, but home.

Her friends and coworkers had been supportive, murmuring their sympathies and moving along. They tried hard, and she was grateful for their words and their intentions, but not consoled. Of the hundreds of Pacific Gas & Electric men who had served in the military, Glenn was the only one who didn't make it back. She was so overwhelmed by the unfairness of it all that sometimes she had trouble breathing. In Glenn's memory, the company president presented Esta with a white enamel gold pin inlaid with a gold star, framed by a black border. It was a thoughtful gesture from a kind and decent man. She would, of course, surrender the pin in an instant in exchange for just one more kiss from Glenn, just one more moment like the morning of April 23 on the front steps of their Portland apartment house. She could hear his tender voice: "*I forgot to kiss you good-bye,*" and knew that the inflection of his words, the warmth of his embrace on that raw April morning, would be seared into her memory no matter how old she grew.

She gazed out over the ship's rail, sun reflecting off the water, and watched as the pull of the ocean swept the memorial wreath farther out to sea. For a brief moment it rode high on a wave crest, a black dot in the distance. And then it was gone.

June 5, 1945
F-21 U-boat Tracking Room
Washington, D.C.

Kenneth Knowles's final official memorandum as commander of the Secret Room was an uncharacteristically tender personal message to his Canadian counterpart, Lieutenant Commander John B. McDiarmid, head of the Royal Canadian Navy OIC Tracking Room in Ottawa. Both Knowles and British Commander Roger Winn had toured McDiarmid's operation when Winn visited the United States in the spring of 1942, and since that time, Knowles and McDiarmid had shared information and intelligence about U-boats operating off the Canadian and United States' east coasts.

Knowles's message to McDiarmid came only after the sub-tracking room had assisted and commented on final post-surrender issues concerning German U-boats.

First, intelligence reports had indicated that several U-boats had been on their way to Japan later in the war carrying German aircraft engineers, turbine engines, and valuable plans for the construction of jet- and rocket-propelled planes that could travel faster than the speed of sound, "built on the V-2 principle with steering apparatus." The tracking room knew that three U-boats were carrying plans—the *U-864*, *U-876*, and *U-234*—and confirmed that two of the subs had been sunk and the third surrendered after V-E Day to U.S. naval forces and was now in Portsmouth, New Hampshire. "There is no other evidence to indicate that the Japanese have been successful in obtaining [these] plans," the May 29 memo to COMINCH read, "although a number of signals containing technical information . . . were sent from Berlin beginning September 1944."

On June 4, a day before Knowles sent his note to McDiarmid, an "Ultra Top Secret" message to Admiral King reported that six U-boats known to be at sea at the time of the German surrender "are still unaccounted for. Three others in the same category have greatly exceeded their endurance and are now presumed sunk." The Tracking Room reported that the length of time these boats had been at sea since May 8 ranged from a minimum of twenty-one days to a maximum of eighty-nine days. "It is evident from the fuel capacity and length of time at sea of these U/Boats that none of them could have proceeded to Japan and it is therefore recommended that the attached dispatch be sent to . . . Buenos Aires," the Tracking Room memo offered. (After the war, Allied intelligence confirmed that indeed, five of these subs had been sunk, and one apparently returned to her home base in the Baltics. One of these unaccounted-for U-boats, the *U-881*, was sunk off the coast of New York on the same day, ironically, as the *U-853* was destroyed off Block Island. This information apparently was either not reported by the escort *Farquhar*, which killed the *U-881* on May 6, was not transmitted to the Tracking Room by OP-20-G code breakers, or else, was mistakenly omitted from the Tracking Room's intelligence reports; the latter possibility seems highly unlikely, given the Secret Room's reputation for thoroughness and impeccable intelligence analyses.)

Now, Tuesday, June 5, with the business of war over in Europe, and with the explosive roar of the Battle of the Atlantic finally stilled, Knowles, in a memo tinged with bittersweet recollections, wrote to McDiarmid:

> Our U/Boat tracking room is being dissolved on 12 June 1945. Upon my detachment from COMINCH Headquarters, may I express to you my deep appreciation for your helpful cooperation during the momentous period our tracking rooms have worked together on our common task, which has now been so successfully completed. Good luck and good-bye. Kenneth A. Knowles.

One week later, on June 12, 1945, as Knowles had precisely noted, the F-21 Sub-Tracking Room and the sealed off F-211 Secret Room officially ceased operations.

Most of America and the world would not know of their existence, let alone their contributions, for decades.

Mid-June, 1945
Blue Mountain, Alabama

Hazel Woods handled the two-page letter from Johnny Breeze carefully, grateful to finally read a personalized account of her husband's death, something more than a newspaper story or an official naval communiqué.

Machinist Mate 2nd Class Ralph William Woods was aboard the USS *Eagle 56* when she exploded on April 23, five months shy of his twenty-fifth birthday. Hazel, a widow now before she turned twenty-two, was left to raise their two-year-old daughter herself; the letter in front of her connected her to Ralph and would give her the strength to go on.

Hazel and Ralph had seemed destined to be together forever. They were both born in nearby Anniston, a valley town in northeast Alabama nestled in the Appalachian foothills. They were high school sweet-hearts—Ralph a few grades ahead of her—and they were married when Hazel was seventeen years old, just four months before the Japanese at-tack on Pearl Harbor would change their lives.

When the *Eagle 56* went down, Hazel and her daughter, Dianna, were living in South Portland, Maine. News was sketchy for days, though most of the talk was that an enemy torpedo had destroyed the ship. On May 11, she received a note from the naval chaplain, along with a clipping from the *Portland Press Herald*, providing a detailed account of the *Eagle*'s sinking. The Navy would have sent the clipping earlier, the chaplain said, but "was unable . . . because of reasons of security."

Hazel and Dianna returned to Alabama, and on June 2, Hazel had received an official letter from another naval chaplain: "It has just come to our attention that your husband has been listed as missing. Please ac-cept our deepest sympathy . . . This office has no information . . . You may rest assured that any new developments in your husband's case will be communicated to you without delay." Beyond that, she had little news about Ralph's death. Had he died quickly? Had he suffered? Was anyone with him when he drowned?

Now, finally, some additional news. Johnny Breeze had sent the let-ter to Ralph's aunt, who had raised him after his mother died when he was fifteen years old. Breeze apparently had the aunt's address, not Hazel's, but it was no matter; Ralph's aunt passed on the letter—Breeze's beautiful, thoughtful letter—and Hazel had read it several times already:

> I don't know how many times I have tried to write this letter, but each time I did, it seemed as though the words were cruel and mean. I vowed to finish this time, so believe me when I say that I mean you no sorrow or anguish.
>
> I knew "Woody" for the few short months he lived on the ship as one of the "Black Gang." Since he and I were both engineers, we got to know each other in just a few days. He was soon kidding me, and laughing with me in our everyday doings, and while I knew him I had fun talking and working with him.
>
> Why God should spare me while he saw fit to take the rest, I do not pretend to know, but I am truly sorry that Ralph did not come with me.
>
> I hope you can get some small measure of consolation when I tell you that "Woody" passed from our earth painlessly and quickly. He

was on watch in the engine room when the explosion occurred, so his fate was quick and merciful. I am sure that Ralph never knew what hit the ship, believe that, please.

The Navy did not come to any definite conclusion of what caused the explosion, but the boys were inclined to think that it was a torpedo. No one will ever know for sure just what happened, so I'm sorry that I cannot give you any more information.

I guess I haven't said much, but words come hard with me at such a time, so I hope you will excuse my clumsiness at writing you with such heartbreaking news.

Please give Mrs. Woods my deepest sympathy, for it's from my heart as one of Ralph's shipmates.

I would stake my life that Ralph died a happy man.

> Very sincerely yours,
> J. L. Breeze

Hazel did not think Johnny Breeze's letter was clumsy at all. It informed and comforted her at the same time. Her broken heart would never truly heal, but she took solace from Breeze's reassurances that Ralph had died quickly and happily. She was deeply grateful that Breeze found the time to write, and would cherish his letter until the day she died.

29

John Scagnelli had spent the last five weeks alternating his time between pushing paper and battling guilt.

In late June, the *Eagle*'s lone surviving officer had been transferred for temporary duty to the Bureau of Naval Personnel (BuPers) in the nation's capital, assigned a desk and a clerical person, and ordered to close the book on the *Eagle 56* story. Now his time in Washington was coming to an end; he would be officially detached from BuPers on July 30.

For Scagnelli, the work was painful and surreal at the same time. Washington and the nation were still celebrating V-E Day and anticipating the end of the war with Japan, while Scagnelli was buried in paperwork and grief. He had arrived in Washington in the midst of an oppressive heat wave, yet the city was still exultant over its outpouring of affection just days earlier for the man who had led the Allies to victory in Europe. More than one million men, women, and children had jammed the sidewalks along Washington's wide avenues to honor General Dwight D. Eisenhower. *Time* magazine described the parade as a "triumphal tour unparalleled in U.S. history . . . People hung from windows [and] perched in trees. As the General passed, the roar of welcome all but drowned out the bands along the street. He stood in his car, arms outstretched, grinning as though at old friends. When police lines broke at 14th Street and Pennsylvania Avenue, he leaned out to shake hands with those who pushed against his automobile." Ike, flushed and perspiring after the open auto tour, then strode into the Capitol to address a joint session of Congress, where he said it was his "passionate belief" that forces capable of crushing "the world's greatest war machines" were also capable of keeping the peace. The next day, Eisenhower had traveled to New York, which welcomed him "with a tumult which dwarfed the memory of receptions for Admiral Dewey, General Pershing, Charles Lindbergh, and Admiral Byrd," *Time* noted. "Along Fifth Avenue and in the high canyons of the financial district, clerks threw cautionings and paper to the winds, sent 77 tons of ticker tape and torn wastepaper fluttering down . . . everywhere the sound of cheering erupted deafeningly."

Celebrating was the last thing Scagnelli felt like doing, then or now. He had spent better than a month filling out benefits and next-of-kin forms, compiling the final sailing list of the *Eagle* and the duties of the men on board, cataloging for his superiors what personal effects and official Navy articles had been lost with the ship—deck logs, account registers, and personnel records. He had to recount the sinking for the Welfare Division so family members could receive benefits. "In view of the extreme violence of the explosion, and of the fact that rescue operations were continued until 2316, it is believed that all personnel not rescued, either living or dead, must now be considered dead, having gone down with the ship or drowned while awaiting rescue," Scagnelli wrote. "In addition to the state of the sea (force), the temperature of the water, and the absence of any response or sighting reports from any other sources, all combine to re-emphasize the inevitable conclusion that survival in the water after the departure of the rescue ship was impossible. In view of the above-mentioned considerations, amplifying reports on 47 men are enclosed changing their status from 'missing' to 'dead' [two bodies were recovered at the scene and pronounced dead there]."

In addition to drafting the official documents, Scagnelli had painstakingly labored over what he believed was far more important work: writing more than sixty condolence letters to send to the wives, parents, uncles, and aunts of his fallen shipmates, officially informing them that their husbands, sons, and nephews would not be coming home. The Navy would not allow Scagnelli to mention, or even imply, a torpedo attack, nor could he explain why the *Eagle 56* was at a dead stop just after noon on April 23, 1945; he simply did not know the answer to the question that had nagged him just before the explosion had occurred. Scagnelli never has suggested, and probably never will, what other naval scholars have said about the "dead stop" issue: Captain Early, had he survived the torpedo attack, likely would have faced a court-martial for this serious breach of regulations. The exact reason why the *Eagle 56* was stopped is a mystery lost with the ship and the officers who were stationed on the bridge when the torpedo struck.

In the boilerplate paragraph that he wrote to each family, Scagnelli recounted the *Eagle* sinking without mentioning any cause for the explosion: "I think that you will want to know what happened to the USS *Eagle*. On the morning of the 23rd we were engaged in carrying out exercises which consisted of towing a spar for aerial torpedo bombing practice. We had completed the morning's exercise and were standing by awaiting another group of planes; meanwhile, noon-chow was put down and the men who were not on watch either rested or sat about talking. At approximately 12:15 the ship was rocked by a terrific explosion which split the ship in half and rendered practically everyone unconscious. The ship sank within a few minutes, and those men who were not conscious were unable to help themselves and went down with the ship."

And then, in every case, Scagnelli struck a personal note about his comrades. "I tried to remember some little bit of something about each person so the families understood that he was being treated as an individual, not just a number," Scagnelli would say years later. He struggled for hours over four weeks to craft the letters, drafting them by hand and then turning them over to his typist.

To Phyllis Westerlund he wrote: "Your husband was known throughout the ship for his amiability. He performed his duty cheerfully and capably and was always ready to go out of his way to do anything for his ship and buddies. 'West' helped us organize and coach the ship's basketball team, which developed into a successful team through his efforts. It is men of 'West's' character around which the Navy is built. We will always remember him as a good shipmate and companion."

To Esta Glenn: "Harold was well liked by both his officers and shipmates. He was continually good-natured and one never saw him aboard ship that he didn't have some cheerful comment. He was a conscientious individual who utilized his spare time in taking correspondence courses given by the Navy so that he might further his station in life. He knew his job and did it well. The quiet manner in which he applied himself was admired by those who worked with him."

Scagnelli addressed most of the recipients formally—"My dear Mrs. Westerlund" or "My dear Mrs. Glenn"—but to the wife of his dear friend, Jack Laubach, he simply wrote: "Dear Ginny." His affection for Laubach was apparent: "His was a commanding personality, yet we all knew him as a warm-hearted friend who gladly shared all of his men's hardships and headaches. We remember him with his inevitable pipe puffing contently on the bridge of the ship working out a navigational problem or at his desk hard at work with his engineering lessons. I spent many an hour with Jack talking about the future and the plans he was formulating to secure a permanent place in the civilian world . . . We lost a great friend and companion in Jack, but may you, Ginny, draw consolation from the fact that he passed into his eternity suddenly, totally unaware of what had happened."

In nearly all of the letters, Scagnelli offered comfort on how his shipmates had died. For those entombed in the ship's bow and stern sections, Scagnelli wrote passages such as, "the force of the explosion rendered him unconscious and he went down with the ship void of struggle or pain." For those who made it to the water but died before they were rescued, Scagnelli chose different words: ". . . the sea conditions and the water temperature exhausted him so that he passed quietly away in the water soothed by the daze of shock and excitement."

For several sailors, Scagnelli had to write more than one condolence letter—one to a wife and a separate one to parents, for example—and in each case he found something slightly different to say about the *Eagle* crew member. For him, the condolence letters were a way to memorialize each man and ease his family's pain. But it broke his heart to omit the story of the U-boat and the torpedo. Would these families ever know the truth? Could they ever forgive him?

And even though he knew with every fiber of his being that a faulty boiler had not destroyed the *Eagle*, the official version of events gave rise to a question that he was almost afraid to ask: Could he ever forgive himself?

During John Scagnelli's brief stay in Washington, D.C., the American capital was abuzz with activity, and major news was occurring across the world.

President Truman presented to the Senate for ratification a charter for a new United Nations, one he hoped would bring world peace for the next fifty years. With that task completed, Truman traveled to Potsdam, Germany, to discuss with the British and Russians the fate of postwar Germany and Europe.

Meanwhile, America was bringing home troops from Europe at a pace of more than 50,000 per month—the *Queen Elizabeth* arrived in New York Harbor on the last day of June with more than 13,000 GIs aboard—and transferring hundreds of thousands more to the Pacific. With his work in Washington completed, Scagnelli himself would be shipping out to San Diego in a few weeks, then would likely board a ship bound for an island base in anticipation of the invasion of Japan. Trains across America were jammed, and the Office of Defense Transportation banned the use of sleeping cars for civilians for trips shorter than 450 miles after an Arizona senator called for an investigation into the "shocking" situation involving troops being "subjected to arduous and uncomfortably long train trips" without adequate facilities. *The New York Times* reported: "There have also been expressions of criticism in the House in the last several days over reports that battle-weary veterans had been moved across the country in coaches lacking ventilation, sanitary facilities, and sufficient space to eliminate conditions of over-crowding."

GIs who were either returning home to or passing through New York City got a taste of fear on U.S. soil when, on July 29, an American B-25 bomber, flying too low over Manhattan, crashed into the Empire State Building, setting it afire at the seventy-ninth floor, killing thirteen and injuring more than twenty-five. "Horror-stricken occupants of the building, alarmed by the roar of engines, ran to the windows just in time to see the plane loom out of the gray mists that swathed the upper floors of the world's tallest office building," reported *The New York Times*. "Its wings were sheared off by the impact, but the motors and fuselage ripped a hole eighteen feet wide and twenty feet high in the outer wall of the seventy-eighth and seventy-ninth floors of the structure."

But American planes inflicted their greatest damage in the Far East, as B-29 long-range bombers repeatedly and relentlessly pounded Japanese cities, including Tokyo. By late July, the devastating attacks from American bombers had dropped a record tonnage of bombs on Japan, and the Twentieth Air Force warned residents in eleven Japanese cities of their imminent destruction by aerial assaults from Superfortress bombers. "In one of the most remarkable challenges ever issued by any air force against an enemy, leaflets were dropped during the night over the eleven designated cities, of which four will be struck in the next few days," reported *The New York Times* on July 28. "Radio broadcasts from Saipan . . . are repeating the warning to the Japanese people at intervals, urging the residents of those cities to flee their homes."

Yet, on July 30, the Japanese officially rejected an ultimatum issued by the United States, Great Britain, and China to surrender or meet destruction, dismissing it as "propaganda" and labeling it as evidence of the "war-weariness" of the Allies. Japanese kamikaze pilots on deadly suicide missions continued to slam into American battleships in the Pacific. Newspapers carried accounts of Japan training a "mass suicide corps" and providing them with a "tremendous volume of secret, suicide weapons . . . [that] a man would ride to his doom during the Pacific war's inevitable showdown on the Japanese home island." Ultra reports revealed a daunting picture of a vast killing ground in preparation. "Nearly 5,000 kamikazes were being stockpiled, with enough fuel to provide all of them with a one-way flight," historian Geoffrey Perret pointed out. "It had cost 50,000 American casualties to take Okinawa . . . if that was the yardstick, then seizing Kyushu would bring a casualty toll of 275,000 dead and wounded Americans."

Americans considered this news with a mixture of pride and fear. American soldiers, sailors, and airmen had vanquished the once-powerful military forces of Nazi Germany and seemed on the verge of defeating Japan. Yet, the ferociousness with which the Japanese had battled on places like Iwo Jima and Okinawa, the tenacity they displayed even as their cities were being reduced to rubble, the exalted martyrdom they bestowed upon their kamikaze pilots—all gave pause to Americans as they pondered the potentially staggering losses an invasion of the Japanese homeland could produce.

In July of 1945, banner headlines trumpeted these issues and events as they unfolded, and Americans must have sensed that they were participants in one of history's most remarkable eras.

Yet, virtually none of them knew *anything* about the biggest story of all that was taking place that month. Thanks to careful planning and execution, unprecedented security, and the isolation that accompanies geographical remoteness, this world-changing news had been kept a total secret.

That fact was about to change.

30

As John Scagnelli was preparing to leave Washington, D.C., at the end of his BuPers assignment, President Harry S. Truman was preparing to leave Potsdam for his return voyage to the United States. The conference had produced a mixture of small victories, tense negotiations, unresolved issues, and maddening frustration. The president wanted Germany's future satisfactorily settled, free elections in Poland, Eastern Europe, and the Balkans, and he wanted Russia to join in the assault on Japan. "But only on this last item could he feel he had succeeded," historian David McCullough wrote. "For the rest he faced ambiguity, delays, and frustration, Stalin having no wish to accept any agreement that threatened the control he already had, wherever the Red Army stood." Despite his best efforts, Truman could make little or no progress with Josef Stalin.

Yet, as the conference concluded and Truman prepared to set sail for America on August 2, he had even larger matters on his mind. In July, the president had authorized the chief of staff to move more than one million troops for a final attack on Japan; thirty divisions were on the way to the Pacific from the European Theater. Japan had amassed some 2.5 million regular troops on the home islands, and McCullough noted that "every male between the ages of fifteen and sixty and every female from seventeen to forty-five, was being conscripted and armed with everything from ancient brass cannon to bamboo spears, taught to strap explosives to their bodies and throw themselves under advancing tanks. One woman would remember being given a carpenter's awl and instructed that killing just one American would do. 'You must aim at the abdomen,' she was told. 'Understand? The abdomen.' Thousands of [additional] planes were ready to serve as kamikazes." Truman foresaw unprecedented American carnage in any attempted invasion. "It occurred to me," he would remark a few months later, "that a quarter million of the flower of our young manhood were worth a couple of Japanese cities, and I still think they were and are."

Truman believed the United States had a weapon that could preclude the need for a bloody invasion of Japan and save thousands of American lives, and he had authorized its use a week earlier. Had the atomic bomb been ready in March and deployed by President Roosevelt, had it shocked Japan into surrender then, it would have already saved fifty thousand American lives lost in the Pacific since. Now it was ready.

On July 21, President Truman had reviewed a powerful report from General Leslie Groves, director of the Manhattan Project, the code name for the development of the nuclear bomb. Just days before, in a remote part of the Alamogordo Air Base in the New Mexico desert, there had been a blinding flash "as bright as a thousand suns," from the first nuclear explosion in history. Groves's report detailed the momentous event in language worthy of epoch-making history:

> For the first time in history there was a nuclear explosion. And what an explosion . . . For a brief period there was a lightning effect within a radius of 20 miles equal to several suns in midday; a huge ball of fire was formed which lasted for several seconds. This ball mushroomed and rose to a height of over ten thousand feet before it dimmed. The light from the explosion was seen clearly in Albuquerque, Santa Fe, Silver City, El Paso, and other points generally to about 180 miles away. . . . A massive cloud was formed which surged and billowed upward with tremendous power, reaching the substratosphere at an elevation of 41,000 feet, 36,000 feet above the ground, in about five minutes, breaking without interruption through a temperature inversion of 17,000 feet, which most of the scientists thought would stop it . . . Two supplementary explosions occurred in the cloud shortly after the main explosion . . . Huge concentrations of highly radioactive materials resulted from the fission and were contained in the cloud.

The test bomb had not been dropped from a plane, but exploded on top of a 100-foot steel tower, which had evaporated, leaving nothing but a crater more than 1,000 feet in diameter. The energy generated was estimated to be the equivalent of 15,000 to 20,000 *tons* of TNT. Its destructive power was awesome, Groves stated:

> One-half mile from the explosion there was a massive steel test cylinder weighing 230 tons. The base of the cylinder was solidly encased in concrete. Surrounding the cylinder was a strong steel tower 70 feet high, anchored to concrete foundations. The tower is comparable to a steel building bay that would be found in a typical 15- to 20-story skyscraper or in warehouse construction. Forty tons of steel were used to fabricate the tower which was . . . the height of a six-story building. The cross bracing was much stronger than that normally used in ordinary steel construction. The absence of solid walls of a building gave the blast a much less effective surface to push against. [Yet] the blast tore the tower from its foundation, twisted it, ripped it apart. and left if flat on the ground. The effects of the tower indicate that, at that distance, unshielded permanent steel and masonry buildings would have been destroyed . . . None of us had expected it to be damaged.

In the report, Groves also included the impressions of his deputy, General Thomas Farrell: "Everyone in that room knew the awful potentialities of the thing they thought was about to happen," Farrell reported, who also wrote of the explosion's "searing light" and a "roar which warned of doomsday." As for the scientists, including J. Robert Oppenheimer, director of the Los Alamos National Laboratory, Farrell added: "All seemed to sense immediately that the explosion had far exceeded the most optimistic expectations and wildest hopes of the scientists. All seemed to feel that they had been present at the birth of a new age . . ." Truman himself wrote in his diary on July 25: "We have discovered the most terrible bomb in the history of the world."

Days after Groves's report, on July 26, the cruiser *Indianapolis* delivered the U-235 portion of the atomic bomb, nicknamed "Little Boy," to the island of Tinian. All that remained was for Truman to give the final go-ahead for the use of the bomb, a decision only he could make, and one that Groves hoped could be made no later than August 1. On the morning of July 31, the president, "writing large and clear with a lead pencil on the back of [a] pink message," according to McCullough,

Truman gave his answer: "Suggestion approved. Release when ready but not sooner than August 2."

President Truman wanted to be away from Stalin and Potsdam when the atomic bomb was dropped on Japan.

At 8:05 A.M. on Thursday, August 2, Truman boarded an airplane at Gatow Airfield to take him to Plymouth, England, to meet the USS *Augusta*. After he lunched with England's King George VI aboard another ship, Truman returned to the *Augusta*, which left for America at around 4:00 P.M.

August 6, 1945
Morning, at sea, aboard the USS *Augusta*

Four hours after the atomic bomb was dropped on the Japanese industrial city of Hiroshima by the B-29 *Enola Gay*, Truman received a decoded message at sea from the secretary of war: "Results clear-cut successful in all respects. Visible effects greater than in any test." Minutes later, a second message arrived: "Big bomb dropped on Hiroshima August 5 at 7:15 P.M. Washington time. First reports indicate complete success which was even more conspicuous than earlier test."

An exuberant Truman announced the attack to his staff and crew, and by 11:00 A.M., Washington time, the text of the president's message was broadcast to the American people:

> Sixteen hours ago an American airplane dropped one bomb on Hiroshima . . . It is an atomic bomb. It is a harnessing of the basic power of the universe. . . We are now prepared to obliterate more rapidly and completely every productive enterprise the Japanese have above ground in any city. We shall destroy their docks, their factories, and their communications. Let there be no mistake; we shall completely destroy Japan's power to make war . . . If they do not now accept our terms they may expect a rain of ruin from the air, the likes of which has never been seen on this earth . . .

Neither Truman nor anyone else at that moment was yet aware of the full force of the bomb's destructiveness. On the ground in Hiroshima, an unimaginable incandescence had swallowed the sky and outshone the sun. The heat in the fireball above the city was later calculated at 540,000 degrees Fahrenheit. At Ground Zero, the temperature reached 11,000 degrees Fahrenheit and air pressure reached eight tons per square yard. Estimates would later put the death count at 140,000 or more—at least 80,000 killed instantly and the other 60,000 in the next several months. Thousands more suffered from thermal burns, shock, and radioactive poisoning. No one could predict that years and even decades afterward, the aftereffects of radiation would continue to claim new victims.

And still there was no word from Japan on surrender.

August 6, 1945
St. Paul Community Hospital
Cushing, Nebraska

Pauline Michelsen—her friends and family called her "Freddie" after her maiden name, Fredricksen—nuzzled her newborn son and listened to the joyous shouting outside her hospital room. Fredrick John Michelsen Jr. had been born at 4:05 A.M. Nebraska time on August 6, 1945, a date that would forever mark the atomic bombing of Hiroshima, but one that Freddie recorded as the birth of her first child, which took place three and a half months after her husband had been killed when the *Eagle 56* exploded.

The Navy hadn't officially acknowledged her husband's death; Mike was still listed as "missing," but Freddie held out no hope. On the day the *Eagle* went down, she and Mike had been living in a tiny apartment on Bracket Street in Portland, no bigger than a closet, really, and she had heard the news immediately. She worked as a registered nurse in a hospital a few blocks away, and she rushed to the docks to help. "Pete" Petersen explained to her how Mike had relieved him just before the explosion rocked the ship. The rescue ships had fished only thirteen survivors out of water so cold that no man could survive for very long.

Then there had been telegrams from the Navy command, the Navy chaplain, and the Navy's Casualty Section all expressing their "deepest sympathy" upon the loss of her "missing" husband. She would not kid herself—Mike was gone and would never see their baby. It seemed to her that Naval Reserve Chaplain Robert Scott had probably violated some sort of Navy protocol when he wrote in his "missing" letter: "Your husband . . . *died* for his country and for its ideals just as surely as if he had gone down in some Pacific battle." Even the language in the letter she had received from Nebraska Governor Dwight Griswold seemed to unofficially confirm Mike's death: "I have just read of the loss of your husband and while I realize that there is little anyone can do which will be of help to you . . . I do want you to know that the people of Nebraska are deeply appreciative of the sacrifice you have made."

Freddie left Portland on May 1, about a week after the *Eagle* sinking, and embarked on a circuitous three-train rail journey, paid for by the Navy, that took her to Boston, New York City, Chicago, Omaha, and finally, to Grand Island, Nebraska, where she returned to her family farm. It was an arduous journey under any circumstances, but in her case, pregnant and alone, mourning the violent death of her husband, she felt as though her trip would never end; that the Navy agreed to pay for a private lower berth made it only just bearable.

Today, on the day her son was born, she had relived memories. She and Mike had grown up on farms in Howard County, Nebraska, met and fallen in love in high school, before he left in 1936 at age twenty to live with relatives and work in Oregon. She moved west shortly thereafter to be with him, living with relatives of her own, until the two were married on April 22, 1939. He worked as a driver for the Westfir Lumber Company, earned $1,600 in 1941, and they felt rich before he enlisted in the Navy in 1942. She remembered how Mike, a product of a broken home, loved her parents, writing them scores of personal letters from the Naval Training Center in Great Lakes, Illinois, in 1942. "Dear Mom and Pops," he had written once to his in-laws, "Take good care of Pauline for me, as I want her all in one piece when I get home." Later he wrote: "Dear Mom and Pops, Don't mind if I call you that, do you? Mr. and Mrs. Fredricksen sounds so formal." Then, just before Freddie had visited him for a weekend trip to Chicago, Mike had written to her parents: "I can hardly wait until Saturday when I can see Freddie; that is really going to be swell." They had spent a wonderful weekend touring Chicago, staying at the Palmer House Hotel, where their room cost $7.20 per night.

And then, more recent memories. Twenty-four hours before the *Eagle* sunk, on April 22, 1945, their sixth wedding anniversary, Mike had brought home apricots and she baked an apricot pie. They ate pie, talked about the baby and their future, and later that night, Mike let her paint his toenails red, the two of them laughing over the likely reaction of his shipmates when they found out the next day.

Now she wondered what would become of her. She was smart, independent, and resourceful, but now she lay in a tiny hospital about the size of a three-room house with a new baby and had no idea what the future held. Mike was dead, but the fact that she had received no official

word made her feel worse, not better. In mid-May she had written to
Navy Chaplain Scott: "Would you be able to tell me if any ship went out
over the area where my husband's ship sank and held memorial services?
It would make me feel better in my heart if I knew they had." The chaplain had yet to answer.

Outside her hospital room, she heard the sounds of ringing bells and
shouts of joy as news of President Truman's message and the dropping
of the atomic bomb spread. Like towns across America, the people of
Cushing, Nebraska, were celebrating what they hoped was the imminent end to the war.

But in her bed, Pauline Michelsen sobbed uncontrollably and
pressed little Fred, now just hours old, close to her broken heart.

Three days later, on August 9, true to President Truman's threat to bring
a "rain of ruin" from the sky upon Japan, the United States dropped a
second atomic bomb on the major Japanese seaport of Nagasaki, a shipbuilding and torpedo-factory center on the southern island of Kyushu.
Another 70,000 people were killed, and estimates were that the damage
would have been far worse if the bombardier had not been off-target by
two miles.

That night, Truman addressed the American people: "I realize the
tragic significance of the atomic bomb," he said. "Its production and its
use were not lightly undertaken by this government . . . Having found
the bomb, we used it. We have used it against those who attacked us
without warning at Pearl Harbor, against those who have starved and
beaten and executed American prisoners of war, against those who have
abandoned all pretense of obeying international laws of warfare. We
have used it in order to shorten the agony of war, in order to save the
lives of thousands and thousands of young Americans. We shall continue to use it until we completely destroy Japan's power to make war.
Only a Japanese surrender will stop us."

Finally, less than twenty-four hours after Nagasaki, it was Emperor
Hirohito who decided that Japan must "bear the unbearable" and surrender. The Japanese government would accept the Potsdam Declaration with the understanding that the emperor would remain sovereign.
On August 14, 1945, President Truman received word that Japan had
officially surrendered.

Massive celebrations broke out in cities and towns across the nation, including more than half a million people in Washington, D.C., where President Truman addressed the crowd outside the White House: "This is a great day, the day we've been waiting for. This is the day for free governments in the world. This is the day that fascism and police governments cease in the world."

The greatest war in mankind's history—one that had claimed more than fifty million military and civilian lives around the world, consumed untold material wealth, destroyed the economies of several nations, and wreaked unimagined death and destruction upon some of the world's great cities—had finally ended. After six years, the guns were silent.

Pauline Michelsen's personal dates of anguish mirrored history's big picture. Her baby was born on August 6, Hiroshima Day. On August 9, the day the second atomic bomb struck Nagasaki, she received the official Western Union telegram that her husband, Fredrick Michelsen, was dead: A CAREFUL REVIEW OF ALL FACTS AVAILABLE . . . LEADS TO THE CONCLUSION THAT THERE IS NOT [SIC] HOPE FOR HIS SURVIVAL AND THAT HE LOST HIS LIFE AS A RESULT OF AN EXPLOSION ON 23 APRIL 1945, read the message from Vice Admiral Randall Jones, Chief of Naval Personnel. And, on August 14, Victory over Japan, or V-J Day, Pauline received a similar message from another Navy chaplain, who said: "It will bring you comfort and justifiable pride, I am sure, always to remember that your husband, when he died, was serving our nation as a member of the Naval forces, and doing his part to bring about victory in our struggle to maintain justice and freedom for all."

In between these messages, Freddie Michelsen received a letter that she cherished most of all, one dated August 2 from *Eagle 56* Lt. John Scagnelli. The letter had been mailed to Portland and rerouted to Nebraska. Scagnelli had explained the explosion, pointed out that Mike was in the engine room at the time, and said "there is no doubt that he died instantly, unaware of what had happened."

But it was Scagnelli's next paragraph—one that described Mike's skills, his special personality, and the respect he evoked in his shipmates—that provided the greatest comfort and solace for Freddie Michelsen:

> Mike was one of the finest men I have been privileged to know.
> He knew the ship, was experienced in his duties, and he earnestly
> endeavored to do the best possible job at all times. The ship, particu-
> larly in the engineering department, was fortunate to be favored with
> the good judgment and skill that Mike possessed. He was the most

outstanding petty officer in his division, and all his associates and coworkers deeply respected and admired Mike. No matter where he was, he could always be seen engaged in conversation; joking, laughing, and enjoying the brighter side of any situation . . . Though you as a nurse must face death constantly, I know your personal loss will not be lessened by your professional tasks, but may the knowledge that Mike died swiftly and without pain help you in your hour of grief.

31

Ginny Laubach read and reread her mother-in-law's poems, despair and grief encircling her like fog tendrils, imbuing her with the indisputable certainty that the hole in her heart would never fully heal. It was her first Christmas without Jack since she was a child, the first in seven years that they would not celebrate the holiday as husband and wife, and the total loneliness she felt pressed on her like a weight on her chest.

More than eight months had passed since Jack's death, every hour dragging, the horizon of every day stretching endlessly before her, the twenty-third of each month elevated to holy status marking the anniversaries of her husband's death. This month, December 23, was perhaps the hardest. Her neighbors were celebrating the first Christmas at peace after four previous ones at war; the country was rejoicing in the return of millions of veterans from distant battles, as the Armed Services moved mountains to bring as many men home as possible for Christmas. Jack would be one of more than four hundred thousand American servicemen who would not be coming home.

Since April, Ginny had heard from John Barr, the former commander of the *Eagle 56* who had transferred to the Pacific three months before the ship had exploded. John and Jack had been close friends, and Ginny admired John Barr as a commander of men. She believed firmly that Jack would be alive today had Barr still been skippering the *Eagle* on April 23, 1945. She knew John Barr felt his own deep guilt about the *Eagle* sinking, but her feelings were not meant to lay blame or assign guilt; they were simply her own deep convictions. Years later, she would share them with others, including Barr's daughter.

She had also grown closer to Jack's mother since his death. They had always been dear friends, but their mutual loss had bound them together in an unbreakable bond that Ginny sensed was permanent. To deal with her grief and honor her son's memory, Jack's mother had decided to write poetry. She had shared the first two poems with Ginny this Christmas, and had vowed to write more. Ginny read the first again, entitled "I See You":

I see you in the dawning sky,
I hear you in each little sigh.
In all life's beauty and greatness, you are here;
In all its sadness and heartache, you are near.
I see you in the trusting eyes of each little child,
I feel you in the small hand they place in mine.
You are part of all that is fine and true
As you are part of all the suffering this world must bear,
For I know that of each, you had a full share.

I am thankful for the short years you were here,
You realized all of the beauty and fullness of life.
All the wonders of the best one in love can know.
Even thankful for the heartaches you had to bear—
The fine way you met them, and the splendid man you grew
* to be, my son.*

I thank God for each year you were here—
For all the memories you have left in my heart
For all the vision growing beauty through the years.
But most of all, for the love I saw shining from your eyes
When last you smiled at me, my dear.
I know now that God was very near.

There was a mother's anguish in her words, Ginny thought, but there was also hope and gratitude and pride—for the joy and beauty Jack brought to their lives, for the man he was, and perhaps for the even better man he would have become. Jack's mother, a deeply religious woman, affirmed her faith and her belief that God would comfort her through her ordeal in her second poem, entitled simply "Christmas—1945":

> *You are the star that guides me, as the wise men were guided*
> *of old.*
> *When I look on your picture I see the beauty of God in*
> *your soul.*
> *'Tis the glory of His sky and sun, so fair*
> *In the blue of your eyes, and the gold of your hair.*
> *The joy of your smile, so kind and tender,*
> *In my way to God, fears and doubts surrendered.*
> *This is the gift you have given me today, my dear.*

Ginny had her own fears and doubts, and did not know whether she had the same ability to surrender them by turning to God. But, like her mother-in-law, there was no doubt in her mind that His comfort was the only way she could get through life without her beloved Jack.

January 3, 1946
Navy Department, Office of Public Information
Washington, D.C.

At a special ceremony at the Navy department offices, Admiral R. S. Edwards, vice chief of Naval Operations, presented the Legion of Merit to Commander Kenneth A. Knowles. The accompanying citation read as follows:

> For exceptionally meritorious conduct in the performance of outstanding services to the government of the United States as head of the Anti-Submarine Section from July 10, 1942, to July 1, 1943, and as head of the Atlantic Section, Combat Intelligence Division, of the Headquarters of the Commander in Chief, United States Fleet, from July 1, 1943, to June 12, 1945.
>
> Commander Knowles expanded and developed the Anti-Submarine Section and later organized the Atlantic Section, Combat Intelligence Division of the Headquarters of the Commander in Chief, United States Fleet. For a period of approximately 35 months he carried out duties of great responsibility by evaluating

enemy combat information pertaining to German, Italian, and other Axis submarine strength, dispositions, capabilities, and intentions.

His estimates were of incalculable value and assistance to the Naval High Command and in direct support of operations against the enemy in the Atlantic. During this period, he continuously carried out his duties in a manner characterized by thorough knowledge, loyalty, perseverance, and zeal, thereby greatly contributing to a clear understanding of the enemy situation in the Atlantic.

Several months later, on May 16, 1945, Commander Kenneth A. Knowles received his simple detachment orders from the Naval Bureau of Personnel: PROCEED HOME; RELIEVED ALL ACTIVE DUTY.

April 3, 1946
San Diego, California

When his temporary work at BuPers and World War II ended in the summer of 1945, Lt. John Scagnelli remained in the Naval Reserves and was transferred briefly to Pacific duty aboard the destroyer USS *Hatfield* in San Diego.

It had been a difficult time for Scagnelli. After the *Eagle 56* incident, he had developed uneasiness around water, perhaps even a fear of it, something he would never have dreamed possible for a swimmer of his ability. But another crisis off the West Coast helped him overcome his new phobia. During exercises one day, two sailors were practicing lowering the *Hatfield*'s lifeboats into the water, when they became tangled in the support ropes and tossed into the water. Scagnelli was on the top deck when he heard the chilling cry, "Man overboard!" Scagnelli saw one of the sailors several hundred yards to the rear of the ship struggling to stay above water, and without hesitation he removed his shoes, dove from the fantail, and swam to his shipmate. He calmed the man and began moving him toward the *Hatfield*, whose crew members pulled them both aboard. The second sailor was also rescued. Scagnelli believed that his fellow sailor's distress was a much more powerful force than the fear he had developed of the water, and was actually grateful for the opportunity to "dive into the water without thinking."

Later, while still in San Diego, Scagnelli received word from home that his mother, Celestina, had passed away. The Third Naval District discharged him and he returned home.

Yet, while he wrestled with and overcame his fear of the water, and dealt with his mother's death, Scagnelli struggled more with a letter he received on April 3, 1946, from Captain H. G. Patrick of the Navy Department Board of Decorations and Medals. Scagnelli had written to the office imploring its administrators to award posthumous Purple Hearts to the forty-nine men who were killed almost a year earlier.

Patrick denied Scagnelli's request, and wrote:

> This office has been informed that, in view of the fact that investigating officers conducting the Board of Inquiry into the loss of the USS *Eagle (PE-56)* stated that the loss of this vessel was due to the explosion of its boilers, there is no authority for changing the status of the personnel from "dead or injured not the result of enemy action" to "dead or injured as the result of enemy action."
>
> In view of the above, favorable action cannot be given to your request for the award of the Purple Heart to the personnel listed.

John Scagnelli was upset but not surprised by the response. He would go on to marry, have children, and enjoy a laudable and fulfilling career working on behalf of people less fortunate than himself. But for the next fifty years, he would be haunted by the contents of the letter and the contention by the United States Navy that his ship was destroyed by something other than an enemy torpedo.

Who would history blame for that?

October 1, 1946
Nuremberg, Germany

After ten long months of testimony, judges of the International Military Tribunal at Nuremberg were about to render their verdicts against military and political leaders of Nazi Germany for war crimes during World War II. The previous day, September 30, judges gathered to begin final deliberations amidst unprecedented security. The entire city was surrounded by U.S. Army vehicles; every road into it was barricaded, every vehicle and pedestrian trying to enter was stopped and searched. More than a thousand extra guards were stationed around the Palace of Justice, where the trial took place, and snipers were stationed at strategic points. According to writers Ann and John Tusa, every room in the palace had been searched the previous night.

Now, on the first day of October, sitting in the defendants' dock on a double row of benches were some of the most notorious members of Hitler's high command: Hermann Göring, Alfred Jodl, Rudolf Hess, Albert Speer, Martin Bormann, Joachim von Ribbentrop, and Wilhelm Keitel.

And with them was Grand Admiral Karl Dönitz, father of the German U-boat service, and Germany's "Last Führer" after Hitler committed suicide.

Many historians believe that Dönitz likely would not have been indicted as a major war criminal had he not served as Führer. On the witness stand months earlier, he had put up a spirited defense. He justified his "fanatical" Nazi speeches at the end as necessary to keep up morale, since the collapse of the Eastern front would have meant death for countless German women and children. He attacked the conduct of the Russians, and denied he'd had any knowledge that millions of Jews were being murdered as part of the Final Solution. However, as historians Samuel Mitcham Jr. and Gene Mueller point out, he refrained from denouncing Adolf Hitler.

While the U.S. judge believed Dönitz should be acquitted on all counts, both the Russian and British justices voted "guilty," and he was sentenced to ten years' imprisonment—the lightest sentence of any of those convicted at Nuremberg (twelve of the twenty-two defendants were sentenced to hang, and three others to life in prison). He served every day of his sentence and wrote his memoirs after his release. His wife died in May of 1962, joining their two sons who had been killed in the war, and the rest of his life was lonely. "He was particularly disappointed with the German people, who, he felt, had unjustly turned against him," wrote Mitcham and Mueller. "He was also annoyed by the Bonn government's continued refusal to clear his name, despite the efforts of various U-boat associations on his behalf. He was also bitterly disappointed when the government refused to grant him a state funeral or to allow uniforms to be worn at a private one."

Karl Dönitz—the leader whose U-boats had terrorized the American coastline during World War II, the admiral who had dispatched the *U-853* near the end of the war to record eleventh-hour kills, the loyal party man who succeeded Adolf Hitler, "a man who had outlived his time"— died on Christmas Eve of 1980 at the age of eighty-nine.

His funeral took place on January 6, 1981, and dozens of his old comrades attended.

Shortly After Thanksgiving, 1946
Baltimore, Maryland

Less than two months after the Nuremberg trials had driven the final stake through the heart of the Nazi regime, Ginny Laubach sat and read the poem her mother-in-law had written in Jack's memory on Thanksgiving night, 1946:

The day is over, sitting here, looking at your picture,
I am trying to be thankful, even though you are gone.
Thinking deeply, I see great reason to thank God for many
*   blessings*
One of the greatest of these, my dear, being just to have had
*   you here;*
Even though your years with us were so short.

When I can hold close to my faith, and know all is well
*   with you,*
And can sense the reality of your presence close to me,
Then the days are not so difficult. It is when the
Things of this world intrude too completely
That I feel alone and lost and you seem to leave me.
Those are the times of my soul's deepest despair.
It is then I know you are the reality I must cling to,
Lest I find myself utterly adrift from God and you.

And so, I'll end this Thanksgiving Day with the prayer
In my heart, that God will let you always stay close to me
As my guide and my guard; and help me live each day
Here, to its fullest and best.
That my son, is the prayer in my heart.

Ginny, too, felt herself in deep despair and adrift when the world became too complicated.

She, too, would keep Jack close as her guide and her guard.

Part III

The Quest and the Truth

32

Lorraine Luttrell handed the urn containing her husband's ashes to the Coast Guardsman, who cradled it carefully in his large hands and moved to the ship's rail. It was a cool, peaceful fall morning aboard the Coast Guard cutter, which rose and fell gently with the swells in the Gulf of Maine, about five miles south-southeast of Cape Elizabeth. On September 21, more than fifty years after the *Eagle 56* had exploded, John Luttrell, the young crew member whom Johnny Breeze had boosted up the ladder as they scrambled to escape the doomed ship, had succumbed to cancer and respiratory failure at the age of seventy-one. Lorraine was now carrying out her husband's final instructions: "Skip the funeral, have me cremated, then call the Coast Guard and ask them to scatter my ashes in the general area where the *Eagle 56* went down, so I can be close to my former shipmates," John Luttrell had insisted.

Lorraine and John had spent more than thirty years together, marrying in 1965 after John's first wife died. John rarely spoke in detail about that horrible day, April 23, 1945, nor did he ever forget. He had heard different pieces of information about his ship through the years; first, from crew members of the *Selfridge* who insisted that a German U-boat had sunk the *Eagle*, which confirmed what many of his own shipmates had been saying from day one. John himself had not seen the sub, but he told the Court of Inquiry that he had been lying in his bunk at the time of the explosion when a "gigantic concussion blew me out of the sack and onto the deck, and I looked up at the escape hatch and there was water gushing through both of them." He later testified that the blast felt similar to the concussive shock produced when he fired an artillery round from a four-inch gun, "that everything in the ship had rattled." Later he had heard, though never officially, that the Navy had ruled the *Eagle 56* sinking an accident and it had gnawed at him; more than once he told Lorraine that the Navy had lied, that he had no doubts his old buddies were correct when they swore that a German U-boat had destroyed the *Eagle*. In fact, a year earlier, in October 1995, John and Lorraine had attended a fiftieth reunion of the USS *Selfridge* crew in Portland—John had been forever grateful to the men who had rescued him—where the aging sailors had shaken their heads in disbelief as they swapped stories about what they knew of the Navy's decision.

John Luttrell had built a good life after World War II, spending forty years as a trainman for the Portland Terminal Company, where he worked as a conductor and brakeman, enjoying golf passionately—he burst with pride when he talked about his two lifetime holes-in-one— and loving his family, including his wife, children, stepchildren, grand-children, and great-grandchildren. Yet Lorraine knew he felt a profound love for the *Eagle 56* sailors who died in April of 1945, a love she could never fully understand or share.

It was not that he worked so hard to keep in touch with them. He exchanged a few letters and calls with Oscar Davis before Oscar died in 1974 at the age of fifty-two. The big man had suffered a massive heart attack ten years before and had participated in an experimental coronary drug project in Madison, Wisconsin, saying, "If I can help others, I want to do this." Oscar had steadfastly and unwaveringly declared that a U-boat had torpedoed the *Eagle*. John Luttrell had also corresponded briefly with Johnny Breeze after Luttrell got word from the VFW that Breeze was attempting to locate *Eagle 56* survivors. "Still in good health . . . walk four miles a day and play golf five days a week," Luttrell had written to Breeze in 1993. "It's been forty-eight years since we took a ride on that pickle. If you ever come out this way, get in touch with me. Your old shipmate, John Luttrell." Other than Davis and Breeze, Luttrell had lost track of any other *Eagle 56* survivors, but Lorraine knew that the memories of his shipmates were always close to his heart.

Life dealt a harsh hand to John Luttrell shortly after his letter to Breeze. He developed colon cancer in 1995, which required a permanent colostomy, and he began a rapid downward slide as the disease burrowed into his body. Esophageal cancer gripped him shortly afterward, and as the summer turned into the fall of 1996, John Luttrell could fight no longer. He died at the Maine Medical Center, and Lorraine knew what she had to do. The Coast Guard had been more than accommodating, which had led to this moment aboard ship in the Gulf of Maine.

Lorraine Luttrell watched now, tears in her eyes, as one Coast Guardsman stood ramrod straight and saluted, while another carefully stretched his arms over the rail of the ship and poured John's remains into the sea. Perhaps one day his ashes would settle upon the wreckage of the USS *Eagle 56*, lying far below the surface, and John Luttrell would be reunited with his beloved shipmates.

John Luttrell was the tenth member of the *Eagle 56*'s "Lucky Thirteen" who had passed away since April of 1945. As his ashes fell upon the waves in October of 1996, none of the three living survivors who remained knew the other two were still alive.

April 1997
Annapolis, Maryland

In a small diner across the street from St. Luke's Episcopal Church in the Eastport section of Annapolis, Ginny Laubach Pettebone took a sip of her black coffee, then placed a stack of stapled pages on the table in front of her. She looked at her close friend, Peggy Eastman, daughter of former *Eagle 56* commander John Barr, and said: "Peggy, I want you to have these."

The cover page was entitled "So Lovingly Remembered," and the pages were dedicated to "John Robert Laubach, Lieutenant USNR. He gave his life for his country, April 23, 1945." Beneath the dedication was the inscription, "A country can live only as long as she has men who are ready to die for her," and beneath that, "This collection of poems is written in memory of my son, Jack. I hope they will strike a chord in the hearts of other mothers who have lost a son."

The pages contained the poems Jack Laubach's mother wrote over a period of five years, from 1945 to the eve of the Korean War, in memory of her son, the *Eagle 56*'s executive officer, who went down with his ship on April 23, 1945. Nearly fifty years after the last poem was written, Ginny, twice widowed now, was turning them over to her dear friend, Peggy, an author, journalist, and poet—and widowed twice herself. As Ginny drank her coffee, Peggy read the poems, "leafing through more than fifty years," she wrote later. "I see that Jack's mother—a woman long dead, whom I never knew—has written poems from the heart. I see that the poems are for all of us, all of us women who have lost their men, whether in battle or not." Peggy read a poem entitled "Men Like You," in which Jack Laubach's mother wrote:

> *When I see the one you left, so bereft of all joy in life,*
> *And know my own ache of longing for you—*
> *How can I say other than "No."*
> *And when I see the world as it is today,*
> *Still more do I protest—No!*
> *The cost was priceless, and we who have accepted the sacrifice*
> *Have proven ourselves less than worthy*

On April 23, 1947, the two-year anniversary of the *Eagle*'s sinking, Jack's mother expressed her pain in a poem entitled "Since You Went Away":

> *At times I wonder which one of us is dead, so much of me died*
> *with you.*
> *I see you, living happy, handsome, and gay,*
> *Walking beside me each step of the way.*
> *I feel you are so much more alive than I, who am so full of*
> *sadness and grief.*
> *For you have gone on to where sadness and grief have no part.*
> *While I face life here with so much pain in my heart.*

And yet, there was more than anguish in these poems, Peggy Eastman wrote. "There is joy and pride, too." In a collection of poems entitled "Memories," Jack's mother described the last time she, her son, and Ginny together visited their favorite little park in Portland, Maine:

> *Remember that Saturday we sat and reminisced, You, Ginny,*
> *and I?*
> *We talked of all the joys you boys had shared while growing up.*
> *How little I dreamed that would be our last time to reminisce*
> *together.*
> *Now I do it alone, but find peace in doing it—*
> *It brings you closer.*

It was such fun that day, you were so handsome in your
uniform, and Ginny always lovely;
I felt great pride in both of you; she wanted an ice-cream
  cone, and how you teased her!
We sat on the banks of the little pond, throwing stones at
  the frogs.
As we talked of all those days gone by,
You seeing things so wisely in retrospect,
I remember the joy I felt in your maturity.

I knew then that no matter what crisis you would be called
  to face,
You would meet it the right way.
Little could I know how soon that time would come.

"I raise my eyes from these pages written by Jack's mother after World War II and look across the Formica-top table and into Ginny's hazel eyes," Peggy Eastman would write later. "I see the eyes of a young bride who loved to eat ice-cream cones her husband bought for her and curl into his arms at night when they went to bed together . . . As I look into Ginny's eyes, it seems I am looking across more than fifty years, more than a hundred, more than a thousand . . . I am looking down the long ribbon of centuries into the eyes of every woman who has ever lost a man she loved."

After the *Eagle 56* disaster, Ginny Laubach turned to others for strength: to her mother-in-law, whom she would one day write was her "stronghold . . . she had always loved me and his [Jack's] death bound us even closer," and to Jack Barr, who, every year on April 23, wrote Ginny a letter recounting his memories of her Jack and describing what a fine man and officer he was. On April 23, 1995, the fiftieth anniversary of the *Eagle*'s sinking, Jack Barr arranged a service at St. Luke's in memory of the crew members who died on that terrible day; Ginny attended and stood beside Jack and Peggy, her "voice quavering" as she tried to sing the hymns. Jack Barr had been hit hard by the loss of the *Eagle*, always believing a torpedo had destroyed the ship, and perhaps thinking that things would have turned out differently if he had remained as skipper.

Eight years after Jack's death, Ginny Laubach married Elliott Pettebone, an old school friend who had never married and still carried a snapshot of Ginny in his wallet. "He was very kind and understanding," she would one day write to Johnny Breeze; but the ache of losing Jack more than fifty years earlier had never gone away, and never would. Jack's mother had the prescience to recognize this in her poem entitled: "To Virginia":

> *When I saw you walking off alone that night in the rain,*
> *Knowing how deep in your heart was the pain of loneliness,*
> *A prayer came to my heart that God would open your eyes*
> *And let you see Jack walking there beside you.*
> *Then I looked again, and saw him there—*
> *His fair head bent so tenderly over your dark one.*
> *And I prayed that you would see him too, and in feeling*
>   *his nearness*
> *Would know that love can know no separation.*

Ginny also turned to God for strength. She and Elliott had been faithful parishioners at St. Margaret's for years before he died, and Ginny tried to live her life according to the best precepts of her deep Christian faith. "Ginny was a tireless and empathetic listener," wrote Peggy Eastman. "She made a lot of friends because she knew how to be a friend. Friends listen; friends accept; friends keep confidences; friends show love. And she certainly did." As for strength, Eastman noted: "Jack Laubach's death could have broken Ginny, but the young war widow went to work, determined to be useful. She spent most of her career . . . in administration in the mathematics department of the U.S. Naval Academy, where she was, thankfully, appreciated for her keen mind, organizational skills, and promptness."

More than fifty-five years after the *Eagle 56* tragedy, at the dawn of a new century, Ginny herself would write to Johnny Breeze: "I thank God each day for His love which manifests itself in so many ways . . . After all this time I cannot think about Jack without inward emotion. It is my faith in God that has sustained me."

33

Doyle's Pub & Grill in Brockton is a friendly working-class establishment with a big horseshoe bar dominating the center and small booths lined in rows along the side walls. The television sets are tuned to CNN or ESPN's *Sports Center*, and the house fare includes clam rolls, hamburgers, fish-and-chips, and turkey club sandwiches. The conversation is lively and the food is good; patrons often choose to eat at the bar instead of booths to take part in the discussion of the day.

Doyle's efficient bar service and physical coziness combined to warm its patrons from the inside out on chilly nights; it was just such a Thursday evening in March of 1998 when Paul Lawton and two of the Westerlund brothers, Paul and Bob, were drinking Yukon Jacks and reminiscing about their friendship. Lawton and the Westerlunds were Brockton natives and had been friends for years. The Westerlund brothers, Bob, fifty-nine, and Paul, nearly fifty-four, were older than Paul Lawton, but Bob had done some work for Paul's uncle earlier in his life, and over the years the two families had gathered together for some swimming, mountain climbing, or other outdoor activities. The three men had been around the water all their lives; they were certified scuba divers—Lawton received his certification as a thirteen-year-old freshman at Brockton High School—the Westerlunds were avid sailboaters, and all of them had enjoyed swimming since they were children. Lawton's earliest childhood memories were of his family visiting Cape Cod. He would spend hours in the water, fascinated first by horseshoe crabs and seaweed, then snorkeling when he got a little older. "I was always part dolphin," he said. Later, after he became a proficient diver, Lawton was trained in underwater archaeological techniques as a member of the Rhode Island Marine Archaeology Project (RIMAP).

Tonight, at Doyle's, the talk turned to both diving and to Lawton's other specialty—German U-boats. The thirty-eight-year-old Lawton, an attorney and military historian, had for nearly two decades researched, and lectured and written on, the Battle of the Atlantic and the U-boat attacks against America. He was acknowledged by World War II military historians as one of the world's foremost authorities on the subject. He had taught numerous college-level courses, delivered countless lectures at museums, diving symposia, colleges, and for the U.S. Navy and Coast Guard groups. Lawton's work in naval history and underwater exploration had been featured in television news specials and dozens of newspapers and magazine articles published in the United States, Canada, and Europe, and he had served as a consultant for several historical documentaries. Currently, he was teaching a course at a local community college called "New England's U-boat Wars," and two of his students were relatives of the Westerlunds.

It was this last, seemingly innocuous, detail that sparked a conversation that would change the lives of Lawton, Westerlund, and scores of other families, and lead to a rewriting of United States naval history.

After the Westerlund brothers told Lawton that their relatives were enjoying his U-boat course, Bob Westerlund uttered the words that sent a jolt of electricity through Lawton:

"I'd like to dive on the *U-853*, since that's the boat that sank my father's patrol ship off the Maine coast."

Lawton wasn't sure he had heard correctly. First, he knew a great deal about the Westerlunds, but until that moment, he did not know that their father had been killed in World War II. He did not know that Phyllis Westerlund's second husband, Bertram Kendrick, whom she married two years after Ivar's death, had raised the four Westerlund children as his own (he and Phyllis also had a child together). Lawton simply had assumed that Bert was their biological father.

Second, Lawton *was* familiar with the *U-853*, and he would swear that it had never sunk an American warship in New England waters. In fact, according to official U.S. Navy records, *no* American warships had been sunk in New England waters during World War II; merchant ships and tankers, yes, but not fighting ships. He knew the *U-853* had patrolled New England waters during World War II, knew it had torpedoed the SS *Black Point* a few days before war's end, and knew its crew members had suffered agonizing deaths from the depth charge and Hedgehog pounding inflicted by American warships just hours before the German surrender.

Lawton knew the *U-853* even more intimately. Unlike the Westerlunds, diving on the *U-853* is not something Lawton just *wanted* to do; he had already done it. In his early twenties, Lawton dove 130 feet to the *U-853* wreck, a popular site for recreational and technical divers. He remembered the sense of awe and reverence he had felt—like he was visiting an undersea cemetery—which was why he despised those divers who plundered the wreck for souvenirs or sport. To him, this underwater wreck was a war grave, as sacred as any military cemetery, and he believed it should never be desecrated; that it was a *German* resting place made no difference to him. Looking at the sunken U-boat was fine, but removing bones and artifacts bordered on the criminal.

But Lawton's feeling about the *U-853* site ran even deeper. As he approached the wreck, it was as if the battle were happening again all around him; he could almost *feel* the concussive explosions of the depth charges and hear the screams of the *U-853* crew as their eardrums split, madness overtook them, and their beloved U-boat became their eternal coffin. He recalled, even now in 1998, the "weird feeling" he'd had nearly twenty years earlier as he maneuvered through the murky water and approached the *U-853* wreckage, a sense that the boat had stories it had not yet yielded up, that he was looking at history, but that there was even more history to learn. He knew, even as he examined the rusting shell and poked his head into its hatches, that the *U-853*, along with several of the final German U-boats dispatched in the winter and spring of 1945, had been the subject of rumors at the end of the war: that it had been carrying secret plans to Japan, or mercury for Japanese weapons systems, or Hitler's gold that the Führer and his henchmen had stolen from Jewish concentration camp victims, or even that Hitler and Eva Braun had slipped aboard seeking to escape the carnage in Berlin. These were all rumors that he and other historians had debunked over the years.

For all he knew about this German U-boat, had he missed something? What was Bob Westerlund saying? The brothers wanted to dive on the *U-853* to view the boat that had torpedoed their father's ship during World War II? Perhaps he had misunderstood Bob's father's role in the Second World War. He asked for clarification: "Your father was a crew member on the *Black Point*?"

"No," Bob Westerlund answered, "on a boat called the *Eagle*." He explained that Paul Westerlund had picked up a book in Rhode Island entitled *The Defenses of Narragansett Bay*, which contained a small footnote saying that the *U-853* may have sunk the *Eagle* off the coast of Maine. "It's been the rumor in our family," Bob said. "My mother always said a torpedo sunk our father's boat. We've even taken the sailboat right over the *U-853* site, which always made us feel a little strange, especially if it was the boat that sunk my dad's."

Thunderstruck, Lawton left Doyle's and rushed home to begin poring through his books and records. To his surprise, several books contained a brief mention that the *U-853* possibly sank the *Eagle 56* subchaser off the coast of Maine. And to his even greater surprise, all of the references tracked back to one source: Jürgen Rohwer, the renowned German historian, whose encyclopedic compilation of U-boat records was the most authoritative source in the world, the bible on German U-boats. Rohwer had spent years collaborating with U.S. naval archivist Bernard Cavalcante to catalog precise Battle of the Atlantic information, drawing on German archival sources and Tenth Fleet anti-submarine and Ultra documents. Cavalcante and Rohwer were as familiar with the original records as anyone in the world.

Lawton pulled out Rohwer's volume, entitled *Axis Submarine Successes, 1939–1945*, and read the short entry on page 195. Under April 23, 1945, Rohwer listed the *U-853*, Commander Froemsdorf's name, and the *Eagle 56*, with a footnote that read: "The *Eagle 56* sank after an explosion. Probably *U-853* operated in this area."

That was it—certainly not a definitive claim by Rohwer; the German historian had written two separate sentences without explicitly stating—although certainly implying—a causal link between each. Rohwer's uncertainty aside, Lawton still couldn't believe the reference. He had looked at Rohwer's book thousands of times, dog-eared page after page throughout years of research, and had never come across this entry, never put two and two together, never speculated as it appeared Rohwer had. How could he have missed it?

But it wasn't only him who had missed Rohwer's clue. Official U.S. Navy records mentioned nothing about a U-boat sinking in the Gulf of Maine in April of 1945. So if the *Eagle 56* had been in the area, what did cause it to explode? And if the *U-853 had* sunk the *PE-56*, then official naval history was wrong, and the *Eagle* crew—including Ivar Westerlund—deserved posthumous Purple Heart medals for being killed in action.

"Holy shit," Lawton whispered as he continued to stare at the page in Rohwer's book. "Holy shit."

34

Paul Lawton had always believed in the honor of military service and especially admired members of the World War II generation. Inspired by the contributions of veterans, especially his own father's bravery under fire and James Lawton's courage afterwards—refusing to let his injuries slow him down throughout a lifetime of personal and professional achievement—Paul Lawton made military history his passion. He also believed deeply in the sanctity of historical truth, supported by documented facts, and turned a skeptical eye toward pop historians who, in their quest for publicity and recognition, often put forth outlandish conspiracy theories and sensational, yet unsubstantiated, claims. In his two decades of research on the Battle of the Atlantic, he had debunked myths and discovered and verified facts by building a case from the ground up, much as he did when practicing law. When Lawton found a subject that interested him, one that he believed required additional research to uncover the truth, he immersed himself in the project. "He's like a pit bull," James Lawton said. "Once he sinks his teeth in, he won't let go."

Which is why, on the day following his conversation with the Westerlunds in Doyle's, on the morning after he discovered the entry in Jürgen Rohwer's book, Lawton called Barry Zerby at the National Archives in College Park, Maryland, a contact he had dealt with for years on different projects, and requested the deck logs for the USS

Eagle 56 and the records of the Court of Inquiry that investigated her loss. The convening of a COI was part of naval protocol when a ship is destroyed and there is loss of life.

Six days later, on March 23, 1998, Zerby wrote back to say he was unable to locate a copy of the Court of Inquiry records, and that the National Archives did not have custody of such records. Zerby suggested that Lawton contact the Navy JAG (Judge Advocate General) in Alexandria, Virginia, to inquire about the COI records. What Zerby *did* send Lawton were a few pages of "formerly confidential" files of the Secretary of the Navy/Chief of Naval Operations relating to the loss of the *Eagle 56*. The documents confirmed that the *Eagle 56* was conducting routine training operations in the Gulf of Maine on April 23, 1945, when she "exploded and sank . . . one officer and 12 enlisted men were rescued and survived." In an excerpt from the administrative report describing the *Eagle*'s loss, Lawton read these words: "It is thought that the cause of the accident was a boiler explosion . . . after a full review of all the evidence . . . it was determined that the subject named officers and enlisted men be continued in the status of 'missing,' not enemy action."

A boiler explosion? Lawton found the explanation plausible but unlikely. And, when he coupled it with the knowledge he had of the *U-853* prowling in New England waters during this time, Rohwer's cryptic entry, and the Westerlund brothers' claim that their mother always believed a torpedo destroyed the *Eagle*, he knew he had another mystery to solve.

The pit bull went to work.

Throughout the spring and summer of 1998, Paul Lawton wrote a flurry of letters approaching the *Eagle 56* mystery from a number of angles. In late March, he took Zerby's advice and wrote to the Navy JAG requesting the Court of Inquiry records. In early April, he wrote to the Henry Ford Museum for documentation on Eagle boats, and whether others had experienced boiler explosions. "In my research, I have failed to find any evidence of any other instances of catastrophic boiler failures on Eagle boats," he wrote, asking for "any information you could provide regarding their engine type, fuel, boiler and valve manufacturer names, diagrams, and whether you have any record of any other vessels of this class having experienced catastrophic boiler failures . . ." The museum sent Eagle boat plans and background information without addressing the boiler issue. In July and August, Lawton requested from

Zerby—and in most cases, received—deck logs, war diaries, and action reports from the *Selfridge, Woolsey, Craven, Evarts*, and other ships in the area, all documents which once had been marked confidential. Most of these records, especially from the *Selfridge*, indicated that positive SONAR contacts had been recorded, indicating the probable presence of an enemy submarine.

But if there was a Court of Inquiry record, Lawton's attempts to acquire it during the spring and summer of 1998 were unsuccessful. On May 4, he received the first piece of disappointing news from the Department of the Navy JAG office:

> We ordered the entire box that the requested investigation should
> have been filed in from our long-term storage facility at Suitland,
> Maryland, and the record was missing and is presumed lost. Because
> [this] determination . . . constitutes a denial of your request, you are
> entitled under the Freedom of Information Act to appeal this deter-
> mination in writing to the designee of the Secretary of the Navy . . .

On July 1, Lawton filed his official Freedom of Information Act Appeal seeking the Court of Inquiry records, and less than two weeks later, on July 13, he received word that his efforts had been thwarted again:

> An index card concerning the loss of the USS *Eagle* was located.
> Many attempts were made to retrieve the court of inquiry [investiga-
> tion] from our long-term storage facility. All searches for the investi-
> gation, however, were negative. The searches were made in good
> faith, using every effort and available method which could reason-
> ably be expected to produce the requested information. I therefore
> conclude these searches were reasonable and adequate. I regret we
> could not be of assistance to you in your search. This letter consti-
> tutes final denial of your appeal.

Lawton was stunned. "I told my father, 'There is something big going on here.' I had obviously raised some red flags," he said. "I thought the letter in response to my Freedom of Information Act request was nothing short of an insult—to say the records were lost was bad enough, but to say there was no appeal process? That the letter consti-tuted a final denial of my appeal? It's an unbelievable response." Lawton knew that the COI records were critical to his search for the truth.

The documents from other ships in the area on the afternoon of April 23, 1945, all indicated the possible presence of a submarine, which Lawton now believed was the *U-853*. But, presumably, the COI records would contain detailed testimony from survivors, and offer some indication as to *why* the Navy determined that a boiler explosion had doomed the *Eagle 56*. Without such evidence, it would be difficult to prove otherwise.

Lawton had done enough research to know that he would *never* get the whole story from a single set of records or from one source, and that the turnaround time to obtain records after he requested them was exceedingly slow. There were several ways to attack a problem, however, different roads that would eventually converge on the truth. With his attempts to obtain the Court of Inquiry records stalled for the time being, Lawton and the Westerlund brothers contacted *The Boston Globe*, requesting the paper to print a small item related to the *Eagle 56* disaster. On September 24, 1998, six months after the Westerlund brothers had shocked Lawton with their suspicions about the *Eagle* in Doyle's Pub, the *Globe* published the following notice in its "Ask the Globe" section, a collection of requests and letters from readers:

> IN SEARCH OF . . . Paul Westerlund of Brockton is looking for survivors of the *Eagle* No. 56 (*PE-56*) which exploded and sank off the coast of Maine on April 23, 1945. His father was among those who died. Contact Westerlund at . . .

Would the item work? Lawton had no idea. By now, he had read the 1945 newspaper accounts of the *Eagle* sinking and knew that the Lucky Thirteen had been rescued—but who knew if any of them were still alive? Who knew if any of them lived in the Boston area and would see the *Globe*?

But until he determined another strategy to obtain the Court of Inquiry records, until he could break the logjam and obtain additional documents related to this story, the newspaper item offered Lawton and the Westerlunds at least a sliver of hope.

35

Johnny Breeze, now two months shy of his seventy-seventh birthday, had been a born-again Christian since he was twenty-nine years old. The young sailor, who, on April 23, 1945, believed for the first time that someone was listening to him as he prayed from the freezing water while clinging to a piece of shoring from the shattered *Eagle 56*, underwent his conversion seven years later in a gospel tent in Ballard, Washington. As the evangelist spoke about Jesus Christ being everyone's personal savior, Johnny felt like someone grabbed him by the "nape of the neck" and guided him toward the front. There were parallels to the time he spent in the water on April 23 of '45. John Luttrell grabbed Breeze by the neck to keep his head above water, and Johnny would say years later that he "firmly believed that God had his hand on me, from beginning to end, and he could hear me." He was not sure whether his *Eagle* experience opened his heart and soul to the possibility of his Christian conversion that night in Ballard, but he *was* sure that his life "really started when I became a Christian."

And it was because of his faith that Johnny Breeze firmly believed that when something seemed like a coincidence, it was most likely God's hand gently steering events in the right direction.

How else could you explain this?

Johnny and his wife, Betty, had traveled from Seattle to Peabody, Massachusetts, to visit John's only daughter, Susanne Clarke, and meet their first great-grandchild. The minute John and Betty walked in the door, Susanne handed him *The Boston Globe* item that another relative had sent her and asked: "Dad, wasn't this your ship?" Surprised and curious, Breeze called the number and spoke to Paul Westerlund, who quickly put Breeze in touch with Paul Lawton. When an exuberant Lawton thanked him for calling and explained the nature of his research, Johnny Breeze sat stunned. He had always assumed that the Navy "admitted that we got torpedoed." When Lawton told him about the "boiler explosion" theory, an indignant Johnny Breeze felt his own blood boil and declared it a physical impossibility. When Paul Lawton asked Breeze if he'd be willing to offer sworn testimony on the *Eagle 56* sinking, Johnny Breeze readily agreed.

After his phone conversation with Lawton, Breeze spent a few quiet moments reliving a part of his life that he hadn't thought about for years. With the exception of exchanging a few letters with Oscar Davis and John Luttrell, Breeze had lost touch with his old shipmates, wasn't sure any of them were even alive anymore now that Oscar and John had passed. Living on the West Coast seemed a great distance from Portland, Maine, and the centers of media and power like New York and Washington, D.C., in more than just a geographical sense. Although Seattle was his home, Breeze had always felt "a little removed from the action" that pulsed along the East Coast, and he had allowed that "Left Coast mindset" to keep him out of touch. He lost contact with his old shipmates, the Navy, and even his memories, and he certainly had no idea about the decision that prompted Paul Lawton to seek him and any other *Eagle* survivors to hear their stories.

After the war, Johnny Breeze had made good on his word to become the finest machinist he could to honor the memory of his father, who had died while Johnny was stationed in Key West. He spent nearly forty years in a distinguished career with Boeing as an expert machinist and tool designer, and taught students at the Edison Technical School—now South Seattle Community College—machine-shop math and machine-shop practice. He sometimes thought he missed his calling by not becoming a full-time teacher, relishing the moment when "the lightbulb went off" in his students' heads.

There was pain in Seattle, too. Johnny's first marriage to Dorothy ended after nineteen years, a wrenching experience that Johnny refuses to discuss fully. He sued her for divorce, but she never appeared in court and did not contest him for custody of their four children, instead returning to Concord, New Hampshire, to live.

Any misgivings or skepticism Johnny may have had about marriage disappeared when he married Betty, "the love of my life," in 1964; the two have been devoted to each other since. "She never lets me get away with anything; when I crack wise, she gives it right back to me," Johnny said. "She's my best friend, my soul mate, and she always makes me laugh."

Like most people, Johnny Breeze had lived his life in stages, with several lines of demarcation along the way. There was his service life and his civilian life. There was his pre-conversion life and his born-again life. There was his first, largely unhappy marriage, and his second beautiful marriage to Betty. In each case, one life closed and another opened.

Now, though, unlike most people, Johnny Breeze would be going back in time to reopen a door he simply had assumed was closed forever. After his discussion with Paul Lawton, Breeze knew he *had* to open that door to help right a wrong that the Navy had let stand for more than half a century. He owed that to his dead shipmates from another lifetime.

Johnny Breeze would step through that doorway to the past and see where it led.

Someone else had seen Paul Westerlund's item in *The Boston Globe* seeking information about the *Eagle 56*.

Mary Alice ("Alice") Hultgren, formerly Mary Alice Heyd, the former Navy WAVE and legal yeoman and stenographer who took shorthand notes during the *Eagle 56* Court of Inquiry, read the *Globe* at her home in Reading, Massachusetts, a suburban community about fifteen miles northwest of Boston.

She called the phone number and agreed to provide sworn testimony to Paul Lawton. Lawton asked her to come into Boston on the same day he would depose Johnny Breeze.

Alice Hultgren's willingness to come forward quickened Lawton's pulse. Up until now, he had pored through deck logs and war diaries from ships that had responded to the *Eagle* explosion, and had located Johnny Breeze, who would no doubt offer critical testimony from a survivor's perspective. But Breeze was only one survivor. Hultgren had been present in 1945 when all thirteen survivors provided their accounts.

Next to the actual Court of Inquiry transcript, which had eluded Lawton up until now, Hultgren's testimony might be the only way to gauge what the Lucky Thirteen had sworn to under oath more than fifty years earlier.

October 5, 1998
Boston, Massachusetts

Paul Lawton and his father, James, questioned Johnny Breeze and Alice Hultgren separately at the offices of the New England School of Law in downtown Boston on an autumn Monday afternoon. Betty Breeze and Paul and Bob Westerlund attended the deposition, which was conducted before John M. Mahaney, a registered professional reporter and notary public in Massachusetts.

Breeze went first, opening with a brief biographical sketch and a recap of his duties on board the *Eagle 56*. Breeze testified that the Eagle was "dead in the water" when she exploded, "considered a violation if you're in a war zone." Lawton quickly homed in on Breeze's knowledge of the ship's boilers:

Lawton:	Can you tell me, you're familiar, apparently, with all of the machinery, including the boilers, would that be fair to say?
Breeze:	Yeah. We just overhauled them ten days before. Went to Rockland, Maine, went into dry dock, and overhauled the boilers.
Lawton:	Did they appear to you in proper running order?
Breeze:	Oh, yes.
Lawton:	During that period of time [February of 1943 through April 23, 1945, when Breeze was stationed aboard the *Eagle 56*] do you ever remember that vessel having any type of problems with her boilers or valves?
Breeze:	None. Ever.
Lawton:	And it's your understanding as well from working on these engines and the boilers that they had numerous built-in safety valves and pressure-relief valves, isn't that correct?
Breeze:	Yes. It's very difficult to make a boiler explode because the only way you can do it is to let the boiler go completely dry of water. No water injection. And the tube that shows the water level is about ten inches long; as long as you keep the water above the bottom of the tube and below the top of

the tube, you're operating okay, because there's only a certain amount of water that can get to the boiler in the first place.

You have to let the tube go completely dry [to cause an explosion], in other words no water at all, and the fire in the boilers is still going, the boiler's still hot, and then inject an amount of cold water into the boiler which hitting the hot tubes would make it explode. Never happened, Paul. Too many men on the watch watching those gauges to, you know, ever happen.

Lawton then focused on Breeze's sighting of the German U-boat as the sailor scrambled to escape the sinking ship:

Lawton: Can you tell me immediately after the explosion occurred, and you made your way up to the deck, what next occurred, who you observed and who you were with at the time, if you recall?

Breeze: When I got up to the after deckhouse, right behind Johnny Luttrell and ahead of Oscar Davis, Davis stepped out of the after deckhouse and we both stepped into about six inches of water. The ship was going down that fast. And Davis mentioned to me, he said, "Hey Breeze, look, there's a sub." And I looked off the port quarter and there was a sub. Now, it's difficult to tell how far away it was, but there was a sub there, Paul.

Lawton: What was your observation of this submarine—that it was completely surfaced, or did you just see what would have been consistent with the conning tower?

Breeze: No, it was completely surfaced but it didn't stay there very long. Because the next time I looked I think it was gone. I think the skipper saw the tin can, the destroyer, coming for us, and naturally, he got out of the way because that's a submarine's nemesis, is a destroyer.

Lawton: Was the submarine close enough for you to actually have seen any type of markings on the conning tower, or was it too far away to see the conning tower?

Breeze: Too far away. All we saw was black. It's all black.

Lawton then questioned Breeze about his rescue and his time aboard the *Selfridge*. Did he hear anything on the rescue ship that indicated its crew thought a submarine was in the vicinity? "Well," Breeze said, "they were carrying me through the wardroom to put me in a bunk and I heard these loud noises and I said, 'What's that?' And one of the crew that was carrying the stretcher I was on said, 'We're just throwing over some K drum [depth] charges. We got a *ping* sound, you know, off of something.' A sub. They thought it was a sub." Lawton asked Breeze to reiterate: "So it's your understanding that they picked up some kind of submerged sound contact and attacked it with depth charges?" Breeze answered: "Absolutely."

Lawton then asked Breeze about his time in the dispensary, his discussion with other crew members, and his questioning before the Court of Inquiry:

Lawton: And can you tell me from your recollection, were there several other crewmen that saw the submarine surface; approach the surface?

Breeze: Oh, yeah, not just Davis and I. I think Petersen did [he did not]. I can't remember who else. But four or five of us saw the sub [six did].

Lawton: And from your conversations with them at the time, did their stories appear to coincide with what you had seen?

Breeze: Absolutely.

Lawton: And can you tell me, did the naval intelligence personnel, or any of the officers there, did they give you any advice or direction relative to what your statement or testimony should be at the Court of Inquiry?

Breeze: Yeah. It seemed to me, and this is my own recollection, of course, that they intimated that it was not a torpedo; that we had struck a mine. But that's the only thing I can recall.

Lawton: After all these years you still have a good memory, I'd imagine, of being torpedoed?

Breeze: I'll never forget it.

Lawton: Did you have any question at the time, or any hesitation, coming to the conclusion that you were torpedoed by that submarine that you saw that day?

Breeze: No, none. None, Paul.

As he neared the end of his questioning, Lawton established that Breeze did not know of the Navy's "boiler explosion" ruling until the two of them spoke just a few weeks earlier. Breeze said his "estimation of the Navy went down" when he found out. "It was hard for me to understand," Breeze testified.

Finally, Breeze pointed out that John Luttrell had died two years earlier, leaving Breeze—he believed—as the lone survivor of the USS *Eagle 56*. "That's what they tell me," Breeze said. "And I think I asked you, Paul, John Scagnelli, Lieutenant Scagnelli, was still alive [recently] and you said he's gone."

Lawton replied: "I believe they're all gone."

Both Lawton and Breeze would soon learn otherwise.

Whereas Paul Lawton questioned Johnny Breeze for close to an hour, his interview with Alice Hultgren was significantly shorter, but no less powerful. Alice acknowledged that she had not seen or spoken with Johnny Breeze since April of 1945, and had never met the Westerlund brothers. Lawton quickly brought Hultgren up to her time in the Grand Trunk Pier dispensary, where the Court of Inquiry interviewed the Lucky Thirteen.

Lawton: From those individuals that were the survivors that were aboard the vessel . . . at the time of her sinking, do you recall anything about their testimony regarding what they believed the cause of the loss of the ship was?

Hultgren: I remember more than one saying that he thought it was a torpedo or a sub . . . I remember one fellow saying that he thought it was a sub because he had been on another ship that had been sunk and it felt to him like the same thing.

Lawton: Would it be fair to say that from the survivors, they all appeared to indicate that it was in fact some type of enemy attack or torpedo?

Hultgren: I would say the majority of them felt that.

James Lawton then asked Hultgren whether she recalled that "some people" made the observation "that they actually saw a submarine in the water?" Hultgren replied: "I think I remember more that they had the feeling that this came from outside, not within. That they were struck from the outside. I don't remember any of the survivors themselves saying that it was a boiler. And I know the consensus on the base, people that I talked to, thought it was a sub."

By the time Breeze and Hultgren had finished their depositions, Lawton knew he was in this quest for the long haul. He truly believed that the Navy had perpetrated a miscarriage of justice on the *Eagle 56* crew members and their families. Even his dad said, "Paul, you have to pursue this. This is not right."

He recognized, however, that he needed to present a case to the Navy that was airtight. For more than fifty years, U.S. naval history read one way. Lawton was trying to change that history, and he knew change would not come easily.

For him to be successful, he still needed more proof. At the very least, he had to get his hands on the Court of Inquiry transcripts—and after that, on documents that showed the Navy believed the *U-853* had sunk the *Eagle*.

He didn't know it yet, but Alice Heyd Hultgren would help him with the first. And renowned naval archivist Bernard Cavalcante, the man who had worked side by side with Jürgen Rohwer re-creating the Battle of the Atlantic, would unlock the mystery on the others.

In the meantime, Paul Lawton would continue digging and continue fighting the bureaucracy searching for answers. He would spend thousands of dollars of his own money on copying, postage, and other incidentals. He would battle his own frustration, government inertia, and political indifference to find the truth.

The only thing he would *not* do is give up.

36

Fall 1998
Wilkesboro, North Carolina

In this picturesque town situated in the foothills of the Blue Ridge Mountains, Phyllis Westerlund Kendrick anticipated Paul Lawton's effort to rewrite history with a mixture of excitement and skepticism. She was excited that the full truth about Ivar's ship might finally be revealed; she was skeptical that the Navy would change its mind after so many years.

Phyllis was also grateful that Lawton had embarked on his quest. Ivar's death, the sinking of the *Eagle 56*, was a chapter in her life that had never really closed. In 1947, two years after the *Eagle* went down, she had remarried a wonderful man named Bertram Kendrick, who had been stationed at Pearl Harbor when the Japanese bombed it on December 7, 1941. Bert loved her and her four children, even offering to adopt them when they married, though Phyllis had refused; she wanted Carol, Bob, Fred, and Paul to carry Ivar's name. "Still, the kids loved Bert and couldn't wait to call him Dad," Phyllis said. "They wanted a dad so much, my daughter, Carol, especially, who was old enough to realize her loss." Phyllis and Bert Kendrick had their own child, Linda, two years after they were married. "I really wanted to give him a child," Phyllis recalled. "He was a good husband to me and such a good father to all of the children."

Bert Kendrick died of cancer in 1972 at the age of 52, leaving Phyllis a widow for the second time. She couldn't believe that she had lived alone for another quarter-century, proud and self-sufficient, if a little lonely. Twenty-five years without Bert and fifty-three years without Ivar; it seemed a little unnatural to her to have lost two husbands and then to continue to live for another full generation. Death stalked her family later in life, too, when Phyllis lost two grandchildren—Carol and Linda had each suffered the pain of burying a child, deaths that left Phyllis heartbroken. Yet, she just seemed to go on. She left her beloved Brockton in 1983 to join her two daughters who lived in North Carolina. Now, at the age of eighty-three, she still loved gardening, walking, and volunteering for the church hospice. She had many friends, was in good health, kept busy during the day, and attributed her vigor and energy level to "good genes."

Her nights were still lonely, as they were in 1945 when she was composing poetry to Ivar, words she still recalled by heart. She lived with many memories, and the resurrection of the *Eagle 56* story had filled her with loving recollections of Ivar and the pain she felt in the immediate aftermath of his death. For all these years, she thought of Ivar at some point virtually every day—now those images had sharpened and become more vivid. She recalled his voice and his eyes and his laugh, she imagined his face still as a young man, a man of strength and good humor who left her on April 23, 1945, running to catch his bus and never returning. The visits from the chaplain, the telegrams, the messages of sympathy all seemed as though they happened just yesterday, not in another lifetime. She remembered a wooden sailboat that her oldest son, Bob, had carved for Ivar, proud of his accomplishment, a jubilant six-year-old anxious to give the gift to his father when he returned home. Bob was sixty now and still waiting for his dad. She remembered her own feelings of despair in April of 1945, just shy of her thirtieth birthday, a mother of four, alone and penniless, the desperation she felt when she discovered that the monthly government benefit she received months after Ivar's death amounted to about eight dollars per child.

All of these memories had come rushing back since Paul Lawton had begun asking questions. She was an old woman now, still spry and active, but she clung to those memories of a half-century ago, embraced them as though she were embracing Ivar. He was her first love and always would be.

She had felt so close to Ivar again, when, in August, with Carol's help, she had turned over a collection of records to Paul Lawton, documents she had kept for more than fifty years, pages so brittle and worn that they were ready to crumble. Ivar's induction notice. The Western Union telegram informing her that there was no hope for Ivar's survival, "and that he lost his life as a result of explosion." The condolence letter from John Scagnelli. The 1945 condolence message from Secretary of the Navy James Forrestal. The documents saddened her, but buoyed her spirits at the same time; not only did their physical touch connect her to Ivar again, but perhaps these records, old as they were, could help Paul Lawton uncover the truth. "Stay well and thanks for all the work you have been doing on this," Phyllis's daughter, Carol, had written to Paul Lawton when they had enclosed the World War II-era records. Phyllis had added: "Dear Paul, I appreciate you thinking of me. I cannot thank you enough for helping my boys on this project."

Phyllis Westerlund Kendrick was not only expressing gratitude for herself. After fifty-three years, Paul Lawton had given her hope that the truth might finally allow Ivar to rest in peace. He and his shipmates deserved that much.

37

By late spring of the following year, Paul Lawton had amassed an impressive array of documents related to the *Eagle 56* sinking, including U.S. Navy deck logs, war diaries, depth-charge attack plots, contemporaneous newspaper articles, Eagle boat specification sheets, photographs, and the transcripts of the Johnny Breeze and Alice Hultgren testimony. But he had been unsuccessful in obtaining the Court of Inquiry records, and without them, he knew his case was not strong enough to convince the Navy to rewrite its own history.

For his part, Lawton believed that the *PE-56* "was almost certainly torpedoed by the *U-853*," and he was now garnering support to help him get the Navy's attention. He enlisted the help of two good friends, Maine maritime historian and fellow diver Chris Hugo, and Jim Fahey, lead archivist at the U.S. Shipbuilding Museum located at the USS *Salem* in Quincy, Massachusetts. Hugo had been involved in the research of many New England shipwrecks, and would serve as Lawton's liaison with Maine historical authorities, and tap his contacts at the Naval Historical Center. Hugo, a researcher for the Massachusetts Board of Underwater Archaeological Resources, would also provide expertise and assistance as Lawton went about the task of assembling a diving team to search for the heretofore undiscovered *Eagle 56* wreckage, a decision he made within the last couple of months. If divers could find the *Eagle*, perhaps they could find additional evidence that she had been torpe-doed. Fahey would provide research help and guidance as Lawton con-tinued to search for additional documents related to the sinking.

Lawton also contacted Gary Gentile, author of *Track of the Gray Wolf: U-boat Warfare on the U.S. Eastern Seaboard, 1942–1945*, and other books, to inform him of his conclusions, as well as newspapers, local television stories, and production companies in an effort to get the *Eagle* story in front of the public. He believed publicity could help in two ways: put pressure on the Navy to find the documents he had re-quested, and, perhaps, help him locate additional survivors.

His exhaustive work and research continued despite "a few months of hell" at the beginning of 1999, the dual pressures of work and fam-ily health problems weighing on his mind; three of his brothers and his mother underwent surgeries during this period. Despite these hardships, in May, Lawton wrote to Johnny Breeze, still the only *Eagle 56* survivor that he'd located: "The operation to search for the wreckage of the *PE-56* has just begun to take off after more than a year of research and networking with a group of naval and maritime historians, technical wreck divers, side-scan sonar experts, and media sources." To another diver he wrote: "Call it a hunch, but I believe the *PE-56* wreckage may be found in the area near where the survivors were rescued, and the *Selfridge* attacked the SONAR contact, and may lie in or near the area designated as a dumping ground." To Gentile he added: "We believe we may have a good idea about the location of her wreckage, and if we are correct, it will bring to light more evidence that the U.S. Navy went to great lengths to keep the circumstances of this loss quiet."

Still, even as he continued to seek records and made plans to mobi-lize a dive search team, Lawton was feeling frustration a year after his discussion with the Westerlund brothers at Doyle's pub. "The families of the forty-nine dead officers and crewmen of the *PE-56* have gotten the runaround by the U.S. Navy since the day of their loss," he lamented to Gentile. "I have faced the same obstacles in my FOIA [Freedom of In-formation Act] requests to the Navy for information regarding this in-cident. I am sure you can relate to this situation . . ."

Though discouraged, and at times angry with the Navy after a year of research, Lawton harbored no thoughts of giving up. "This sounds corny, but when things got tough, I thought of my dad and I thought of my uncle [who was killed in action in North Africa in 1943]—this could be either of them at the bottom of the ocean," Lawton would say later.

"These *Eagle 56* guys didn't know what hit them, and the official Navy account was a complete slap in the face to them. I was going to see it through, one way or another, no matter what. The Navy could write a hundred letters to me telling me they couldn't find records—I wasn't going anywhere."

May 1999
San Diego, California

Sitting alone much later that night, hours after it had happened, eighty-two-year-old Esta Glenn Smith recalled how she knew immediately that the loud crack she'd heard earlier couldn't have been anything but a gunshot. She was comfortable around guns and skilled at firing them; for years she had participated in competitive dove hunting, quail hunting, and trap shooting, and the sharp report of a gunshot was a familiar sound to her. Tonight, it still startled her, the single shot shattering the quiet of the Southern California evening and jolting her body like an electric charge; she imagined that the echo of the after-blast carried for miles on the cool night air. She had been in the living room when the shot rang out from the patio, and almost before she reached the doorway she knew the worst had happened—that Smitty had taken his own life. It was a shock to her system, but not a surprise, when she reached the patio and saw her third husband, Vernon Smith, lying dead by his own hand.

Smitty was seventy-seven years old and battling against enormous health issues: diabetes, leukemia, congestive heart failure. He had recently suffered a stroke and lost vision in his left eye. Then, doctors had found cancer in Smitty's prostate. He had been scheduled for surgery the next morning. He had hinted to Esta that his action tonight was a possibility; he feared dying on the operating table and told her that he would much rather die at home. Brokenhearted that he was gone, Esta didn't blame him for taking his own life. The man had suffered more than one man ever should.

Esta and Vernon Smith had married on November 22, 1952, one day after Esta's thirty-sixth birthday, in a chapel ceremony in Las Vegas, Nevada. Esta told people it was a full-fledged service, "not one of those quickie Las Vegas things." Their wedding came just a few years after Esta's second marriage, to Paul Rollin, had ended. "It was a mistake and didn't last long," she said, although the marriage did produce something beautiful: Esta's only child, a son, Bill Rollin, who was born in January of 1948. "You couldn't ask for a better son," she said.

Smitty and Esta had met on a blind date that Esta reluctantly agreed to after a girlfriend begged her to double-date. "Smitty and I clicked right away, talking and having fun," she said. They had a common love of sports and the outdoors, and it was Smitty who convinced Esta to try trap shooting. "Have I got something for you!" he exclaimed that day. They both became proficient at it, and found it was something they enjoyed doing together.

As they grew older, Smitty's health problems slowed them down first, and then Esta developed serious lung complications which doctors diagnosed as Chronic Obstructive Pulmonary Disease (COPD), for which there is no cure. Esta was "terminal," and doctors had told her it was simply a matter of time. Once an active and proficient sportswoman, she was now homebound and required a caregiver and a walker to simply move from room to room. Her son, Bill, who lived with his wife about a mile away, was kind enough to take her out for drives on weekends.

Tonight she thought of Smitty, of course, but the memories and images of her first husband, Harold Glenn, also flooded her mind: his beautiful sky-blue eyes, his long eyelashes, and ruddy complexion. Their time together was so short, only twenty months, yet their love seemed as deep as the ocean in which he had died. It was not lost on her that two of her husbands had died in violent ways, one young and healthy and full of plans for their future who would have given anything to live; the other elderly and wracked by one serious illness after another, who had chosen to die to end his pain. Loneliness had consumed her after Glenn's shocking death. She would miss Smitty terribly, and she was alone again, but the loneliness was not as profound. Smitty's death was not so unexpected, and she was older now and ill herself, and realized her own time was limited, so she would make the best of it. Other people suffered tragedies—something else she had learned as she aged—but their lives went on. "What else can you do but live each day?" she asked.

She had thought of Glenn every day since his death fifty-four years earlier, thought of him even now as she mourned for Smitty. She had never forgotten, and never would, the way Glenn bounded back up their front stairs to kiss her good-bye on the morning of April 23, 1945, before he boarded the bus for the docks. It seemed like yesterday—did it all happen so long ago? Now, in 1999, alone with her thoughts and uncertain about her future, those memories of 1945 comforted her. She closed her eyes, saw Glenn's smiling face in her mind, and longed to hold him just once more.

May 30, 1999
Brockton, Massachusetts

Fifty-four Memorial Days after Esta Glenn had dropped a wreath into the Pacific Ocean to honor her dead husband, the *Brockton Enterprise* covered the *Eagle* story, and Lawton's struggle to convince the Navy to rewrite history, as its Sunday front-page lead.

It was the first major newspaper article on the subject—it would not be the last—and it would compel several individuals, including sailors who were stationed aboard the USS *Selfridge*, to contact Paul Lawton with more information. Lawton sent the article to Alice Hultgren, who replied with a handwritten thank-you and posed the question Lawton had asked himself: "Wouldn't it be great if another survivor were still alive and read it?"

After more than a half-century, the *Eagle 56* story had finally gone public. Paul Lawton wondered: How would the Navy react now?

38

Summer 1999
Brockton, Massachusetts

Despite the *Enterprise* front-page story, the Navy and the Pentagon remained silent.

Frustrated but undeterred, Paul Lawton spent most of the summer of 1999 reviewing the records he had, seeking new ones, corresponding with *Selfridge* crew members and Johnny Breeze, and writing letters to experts informing them of his progress and his plans to organize a diving mission for the *Eagle 56* wreckage the following season. He was convinced that a visual inspection of the subchaser would prove that a torpedo had torn her apart, and would be the best chance he and his team had to force the Navy to listen and respond.

"We hope to locate the wreck after conducting side-scan SONAR and/or magnetometer search for her wreckage," Lawton wrote to Professor Joel Eastman at the University of Southern Maine, one of the foremost experts on Portland Harbor defenses during World War II. "We hope an inspection of the wreckage will provide evidence of the true cause of her [*Eagle 56*] loss, and may help rewrite this chapter of U.S. Naval history."

As leader of the soon-to-be-formed dive team, Lawton reassured Eastman that while his primary mission certainly was to locate the *Eagle 56* wreckage, his respect for the deceased World War II sailors and his personal connection to the *Eagle 56* would be uppermost in the divers' minds: "Neither the wreck, nor any of her contents, will be disturbed in any way, as we intend to conduct a noninvasive video survey of the wreck, particularly the blast area. This vessel remains U.S. Naval property, and is also the grave site of a close family friend, Seaman 2nd Class Ivar A. Westerlund."

Lawton also stressed this point in a letter to Dr. Kathy Abbass, president of the Rhode Island Marine Archaeology Project, to whom he had written for advice. "The sanctity and integrity of this wreck is of particular importance to me," he said, citing the Westerlund connection. "We fully intend to conduct this operation in the appropriate manner in order to preserve the archaeological integrity of any such survey, and to insure the dignity of the forty-seven officers and crewmen who rest in or around the wreck [the bodies of two *Eagle 56* crew members were recovered]."

With or without the Navy's help, Paul Lawton was moving ahead. "I knew it was a long shot [to convince the Navy to change its decision on the *Eagle* sinking]," he said. "But we had to try, because with every fiber of my being, I also knew that it wasn't a boiler explosion that sunk that ship. After talking to the Westerlunds, examining the deck logs and diaries of the other ships, interviewing Johnny Breeze and Alice Hultgren, it made perfect sense that it was the *U-853* that torpedoed the *Eagle*. What was frustrating was the Navy's indifference to the whole thing. I was convinced that those *Eagle* crew members had died in enemy action and deserved posthumous Purple Heart medals. So, long shots be damned—I was interested in the truth. In the summer of 1999, diving on the *Eagle* wreck was our best chance to learn the truth."

Late that summer, on August 23, 1999, Alice Hultgren, the former Navy WAVE stenographer during the *Eagle 56* Court of Inquiry, received a package at her Reading, Massachusetts, home that suddenly, dramatically, and irrevocably reduced the long-shot odds that Paul Lawton was fighting against.

The package arrived on Alice's seventy-seventh birthday. She described the contents of the envelope as "a great birthday present." It could also be described as a mail delivery that helped change history.

Alice Hultgren tore open the package and read the note from retired Navy captain Edward J. Melanson, a family friend now living in Virginia with whom she had once discussed the *Eagle 56* case. Excited, she next read the cover page of the thick stack of documents she held in her hands:

Records of Proceedings of a Court of Inquiry
Convened on Board the U.S. Naval Station
Portland, Maine

By Order of
Commandant, First Naval District and Navy Yard
Boston, Massachusetts

To inquire into all the circumstances connected with the loss of the
USS *Eagle (PE-56)* off Portland Harbor, Maine, at about 12:17 P.M.
23 April 1945

Alice read the small notation at the bottom of the cover page that
read CLASSIFICATION CHANGED: FROM CONFIDENTIAL TO RESTRICTED.
Attached to the front page were nearly eighty pages of testimony, plus the
court's finding of facts and its decision. Included in the package was Rear
Admiral Felix Gygax's June 1, 1945, letter questioning, but not overturning, the Court of Inquiry's findings. Alice couldn't believe it. She had described to Captain Melanson the lack of response from the Navy when
Lawton had requested the COI records, including the claim that the testimony had been lost. "He [Melanson] asked me, 'Did you try here and
did you try there?' " Alice recounted. "I told him I wouldn't know where
to start. I never asked him to do anything and he never promised anything. The records simply arrived in the mail. He had apparently made a
few calls and shaken those records loose."

Despite months of claims to the contrary by the Navy, the fifty-four-
year-old records were not lost to history after all.

Alice wasted no time. She called Lawton, whom she described as
"speechless . . . probably for the first time in his life." She followed up
with calls to Johnny Breeze in Seattle and Paul Westerlund in Brockton.
"I was especially thrilled for the Westerlund brothers because they had
lost their father," Alice said.

She quickly made copies of the COI transcript, which she mailed
out the next day, August 24. To Breeze she wrote: "Ta da!!! Here it is!
Enjoy! . . . The day it arrived was my birthday and such a great present.
My present to me was talking to you and Paul." In her cover letter to
Lawton, Alice said: "Enjoy—I'm sure you will still have many ques-
tions, as I do, but maybe you will have luck with your dives."

Alice Hultgren knew the Court of Inquiry records were important, but also knew that the court's conclusion differed from her own recollections from more than fifty years ago. "I remember that more of the men thought it was a sub," she said. "There was one officer [doing the questioning] who kept pushing this idea of an engine or boiler explosion, but there was no reason to think that way." She hoped that the records would provide the information Lawton needed to move his own investigation forward and offer clues that would help him piece together the truth.

"I remember the day it happened," she said, nearly sixty years after the *Eagle 56* was sunk. "They were unloading some of the fellows [*Eagle* survivors] on stretchers back at the base. I didn't know anyone on the ship personally, but many of us were pretty frightened. This was the first time something bad like this had happened to a group of guys that many people on the base knew. Then their story got lost at the end of the war. For the sake of those men, the truth needed to be told."

Sixty-four-year-old Ed Melanson said he made a "cold call" to the Navy JAG to obtain the Court of Inquiry records. "I knew it had to exist and I doubted it would be classified any longer," he said. "I talked to JAG, told them I was a retired Navy captain, told them what I was looking for, and a while later, they sent it to me."

Melanson's modesty notwithstanding, he can best be described as a player in and around Washington and the Pentagon, and his name likely triggered some recognition within the JAG command structure. He had spent thirty years in the Navy, first in numerous early assignments on cruisers and destroyers of the 2nd and 6th fleets in the Atlantic and Mediterranean, and in 7th Fleet amphibious forces in the western Pacific during the Vietnam War. He also served as the forty-first commanding officer of the USS *Constitution*, moored in Charlestown, Massachusetts.

But it was Melanson's post-shipboard duty that almost certainly spurred such rapid cooperation from the Navy JAG in releasing the COI records. He worked on assignments for the Office of the Joint Chiefs of Staff, the Pentagon, and the Office of Secretary of Defense. These included serving as a senior defense advisor to the U.S. Delegation during Nuclear and Space Arms Talks with the Soviet Union, as a deputy for International Intelligence Policy, and as manager of Defense Peacekeeping Support in the Middle East. Following these active-duty assignments,

Melanson served in the first Bush administration as an assistant for national security in the White House and as a U.S. ambassador and chief arms negotiator for the State Department during talks with the Soviet Union in Geneva, Switzerland.

In short, Captain Ed Melanson's name carried some clout.

He stated emphatically that he did not call in a chit or a favor, that "maybe [he] simply found the right person in the JAG office" willing to pursue the COI records further. Perhaps they recognized his name or perhaps not, he said—he didn't ask and they didn't volunteer the information. No one knows, or ever will know, for certain.

One thing was clear: With a single phone call, Melanson had secured the records that helped Paul Lawton breathe new life into the *Eagle 56* case.

Infused with energy by this stunning turn of events, Lawton devoured the COI records, reading each page over and over again, making notes and underlining passages. The court documents invigorated his investigation in so many ways: six *Eagle 56* crew members reported seeing the German U-boat; one testified that he saw red-and-yellow markings on the sub's conning tower; the COI records provided a complete list of missing crew members and survivors; the testimony listed additional ships that responded to the explosion of the *Eagle 56*; and testimony from the commanders and personnel of those ships provided Lawton with names of additional people to seek.

And perhaps just as importantly, the COI documents offered a more exact location of the *Eagle 56* when she exploded.

Throughout the fall of 1999, Lawton used the Court of Inquiry records to fuel another round of letters and requests for information. He wrote to Barry Zerby at the National Archives for the deck logs of additional ships that the court records referenced. To author Gary Gentile, Lawton wrote: "This new [COI] information gives us more than twice as much information regarding the position of the *PE-56* at the time of her loss, including bearings and range estimates from two fixed naval bases on land [Portland Harbor Entrance Control Post at Fort Williams and the U.S. Naval Unit Cape Elizabeth Loop Receiving Station], and two additional ships at sea, the USS *Nantucket* [which plucked Harold Petersen from the water] and the U.S. Navy minesweeper *AMc-62*. This new information has narrowed our search area significantly." Later in the year, in a letter to the production company that intended to accompany the dive team, Lawton again stressed the sanctity of the *Eagle* wreckage site: "I ask that you keep these documents [coordinates, bearing, and range estimates] closely guarded from public disclosure, as we wish to avoid the danger of unscrupulous salvage divers and grave robbers from tampering with the wreck site and compromising the archaeological integrity of our operations next season."

Armed with information from the COI transcripts, Lawton, in mid-October, also contacted Horst Bredow, a former U-boat ensign and founder and director of the German U-boat archives in Cuxhaven-Altenbruch, the world's most comprehensive repository of U-boat and *U-Bootwaffe* records. Bredow was the foremost authority of the German U-boat service and had made the archives his life's work. His dedication to this mission had its genesis in another mission that Bredow missed in April of 1944. Wounded in an air attack while serving on the *U-288*, Bredow was hospitalized and his U-boat left on its next patrol without him. On April 3, 1944, she was lost at sea and her entire crew—all except Bredow—died. "As *U-288*'s second watch officer, or third in command, he became part of the crew," author Jordan Vause wrote. "He fought with them, bled with them, sang with them, enjoyed the friendship and camaraderie which so many who have never served cannot understand." Haunted by his memories as a U-boat officer and a "fate he should have shared but did not," Bredow devoted himself to the archives.

Lawton explained his investigation, asked Bredow for any evidence to support his contention—and Jürgen Rohwer's speculation—that the *U-853* was operating "in or around" the area of the Gulf of Maine on April 23, 1945, and sought to corroborate the testimony of *Eagle 56* crewman Daniel Jaronik: "One survivor in particular stated that he saw what looked like a red-and-yellow marking on the submarine's conning tower. We know that the *U-853* conning tower insignia bore a galloping red horse, but we do not have any information on the color of the shield-shaped background on the insignia. Could it have been yellow or gold in color?"

Toward the end of 1999, Lawton pieced together reports that he had gathered from the U.S. Navy Bureau of Ships (BuShips). He wrote in his own brief history of the *Eagle* case: "Apparently the Navy was not genuinely convinced of the boiler-explosion theory, as it neglected to issue any BuShips advisories regarding their inspection, servicing, repair, or replacement of the Navy's many Thornycroft Bureau Express-type water-tube boilers, which were installed in a number of other small-surface combatants in active service at that time." Moreover, the BuShips' Construction and Repair, Statistics Division offered this explanation about the loss of the *Eagle 56*: "Exact nature of cause of explosion is undetermined. Might have been an enemy mine or torpedo." The words "boiler explosion" do not appear on the BuShips USS *Eagle 56* Information Sheet.

Spring 2000

The Boston Globe broke the *Eagle 56* story wide open with a major Sunday feature story by reporter David Arnold, headlined WHAT SANK THE *EAGLE*?: A DIVER YEARNS FOR A CHANCE TO PROVE IT WAS A TORPEDO, NOT A FAULTY BOILER.

The story detailed the *Eagle*'s explosion and the progress Lawton had made in disproving the Navy's official ruling. "The force of the blast lifted the 200-foot-long ship three feet in the air and snapped it in half," Arnold wrote. "The blast continues to reverberate fifty-five years later as relatives of some victims continue to suspect a Navy cover-up." While the press gravitated to the phrase "cover-up," Lawton, if he used it at all, continued to do so in the context of Portland base commander Ernest Freeman's embarrassment, not a full-scale Navy conspiracy. "Here was a U-boat that penetrated defenses at the end of the war, practically docked in Portland, inflicted casualties, then scooted away," Lawton was quoted in Arnold's article. And it is noteworthy that Lawton was consistent in a clarification he sent to Arnold after their phone interview: "I do not think the Convening Authority in the Court of Inquiry into the sinking of the *PE-56* considered their theory of a boiler explosion as much a so-called 'cover-up' as a convenient instance of plausible deniability."

After the *Globe* story, Lawton continued to receive correspondence from divers and others interested in the *Eagle 56* case, each with their own theories and hypotheses, but with little additional evidence to further his case. There was also no further response from the Navy.

For his part, Lawton finally found the time to review the Court of Inquiry records again, particularly the list of survivors. Additional testimony from survivors would bolster the argument, like a news reporter getting a second source for a story or a lawyer finding a second eyewitness to a crime. Lawton wasn't sure any other survivors were alive; Breeze had already informed him that the two men he knew about, Johnny Luttrell and Oscar Davis, had died. Lawton began to search the records for the hometowns of the survivors and match them against contemporary telephone directories. Of course he couldn't be sure that any of these men had returned to their hometowns, but it was the only place to start. Breeze had made the three-thousand-mile trek back to Seattle after the war, hadn't he?

The first match he got was a Lucky Thirteen survivor who had hailed from Henrietta, New York, during World War II. A man with the identical name was listed in Henrietta's current directory; no guarantee certainly, but it offered Lawton a glimmer of hope at least. On the evening of May 2, 2000, Paul Lawton dialed the number, and on the other end of the phone an elderly man's voice, slightly gravelly, nearly shouted a "Hello?" back at him. From the tone of the greeting, from that single word, Lawton knew he had struck pay dirt. More than a year and a half after Johnny Breeze had stepped forward, Paul Lawton knew that he was talking to another *Eagle 56* survivor.

He had found Harold "Pete" Petersen.

39

The bucolic Henrietta of Harold Petersen's youth—with its sprawling dairy and wheat farms, one-room elementary schools, corner groceries, Bly Martin Feed Store, Family Theater, and Pappas Soda and Candy Sweet Shop—had largely disappeared by the start of the twenty-first century. The center of this Rochester, New York, suburb now consisted of a collection of fast food stores, auto dealerships, strip malls, and restaurants lining a busy boulevard with two travel lanes in each direction separated by a left-hand turning lane. Like everywhere else in America, life's pace had quickened in downtown Henrietta. There was no longer any place for the horse and wagon Harold once guided as a boy, from the Brockett farm, where he hand-planted crops for fifty cents a day, across town to purchase supplies. Even the postwar neighborliness ingrained in Henrietta's character, strong enough to support the Petersens' door-to-door business of selling eggs, chickens, and fresh chicken pies that Alice had prepared, had slowly faded over the years.

And yet, on the outskirts of town the remnants of its past quaintness were still evident. Large farms spread along rolling hillsides, and horses, cows, and lawn mower repair shops outnumbered people. It was as though Henrietta—described in its official town history as "the crossroad of Monroe County"—would not surrender the *entirety* of her physical acreage to creeping overdevelopment, but had declared that her outer fringes were off-limits to steel and asphalt and would instead remain a throwback to an era long past.

As he approached his seventy-eighth birthday, Harold "Pete" Petersen was something of a throwback himself.

He lived modestly with his second wife, Mary, and two dogs in the sturdy Henrietta Road house that he and his father built, the home he and Alice had returned to after the war, the home in which they had raised two sons and a daughter. His beloved Alice had died in 1970 at the age of forty-five from what Harold called "complications" from menopause, his pain from the loss so profound that he is incapable of discussing it further. He married Mary in 1974; she had been a tenant in the apartment house that Pete managed. Now, more than twenty-five years later, she was in the beginning stages of Alzheimer's disease, and Pete knew he would be unable to care for her alone much longer.

Pete's house was the sole residence along a busy business strip, traffic flying by, his four acres, including a barn, flanked by the tower of a local television station and a delicatessen. Inside, years of accumulated memorabilia and photos gave the rooms a cluttered feel, but a pleasantly nostalgic one at the same time: a warm cocoon of security against the outside world, strengthened with each log Pete tossed on the flames crackling in his fireplace.

There was history in this house. Right after the war, Pete himself had acquired most of the material to build it when he received permission from the East Rochester Car Barns to tear apart a discarded wooden boxcar and transport the lumber to Henrietta Road. Pete was proud that he and his dad had done all the work; they needed no help from contractors to complete the house. On August 18, 1946, a year after the war ended, the Petersens' first son, Ronald, was born. Nearly two years later, on June 29, 1948, Richard was born, and Barbara came into their lives on February 2, 1951. Pete and Alice watched their children grow, become excellent athletes, and do well in school. Pete had the good fortune to coach his boys in baseball, football, and basketball. In 1967, he coached Richard's American Legion team to the New York State Championship, and he swelled with pride when Ronald was drafted by the Baltimore Orioles right out of college.

Pete's own dream of playing in the majors ended shortly after the war, when he had been transferred from Portland to the Boston Naval Yard. He had played several games for a Navy team in the late summer of 1946, when the leg and back injuries he had sustained during the

Eagle ordeal became so painful that he could barely walk. He dragged his right foot behind him, found it excruciating to climb stairs, and just as painful to sit down. He was admitted first to the Boston Naval Hospital, and then transferred to the Philadelphia Naval Hospital for more advanced treatment. Doctors did all they could, but finally concluded that Pete was no longer fit for active duty and he received a medical discharge. The experts told him he would be hard-pressed to walk normally again, and would need to "work inside" for the rest of his life. Pete proved them wrong; he recovered, exercised regularly, and was actually able to play semipro baseball—as a catcher—for seventeen years, and semipro football for six years. From time to time, pain flared in his back and legs, but Pete refused to slow down, drawing strength from Alice's support and encouragement.

Always, Alice was by his side. When a 1949 fire nearly destroyed their barn and poultry business, Alice and Pete worked out of the house, candling eggs in the closet and using the front room as an office. They spent twenty years in the chicken business, as partners and best friends, and Alice was a wonderful mother. She generated the energy in the house, filled it with light and spirit, and lifted Pete's heart when she walked into the room. She loved the holidays; Pete called Christmases "the wonder of our lives . . . we decorated completely; it was the time we could see the full joy and happiness in our lives and the children's lives." Her death cleaved his heart, a fissure Pete did not believe would ever close. Years after her death, in a poetry tribute to her entitled "Alice," Pete wrote: "Alice, a very precious name to me, A name I shall remember to eternity."

He considered Mary the third miracle in his life, preceded only by his love for Alice and his survival of the *Eagle 56* sinking. He married her when he was fifty-two years old, and she offered him a second chance for love and companionship that humbled him. She was smart, capable, kind, and beautiful; Pete thought the onset of this dreaded disease was the cruelest blow she could suffer.

Yet, through the most difficult times in his life—his own injuries and the end of his baseball dream, the fire in his home, Alice's death, Mary's illness—Harold "Pete" Petersen refused to brood, refused to be dragged down by the weight of disappointment. How could he? He considered himself lucky to be alive. He never forgot his shipmates who died on April 23, 1945, though he rarely spoke of that day. Anytime he watched a war movie or saw a television program about the sea, the memories flooded back. "I think about the *Eagle* all the time," he would say later, "how if I had spent another three or four minutes in the water I would have been gone, how my three kids, six grandchildren, and four great-grandchildren—with one on the way—wouldn't be here if I hadn't made it out of that water. I see the faces of my shipmates, and they still look so young—they never had the chance I had. I always say, 'I'm glad I'm still here; I can deal with anything.' I'm so grateful for the second chance I got after they pulled me out of that water. It's why I try to help people, do things for them, and stay positive. I got another chance—so I try to give back what I can."

Unlike Johnny Breeze, Pete had heard that the Navy believed a boiler explosion had sunk the *Eagle 56*. He and some of the fellows, including Johnny Luttrell, had talked about it at the *Selfridge* reunion in Portland in 1995. Pete had been aghast at the official version of events. For years he asked himself: "Did I have anything to do with all those comrades who went down with the ship? After all, I had just left the engine room." And yet, he knew he had not. The engines were "working beautifully" when he left the watch just before "Mike" Michelsen relieved him. The question that haunted him more was the one he believed the family members of his dead shipmates had been asking for years: "What kind of incompetence on that ship caused my loved one to die?"

Which was why Harold Petersen would never forget the phone call he received on the evening of May 2, 2000.

"Mr. Petersen," the voice on the other end said. "My name is Paul Lawton, and I'm so glad I've finally found you . . ."

For Pete Petersen, here was another second chance, this time to set the record straight. This was not just for his own sake, but for the benefit of his long-departed shipmates, those men whose young faces Petersen saw in his memories, those men who—unlike Pete—never had an opportunity to grow old.

June 9, 2000
Kensington, Maryland

Another sailor who also had a second chance, former *Eagle 56* skipper, John L. Barr Jr., died on June 5, 2000, at the age of eighty-two, from congestive heart disease and kidney failure. His death came fifty-five years after his old ship exploded. Longing to contribute to the war effort against the Japanese, Barr had relinquished command of the *Eagle 56* three months before the torpedo destroyed her.

A deeply religious man, Barr, who had graduated from Harvard University before the war, went on to earn a law degree in 1947 from George Washington University law school. He practiced general law for forty-five years in the Washington law firm of Ogilby, Huhn, and Barr, before he retired in the early 1990s. He and his wife, Isabelle, had been married for fifty-nine years when he died. They had two children, his daughter Peggy Barr Eastman, and his son, Dr. John "Jack" Barr III, as well as two grandchildren. But for his unlikely request a lifetime ago—*volunteering* to leave cushy stateside duty to help his Navy comrades in the Pacific—Barr's full and happy life may never have happened had he been aboard the *Eagle 56* on April 23, 1945.

But Barr never forgot the *Eagle*. Every year, on April 23, he wrote a letter to Ginny Laubach Pettebone extolling Jack Laubach's virtues, and Ginny and the Barrs had been close friends for years. Unaware of Paul Lawton's findings when he died, Barr always believed that a torpedo had sunk the *Eagle*. He struggled through the years about whether his decision to leave Portland was the right one—partially from the guilt he felt about the fate of his former shipmates, but perhaps also believing, as Ginny did, that he might have saved the crew had he been at the *Eagle*'s helm.

Today, at the Christ Church Parish in Kensington, Maryland, friends and loved ones gathered to honor and say farewell to John Barr. Throughout his life, he had loved the night sky and he loved the sea, and had left instructions that he wanted Robert Louis Stevenson's "Requiem" read at his memorial service. His son, Jack, who delivered the eulogy, first recalled that his father gave him and his sister, Peggy, a great gift: the love of reading. "When we were young, he took us into the worlds of Arthurian legend, reading from Tennyson's *Idylls of the King*," John Barr III opened, quoting familiar passages from the verses uttered by Arthur and Sir Bedivere. Then Jack Barr read the Stevenson poem:

> *Under the wide and starry sky*
> *Dig the grave and let me lie:*
> *Glad did I live and gladly die,*
> *And I laid me down with a will.*
>
> *This be the verse you 'grave for me:*
> *Here he lies where he long'd to be;*
> *Home is the sailor, home from sea*
> *And the hunter home from the hill.*

John Barr, who loved his officers and his crew, who never forgot them, who commanded their ship and their respect, who was devastated by their sudden and terrible loss, was finally reuniting with them after more than half a century.

Home was the sailor, home from the sea.

40

It had been a summer of highs and lows for Paul Lawton in his efforts to uncover the truth about the *Eagle 56*.

He was euphoric after locating and talking with Harold Petersen, who, like Johnny Breeze, completely discredited the boiler-explosion theory and insisted that the *Eagle 56* explosion had been caused by an external force. Petersen had not seen the sub, but believed a torpedo had sunk the *Eagle*, and was outraged at the official Navy ruling.

Shortly after his discussions with Petersen, Lawton had confirmed the dates for the *Eagle 56* dive-search operation. Through letters, he had begun to inform a growing list of people interested in the *Eagle 56* story on his progress—diving experts, historians, elected officials, family members, and others. In June, he began using letterhead entitled USS EAGLE 56 (PE-56) SEARCH TEAM and under that heading, the words, "Diving for the Truth." In a June 30 letter to Bob Westerlund, Lawton wrote: "As we discussed, *Salvage One* will sail from Newburyport [Massachusetts] . . . for Portland, Maine, on the evening of July 10, 2000. They expect to arrive in Portland on the morning of Tuesday, July 11. I am driving up to Portland on the morning of the 11th . . . As you know, we have to transport a great deal of supplies, provisions, and equipment to be loaded aboard *Salvage One*."

For the two-day search, Lawton had enlisted the assistance of Garry Kozak of Klein Associates, one of the world's leading side-scan SONAR experts, and navigation expert Tom Mackie. On July 11 and 12, using highly sophisticated computer and scanning equipment, the search team covered more than six square miles off the Maine coast, exploring most of the *Eagle 56*'s known positions. Both a documentary production company and a Portland television news team were aboard *Salvage One* filming the search. Lawton knew that if they found the *Eagle* wreck, they could dive on her and visually determine whether she had been torn apart by a torpedo. Like mowing a lawn, the *Salvage One* traveled north for one leg, south for another, then crisscrossed east and west, careful to cover every square foot of the target area, the experts on board searching and straining for some sign of the *Eagle 56* wreckage.

But the mission was unsuccessful—the *Eagle* was nowhere to be found.

Lawton was disappointed and stunned. He had used Navy records and nautical maps to plot the *Eagle 56*'s location. Walls and tables in his Brockton home were covered with maps, charts, official documents, and witness accounts as he triangulated and calculated the area in which the *Eagle* went down. The ocean-floor topography in the area in which she sank was rocky, not sandy, meaning it was highly unlikely that the wreck could have been buried as the tides and shifts of the North Atlantic ebbed and flowed over the past fifty-five years. While the *Eagle*'s two large pieces may have drifted as they sank, they would have plummeted to the bottom quickly, and once settled on the ocean floor, their weight should have prevented further movement. And less than sixty years was far too short a time for the *Eagle 56* hull to have deteriorated to the point of *disappearing*.

Everything that Lawton knew about shipwrecks, diving, oceanography—extensive knowledge that was the product of two decades of study and experience—told him that the *Eagle 56* wreck *had* to be there.

So where the hell was it?

There were rumors that the Navy had dredged the area in a demining operation in 1945, and that perhaps the Navy had buried the *Eagle 56* pieces shortly after the war in an effort to discourage a fledgling diving industry from disturbing the site. Yet, Lawton had been unable to uncover documentation to support rumors of any kind. "Everyone had a tremendous time in the search and all members of the team volunteered to return for a follow-up search," Lawton said. "But we had to regroup and figure out if we had made mistakes. The wreckage of a 200-foot sub-chaser sunk in relatively shallow water [130 feet] doesn't just disappear."

The unsuccessful search for the *PE-56* was demoralizing, but certainly not a wasted trip. At least the search team had succeeded in *eliminating* a six-square-mile chunk of ocean floor. And, the team members, which included the Westerlund brothers, did their part to honor the *Eagle 56* crewmen who died fifty-five years earlier. They attached a small brass plaque to a floral wreath, tied it to a brick for weight, and, after a brief ceremony, dropped it into the ocean at the approximate spot where the *Eagle* went down. The plaque read: IN MEMORY OF THE 49 U.S. NAVY OFFICERS AND CREWMEN LOST ABOARD THE *EAGLE 56* (PE-56) DURING WORLD WAR II, ON APRIL 23, 1945.

Refusing to slow down after the unsuccessful search off the Maine coast, Paul Lawton requested his father's help next. James Lawton was friends with Boston congressman Joseph Moakley—could congressional pressure help reopen the *Eagle 56* case? On August 7, the Lawtons met with Moakley, who, to Paul's delight, pledged his support in presenting the case to the Navy. Moakley fired off letters to Secretary of Defense William S. Cohen and Secretary of the Navy Richard Danzig, requesting an investigation into the *Eagle 56* matter. Lawton's roller coaster of emotions continued: The high of finding Harold Petersen had dissipated with the emotional letdown of the fruitless search for the *Eagle 56* wreckage; now he had reason to hope again.

Yet, by late August, Lawton experienced more frustration. The Secretary of the Navy had referred Moakley's request to Captain Marshall Hall, deputy director of Naval History. Hall replied to Moakley: "The question of reconstituting a court of inquiry on the loss of the *PE-56* is a legal matter under the jurisdiction of the Judge Advocate General (JAG) of the Navy. I am forwarding a copy of your inquiry to that command for appropriate action." Lawton couldn't believe the bureaucratic runaround. He quickly prepared a response to Captain Hall, copying Moakley, Danzig, Cohen, and President Bill Clinton. He enclosed copies of the voluminous research he had already gathered in the *Eagle* case and wrote: "For the record, we have long ago made Freedom of Information Act (FOIA) requests, and appeals to the Judge Advocate General (JAG) of the U.S. Navy, only to receive multiple denials from USN/JAG claiming all records pertaining to this tragedy were lost from their long-term storage facilities. It was not until a year ago that a sympathetic source [Retired Captain Melanson, Alice Hultgren's friend] provided us with the copies of the missing Court of Inquiry records." Lawton then varied from his more deferring style and injected passion into his case: "As information has been gathered and witnesses interviewed, it became increasingly clear that a grave mistake may have been made 55 years ago, which has since tarnished the names and memories of the unfortunate 49 young men killed aboard the *PE-56*, and the reputation of the U.S. Navy. After reviewing the technical data on the ship's boilers and machinery, as well as eyewitnesses' accounts regarding the tremendous effects of the explosion that tore the ship in half, every expert I have questioned about this incident has responded with utter disbelief when told of the Navy's explanation: 'boiler explosion.' "

And then Lawton clearly articulated what he wanted: "We were hoping the Navy would be objective in reviewing all of the facts surrounding this incident and do the right thing after 55 years by issuing those 49 casualties posthumous Purple Hearts. The families of those men killed would not be entitled to any additional monetary benefits, as they were admittedly killed *'in the line of duty.'* The highly questionable determination that the 49 deaths were *'not the result of enemy action'* is the conclusion that we are seeking to have revisited, and reversed."

A week after his letter to Hall, Lawton wrote to Secretary of Defense Cohen: "Those 49 men gave the ultimate sacrifice for their country, and the appropriate recognition for their loss in the form of posthumous issuance of Purple Hearts is long overdue . . . For the U.S. Navy to continue to pass the buck and delay acting on this matter until these witnesses have all passed on, would do a great disservice to those men and their families, and cast an ominous shadow on the honor and reputation of the U.S. Navy. Inevitably, the full and complete account of this incident will be revealed. The cooperation of the Navy would certainly mend old wounds and bring closure to the families of these unfortunate men."

Tough language? Yes, Lawton thought. Unfairly tough? Absolutely not. He had provided the Navy with deck logs, battle diaries, the Court of Inquiry documentation, and contemporary press interviews, as well as witness statements from sailors aboard other ships, COI stenographer Alice Hultgren, and the two Lucky Thirteen living survivors, Johnny Breeze and Harold Petersen. He had enlisted the support of diving experts, maritime historians, and authors, all of whom agreed that an injustice had been done in the *Eagle 56* case. He had spent thousands of hours on research and thousands of dollars of his own money seeking the truth. He had done all of this while attempting to manage his law practice—his profession and the way he made his living—which he acknowledged had suffered due to the time, energy, and resources he had diverted to the *Eagle 56* project.

And through all of this, the United States Navy had basically ignored him.

Now, two and a half years into his quest, Paul Lawton was not going to get squeamish over some forceful language in his letter to the Secretary of Defense.

He viewed it as the only way to get results.

October 2000–February 2001
Brockton, Massachusetts

Throughout the fall of 2000, Lawton's efforts brought additional frustration. First, in October, the Secretary of the Navy's Award and Special Projects Office rejected the Purple Heart request until and unless the official Navy record was changed. "Currently, the cause of the sinking has been determined to be the result of a boiler explosion," wrote B. A. Wilson, head of the office. "Until such time that determination is changed to reflect that the *Eagle* was actually torpedoed . . . the crew members would not be eligible for the Purple Heart. Unfortunately, that determination does not fall under the cognizance of this office."

Then, on December 6, 2000, the Navy JAG office wrote to Congressman Moakley: "The Judge Advocate General is not involved in ordering or conducting investigations. The command or chain-of-command involved directs what type of investigation is required . . . Captain Hall of the Office of Naval History is currently reviewing the additional information Judge [James] Lawton provided to that office [and] may expect a direct response from that office in the near future." The JAG response also noted that the Court of Inquiry ruled that the *Eagle 56* sinking was due to a boiler explosion, a statement that "was supported by the Judge Advocate General" in 1945.

The Navy JAG office sent along one enclosure with its response to Moakley, which the congressman promptly forwarded to Paul Lawton. It was a document the JAG office had been unable to locate as part of Lawton's original Freedom of Information Act (FOIA) request, claiming that the records were lost. Eighteen months after Alice Hultgren opened her birthday package from her retired Navy friend, the Navy JAG office had sent along the *Eagle 56* Court of Inquiry records to Moakley. While the COI records were identical to the ones Hultgren had supplied to Lawton, the JAG package also included a more complete chart of the *PE-56* wreck site. The new chart revealed that the USS *Nantucket* was actually a bit further to the northwest, and gave Lawton new hope that the *Eagle* wreck could lie slightly to the north of the *Salvage One* search area.

The country's mind was on other matters during the fall of 2000. The tightest presidential race in history, between Vice President Al Gore, the Democrat, and Texas governor George W. Bush, the Republican, was not settled on Election Day, but would continue into December, and include an astounding recount in Florida and an historic decision by the United States Supreme Court. When George W. Bush was sworn in as president on Inauguration Day, Lawton wondered if the change in administration would change the Navy's attitude toward the *Eagle 56* case.

On February 2, he received a letter that, once again, offered a glimpse of hope. Captain Marshall Hall, deputy director of Naval History, finally responded to Lawton at the request of the Secretary of the Navy. First, Hall offered Lawton a brief tutorial on Navy history bordering on the pedantic: "Historical matters, such as the case of the loss of *Eagle 56 (PE-56)*, are not settled by official decree. They are, rather, approached by evaluating the available evidence, both documentary and archaeological, to determine if they point to a conclusion. This is by no means an absolute process, and in many situations, the best that can be said is that '*this*' is what is known, and it appears that '*that*' may have happened. The loss of *Eagle 56* is a case in point."

The procedural lesson notwithstanding, it was Hall's next paragraph that Lawton would always remember, words that registered on his brain like a jolt of electricity:

"The Naval Historical Center has assigned Mr. Bernard Cavalcante, Senior Archivist, to collect, investigate, and validate all available documentary evidence surrounding the loss of *Eagle 56*, which we hope will result in adequate evidence to provide a historical resolution of the case."

"Finally!" Lawton shouted. It had been nearly three years since he had shared drinks with the Westerlund brothers at Doyle's Pub & Grill and learned about the *Eagle 56* story, nearly three years since he had embarked on this journey—and finally, the U.S. Navy had officially assigned someone to review the case.

As Paul Lawton would soon find out, Bernard Cavalcante—"Cal" to his friends and coworkers—was a very special someone indeed.

41

February–May 2001
Washington, D.C., and
Brockton, Massachusetts

Bernard Cavalcante had worked for the Naval Historical Center since the Eisenhower administration, and in more than forty years he had never been as sure about anything as he was about this: A torpedo from the *U-853* had sunk the USS *Eagle 56*.

The sixty-seven-year-old senior archivist knew this before he had plunged into the records that had become so familiar to him over four decades of immersion and cataloging. He knew it before he had delved into the previously classified and Top Secret Ultra intercepts that he had known existed since the 1960s, but had been forbidden to speak about for reasons of national security. He knew it even before he had finished reading the first few pages of the extensive documentation Paul Lawton had sent him.

Cavalcante knew it the way archivists often know things—by sifting through their memory banks for little known scraps of information, seemingly unrelated nuggets that at first swirl unconnectedly just beyond the conscious grasp and then suddenly crystallize into a coherent picture as sharp and clear as the late autumn sky.

For Cavalcante, the random memory was from the 1960s.

The Historical Center had been working closely with noted German historian Jürgen Rohwer documenting U-boat attacks on Allied ships, and U-boat kills during the Battle of the Atlantic. Cavalcante had been the lead archivist on the project on the American side and had come across records of an anti-submarine task force searching in the Gulf of Maine near the end of the war. What was memorable for Cavalcante was that one of the ships was the *Uniontown*, identical to the name of the town in southwestern Pennsylvania where Cavalcante had grown up. "I remember filing it away at the time, because I never knew there was a ship called the *Uniontown* until that moment in the '60s," he said. "Then, forty years later, when I came across the same ship in the material Paul Lawton sent me, something clicked. I knew there had been ASW (anti-submarine warfare) action in the Gulf of Maine and that the *Uniontown* was involved. What I *didn't* know was that the *Eagle* had been sunk. When I read Paul's information, a lightbulb went on—the *Uniontown* must have been chasing the *U-853*. Now I had to prove it."

Cavalcante would have his chance. By now, with Lawton's continuous inquiries, his father's well-placed phone calls, and the political pressure exerted by Congressman Moakley, the *Eagle 56* case had become a priority. Captain Marshall Hall, deputy director of naval history, whom Lawton had written to seeking information, told Cavalcante to put everything else aside and pursue the *Eagle* case. "He said, 'I'll give you two months; go anywhere you need to go, just work on this,' " Cal said.

Up until now, Cavalcante had not been involved at all in the *Eagle* inquiry. He had been out of work on medical leave for nearly five months with a severe case of neuropathy, a disease of the nervous system, which had attacked Cal's legs and disabled him almost totally. The pain had been so severe that Cal could not walk, and doctors feared he would never be ambulatory again, a real blow for this former Marine who had once been a runner and an athlete. But physical therapy, swimming, and the stationary bike strengthened Cal's legs, and eventually he regained the capability to walk and then "learned to climb stairs again." He had lost fifty pounds during his ordeal and was "skin and bones" when he finally returned to work late in 2000, walking without a limp, but also without feeling in his legs.

He had returned and was catching up on correspondence when he came across "ten or more letters" on the *Eagle 56* case, "three or four of them, at least, from Paul Lawton." Staffers at the Naval Historical Center who were not as versed in the records "had given out some negative information without really knowing fully what they were talking about," Cal said. "I knew we could do more than we had done."

Once Captain Hall had given him the green light to pursue the *Eagle 56* story, Cavalcante called Lawton to tell him he had been assigned to the case and would begin working on it virtually full-time. "Paul went on about the *Eagle* and the *U-853*, reviewed all the work he and his team had done, and was excited," Cal recalled. "His enthusiasm made the hair on the back of my neck stand up. I said to myself, 'I've got to find something that can help this guy.' "

If anyone could help Paul Lawton crack the *Eagle 56* case, it was Bernard Cavalcante. Since February 29, 1960, when he started with the Naval Historical Center Archives after six years in the Marine Corps, he had plied his craft in the Top Secret vault on the top floor, learning and working with the Navy's most sensitive documents and records. He became the foremost expert on World War II Battle of the Atlantic documents, including records of the Tenth Fleet, ASW reports, war diaries, convoy routing reports, survivor summary statements, action reports, German U-boat records—and perhaps most importantly, the Top Secret Ultra records detailing the operations of OP-20-G and Commander Kenneth Knowles's "Secret Room." Cavalcante knew about the Ultra records more than two decades before the rest of the world, until Great Britain and the United States jointly agreed to declassify them in 1987. "We were not allowed to talk about those records back then," he said. "If anyone asked how I knew where a ship or a submarine was when we were plotting them, I simply said it was through Huff-Duff records or war diaries."

Cavalcante loved the work. Like most archivists, he felt a reverence for the records themselves, in the stories they told and the pictures they painted, and he reveled in the search-and-discovery process when he tackled a project, the joy of setting the historical record straight. Perhaps forming the core of his belief in the sanctity of preserving history was his pride in his own genealogy and family history. Cavalcante could trace his paternal lineage back seven hundred years to an ancestor, Guido Cavalcanti, an Italian poet who was a contemporary and friend of Dante Alighieri's. The two poets eventually had a falling out, and Dante condemned Cavalcanti to hell in the "Inferno" section of his epic poem, *The Divine Comedy*.

Now Cavalcante would call on his years of experience and his knowledge of the records to buttress Paul Lawton's research on the *Eagle 56* case. "I felt so bad for those guys [Breeze and Petersen]," Cavalcante said. "To have the Court of Inquiry ruling that a boiler explosion sunk their ship, when they both knew that the boilers had just been overhauled and the *Eagle* was shipshape—it was really a personal thing. It's like the COI was calling those men liars. I was anxious to dive into this case."

By March 20, 2001, Cavalcante had gathered enough information from the Eastern Sea Frontier War Diary and Ultra records to prepare a detailed letter on behalf of William S. Dudley, director of naval history, to send to the Secretary of the Navy (SECNAV). "I had what I was looking for in a matter of days, but I kept looking to make sure I hadn't *overlooked* anything," Cavalcante remembered. "I didn't want to leave a single stone unturned."

The subject line of Dudley's letter to SECNAV read: "Correction of Historical Records ICO (in case of) USS *Eagle (PE-56)* and recommendation of award of Purple Heart Medals." The first section of the letter began boldly: "The Director of Naval History . . . has determined compelling evidence and facts support the correction of the historical record in the case of the loss of the USS *Eagle (PE-56)*, sunk on April 23, 1945, by enemy action. It is further strongly recommended that . . . the 49 crew members of the USS *Eagle (PE-56)* killed and those 13 eligible survivors, be awarded the Purple Heart Medal for death and wounds suffered in combat."

The letter then proceeds to make a point-by-point case, citing the Eastern Sea Frontier war diary and specific Ultra documents that Cavalcante ferreted from the Naval Historical Center archives. "The U-boat Tracking Room continued to track one U-boat in the Gulf of Maine throughout April 1945," the letter continues. "At the time of the deliberation of the Court of Inquiry, the highly classified Ultra information was not shared with the members of the court." In addition, the letter points out that several of the *Eagle* survivors saw the U-boat surface, and that at least one man saw red-and-yellow markings on the *U-853*'s conning tower. "At the time of the sinking of the *PE-56*, German snorkel fitted IXC/40 Type U-boats, such as *U-853*, were painted black, and no one had any way of knowing that one particular U-boat operating in the Gulf of Maine bore a conning tower insignia of a red trotting horse on a yellow shield, as did the *U-853*. The information on the conning tower insignia was obtained from the U-boat archives in Cuxhaven-Altenbruch, Germany."

Dudley made some minor changes to the letter, and the official document was sent to SECNAV on May 1, 2001, more than three years after Paul Lawton had begun his quest to change naval history. The letter was addressed to interim SECNAV Admiral Robert B. Pirie Jr.

Meanwhile, sensing that he was getting closer to his goal, Lawton contacted Congressman Moakley and sent a lengthy update letter to the USS *Eagle 56* search team that said, in part: "Mr. Cavalcante stated to me in no uncertain terms that they are now convinced the *PE-56* was torpedoed by the *U-853*, and that the idea of a boiler explosion was not genuinely a credible explanation . . . We hope the Navy will take appropriate action and I am personally confident that Purple Hearts will be issued to the *PE-56* casualties some time this year . . . appropriately, this year is the '56th' anniversary of this naval tragedy."

Paul Lawton had done what he could do. With Bernard Cavalcante's discovery of Ultra records and Eastern Sea Frontier war diaries to augment his own voluminous documentation on the *Eagle 56* case, and with William Dudley's agreement to petition the Secretary of the Navy to officially change the record, matters were largely out of Lawton's hands. SECNAV Gordon England would either concur with the overwhelming evidence and grant the request, or rule that even in the face of such evidence, the Navy simply could not take the unprecedented action of overturning a Court of Inquiry—especially more than half a century after the fact.

Already impatient for results, weary from three years of research and more than occasional frustration, anxious as the *Eagle 56* case neared resolution, Paul Lawton was now forced to do the one thing he least wanted to do.

He waited.

On Sunday of Memorial Day weekend, May 28, 2001, Congressman John Joseph "Joe" Moakley died at age seventy-four of complications from leukemia. He did not live to see the Navy's decision on the *Eagle 56*.

On May 30, Lawton wrote to his archivist friend, James Fahey:

> Though we were all hoping interim SECNAV . . . Pirie was going to
> act on the . . . recommendation to issue Purple Hearts to the *PE-56*
> casualties while Congressman Moakley was still with us, he [Pirie]
> apparently left it up to the new SECNAV appointee, Gordon R. Eng-
> land [sworn in on May 24, 2001]. We all hope Secretary England
> will do the right thing and set the record straight, before more of
> those involved pass away.

42

Spring rolled into summer without an answer. James Lawton gave Gordon England about a month and a half to become acclimated to his new position before the judge decided to roll out the big guns to help expedite a final decision in the *Eagle 56* drama. To reverse the Court of Inquiry, Secretary England basically had to concur with and approve William Dudley's recommendations—nothing more—and James Lawton believed that decision needed to happen sooner rather than later.

"I had seen how long and how hard Paul had worked on this, and I was damn proud of him," James Lawton said of his son. "Paul is not the type to ask for help, but in this case, it was a small gesture I felt he deserved—and the *Eagle 56* family deserved it, too."

On July 11, James Lawton wrote to his friend at the White House, Andrew Card, chief of staff for President George W. Bush. Card was once a state representative from Massachusetts, where Judge Lawton had served on the bench for years before he retired.

After beginning his letter "Dear Andy," Lawton briefly laid out the details of the *Eagle 56* case and his son's involvement in this chapter of naval history. Then he got to the crux of the issue:

"Since the research into this tragic event began . . . several of the survivors and other individuals involved in that event have passed away. At present, there are only two of the original 13 survivors of the *Eagle 56* still known to be alive, and these fine men are approaching their eighties. Additionally, several surviving spouses, brothers, sisters, and children of those crewmen killed and injured are anxious to have this record corrected, once and for all . . . we would greatly appreciate any assistance you might be able to provide in bringing this matter to the Secretary's attention, before any more of those parties involved in this request, including the late Congressman John Joseph "Joe" Moakley, also pass away."

In addition, Lawton addressed two other issues "that may be of concern to Secretary England." First, James Lawton said, approval of the recommendation "would not be seen as an admission by the Navy of a cover-up fifty-six years ago," but rather a "mistaken conclusion," since the Court of Inquiry did not have access to Ultra decryptions. Second, England's approval of the recommendation would not expose the Navy or the federal government to any further financial burden. "The survivors of those men killed and injured aboard the *Eagle 56* long ago received all benefits that would have been due them, even had the original Court finding been 'enemy action,' " James Lawton assured Andrew Card. "The gesture is long overdue and should be acted upon as soon as possible, while the last few survivors are still with us to see this injustice to their loved ones made right."

His son's indefatigable determination to set the record straight, coupled with pressure from an influential congressman and generous assistance from a legendary naval archivist, had landed the *Eagle 56* investigation squarely on the desk of the Secretary of the Navy.

James Lawton hoped that pressure from the White House could now move it *off* Gordon England's desk and onto the pages of history.

It is worth noting that James Lawton's reassurance to Andy Card that the Navy would not be admitting a "cover-up" by overturning the *Eagle 56* Court of Inquiry was an opinion shared by Bernard Cavalcante. The senior archivist believed the *Eagle 56* story had been overshadowed by the end of the war and then forgotten, a painful and unfortunate injustice, for certain, but not a cover-up. "I've spent too much time in these records to know that cover-ups usually come uncovered," he said. "They just don't wash. There are certainly secrets in these records, but most of them are not cover-ups—they are stories that haven't been told yet."

Cavalcante acknowledged that the Court of Inquiry's boiler-explosion conclusion was "far-fetched and unrealistic, and it's inexcusable that the court ignored the crewmen's testimony" about seeing a submarine. Yet, his belief is that, with no "hard documentary evidence" of a U-boat in the area in 1945, the COI was predisposed to attribute the *Eagle* explosion to an internal mechanical failure. "Their [the Court] ruling was based more on ignorance than any deliberate attempt to cover up," Cavalcante argued. "They did not have the Ultra information available to them, and they had no way of knowing the *U-853* was in the area. The COI might have been sloppy, but I don't see it as any active cover-up. That doesn't make their decision any less difficult for the survivors, though. For years, those guys suffered thinking they may have been responsible for the deaths of their buddies. That's the most important reason the truth had to come out."

While Cavalcante had nothing but admiration for Paul Lawton's determination to set the record straight, he also disagreed with Lawton on the motives of Ernest Freeman, Portland base commander. Lawton believed that Freeman likely influenced the Court of Inquiry's decision in an effort to protect his own reputation, one that faced scrutiny and possible damage due to the loss of an American warship so close to shore so late in the war. Yet, Cavalcante maintained that no harm had come to the reputations or careers of other base commanders who lost ships on their watch. "Ships were torpedoed, these things do happen in wartime," Cavalcante said, "although I have to say that Paul does have a point about how close to shore this ship was when it was destroyed—it was extraordinarily close. Given that, I can see how someone could hold the opinion that Freeman was trying to cover his own butt by nudging the COI away from a torpedo ruling. It's just not an opinion that I hold."

Nonetheless, Cavalcante said there was no excuse for the *U-853* creeping so near to shore in late April of 1945. By that time, the East Coast of the United States was well protected and ships traveled almost freely from Canada to Florida, despite vigilance against the occasional U-boat. For Froemsdorf to have maneuvered his boat to just a few miles off the Maine coast, for the *U-853* to have closed to within a few hundred yards of the *Eagle 56* without detection—it meant mistakes had been made. Was it overconfidence that caused Freeman to ignore the general U-boat warnings? Was it incompetence that caused *Eagle 56* skipper Early to grind his ship to a dead stop in a war zone and miss the presence of a lurking submarine? Perhaps yes, said Cavalcante.

"A colossal mess-up? Yes. But a deliberate cover-up? No, I don't believe so," he said.

43

August–September 2001
Washington, D.C., and
Brockton, Massachusetts

More than fifty-six years after the *Eagle 56* exploded and sank, and forty-nine of her officers and crew members were killed, Secretary of the Navy Gordon England officially concurred with Bernard Cavalcante's findings that a torpedo had sunk the American subchaser. In so doing, Secretary England went along with Naval History Director William Dudley's recommendation to take the historic and unprecedented step of reversing a Court of Inquiry decision that had stood, however shakily, for more than a half-century.

Paul Lawton's three-and-a-half-year fight had ended in victory—for the *Eagle 56* survivors, for the families of her lost crew members, and for the sake of U.S. Naval history.

Actually, Secretary England had rendered his decision weeks earlier, but no one knew about it. He had approved Dudley's recommendation in mid-summer, yet it wasn't until the call from White House Chief of Staff Andy Card, at James Lawton's request, that the SECNAV's office shared England's action.

"We waited and waited," Cavalcante recalled, "and there was no answer. Finally, a lieutenant at SECNAV called and said that Secretary England concurred with my findings and that our recommendation had been approved. The *Eagle* Court of Inquiry had been reversed. I called Paul immediately and told him. He set the phone down and started yelling and jumping around. He was thrilled and I was so happy—for him and for all the others."

On August 28, James Lawton received official word from Christopher Rouin, Director of the SECNAV White House Liaison Office, responding to Lawton's letter to Andy Card.

"You will be pleased to know that the Secretary of the Navy recently reviewed and approved the Director of Navy History's recommendation regarding the sinking of the USS *Eagle*," Rouin's letter said. "As a result, personnel at the Naval Historical Center are currently in the process of correcting the historical record of the USS *Eagle*, to indicate that the ship was lost due to enemy action."

Rouin's letter went on to say that the Navy's Board of Decorations and Medals was "taking appropriate steps to award the Purple Heart Medal to the crew members who were killed or wounded on 23 April 1945 . . . [and] the Board will forward Purple Heart Medals to the service members or their appropriate next of kin."

As soon as he received word about the Navy's historic decision, the first people Lawton contacted were the Westerlunds, before spreading the word to the entire *Eagle* search team. He was jubilant, but emotionally drained after more than three years of digging for records and assembling the narrative of the *Eagle 56* and *U-853* stories.

"I viewed the decision as a victory for the truth, a vindication of the survivors, and justice for those brave sailors who were lost on April 23, 1945," Lawton said. "Getting the call from Cal was amazing, although the decision was still long overdue. But he really reignited our efforts. It looked like we were going to stall, but he believed in the cause. Cal made me believe we could rewrite history."

For his part, Cal said Lawton's enthusiasm and determination drove the archivist to prove the case. "I wasn't going to take no for an answer," Cal said, "not after what Paul had been through. I've been involved in other cases before, but none as important as this—because of the survivors, their families, Paul Lawton and his dad, the Westerlunds. God, I felt like they deserved so much to know the truth. And Paul, he was unbelievable—the amount of research and work he did. I never had a son, but if I did, I would want him to have the same integrity and dedication to the truth as Paul Lawton."

✪ ✪ ✪

Even before Rouin's letter reached James Lawton, the *Eagle 56* story began to spread.

Paul Lawton contacted the media, including the Associated Press, to inform them of Secretary England's decision, and by August 30, 2001, a major AP feature story by Melissa Robinson began running in newspapers and on Web sites across the country and the world. The article credited Paul Lawton for gathering the evidence to convince the Navy. Johnny Breeze's remarks and Harold Petersen's photo and quotes appeared in dozens of publications, large and small. "The AP photographer came to my house and shot a hundred pictures," Petersen said. "He said he had orders to take a large number, that they would pick out the best one and it would go all over the world." Identified as one of two survivors still living, Petersen said he was gratified by the Navy's decision, but sorry it took so long. He said he still thought of the parents of the sailors who died and wished they could have known the truth. "They had to think all these years, 'Who was so negligent that they allowed the boilers to explode and kill my child?' " the seventy-nine-year-old Petersen was quoted by the AP.

The story also appeared in the *Rochester Democrat and Chronicle*, which also covered Petersen's hometown of Henrietta, New York. The piece in that paper prompted a letter from New York Senator Hillary Rodham Clinton to Gordon England, urging him to review the service records of the *Eagle 56* sailors to determine if they were eligible for Purple Hearts, a process that was already under way.

Over the next week, after the AP story began showing up in more and more publications, Petersen received letters from around the country, and from as far away as Holland. And the *Eagle 56* story and Pete's photo truly went "national" when *The New York Times* picked up the AP feature on September 4, 2001.

Within a matter of days in early September, it is likely that hundreds of thousands of people—perhaps millions when the *Times* story is factored in—learned about the *Eagle 56* sinking and the Navy's reversal of the Court of Inquiry decision. Some of those newspaper and Internet readers may have glanced at the headline, thousands of others might have perused the body of the story in a cursory manner, untold thousands more may have finished reading until the final paragraph, where Fred Westerlund was quoted as saying: "We always wondered what really happened. It shouldn't have taken fifty-six years to get this straight."

But one eighty-one-year-old man, sitting in his cozy, wood-paneled study in Morris Plains, New Jersey, read the AP story in the September 4, 2001, edition of *The New York Times* with a mixture of euphoria and stunned disbelief. He read through the article twice, still unable to fully comprehend it, thunderstruck not only by the *content* of the piece, but by the serendipity that allowed him to see the news that changed his life the instant he read the headline: IN SWITCH, NAVY SAYS GERMAN SUB SANK SHIP OFF MAINE IN '45. After all, he read the *Times* frequently, but certainly did not devour it every day. What if he had missed this article? What if he had missed Harold Petersen's proud photograph, along with the caption underneath identifying the Henrietta native as one of two living survivors of the *Eagle*, with Johnny Breeze being the other? *What if?*

But he *had* read the *Times* that morning. And when he finished scouring the article and the caption, finished staring slack-jawed at the photograph, the tall man with the proud bearing leaned back in his chair, sipped his coffee, and whispered hoarsely to himself.

"I'm still here, too," John Scagnelli said. "I'm still here, too."

44

John and Bea Scagnelli were married in 1949, fifty-two years before John saw *The New York Times* that morning in September of 2001, yet she had only known about his *Eagle 56* experience since the late 1990s. "For all those years, I think he didn't talk about it because he thought he may have been at fault, and it bothered him deeply," she said. Like the other *Eagle* survivors, Scagnelli had put the events of April 23, 1945, behind him, but never beyond the reach of his memories.

Indeed, his *Eagle 56* experience had influenced and defined his professional and community life afterwards. Fifty-six years earlier, as he treaded water and watched the *Eagle*'s bow section plunge beneath the surface, Scagnelli vowed in a prayer that if God spared him, he would devote the rest of his life to helping people. He had kept his promise from the beginning of his postwar life, when he abandoned a likely career path in engineering, and earned a master's degree in social work from Columbia in 1949.

He began work for the Children's Aid Society in New York, and eventually became director of the agency's settlement houses; his first assignment was in Little Italy, not far from his boyhood home. Later, he accepted a job with the Boys Club of America—whose name John helped eventually change to the Boys and Girls Clubs of America—where his first responsibility was to raise funds to build a new facility in Queens, and then work closely with youth gangs in the neighborhood, "to try to change their attitudes and behavior." John Scagnelli did his job so well that he became assistant director of national programs, working to meet the needs of adolescent boys by designing programs that focused on neighborhood outreach and preparing troubled youths for jobs.

One of the highlights of his tenure with the Boys Club was a trip to the White House to receive an award, and attend a meeting in the Oval Office with President John F. Kennedy. When Scagnelli told the president he had been a Navy officer, the two exchanged stories of their war experiences; both men had spent time in the water after attacks by enemy ships, and it was the first time in years that Scagnelli had talked about the *Eagle 56*. During the conversation, Scagnelli noticed that President Kennedy was wearing a tie clip with "109" engraved on it, the number of JFK's PT boat during World War II. "I told him how much I admired the clip and without another word, he took it off and presented it to me as a token of my visit," Scagnelli said. "I was shocked at this gesture by the president! What saddens me is that I lost it years later. I've tried so hard to find it, but it's lost to this day—I regret I didn't take better care of it."

When he and Bea moved to Morris Plains shortly thereafter, Scagnelli switched careers briefly and became director of community affairs for the Newark Museum, where he was responsible for fund-raising and endowments, associating with CEOs and community luminaries, but missing the "human contact and satisfaction" he had enjoyed with social work. After four years with the museum, he resumed his career in human services, this time with the Association of Retarded Citizens (ARC), which primarily provided advocacy programs and assistance for the parents of mentally retarded children. Scagnelli relished and excelled at the work, and eventually became director of the New Jersey ARC.

Scagnelli felt at home again, contributing in a special way. "These were kids who were forgotten, kids nobody wanted to deal with, kids who had needs but no one to go to bat for them. Our job was to educate people that these children had worth and that society owed them the chance to grow and exercise their potential. Why should they be excluded from society? I started with this organization at the ground level of this movement, to begin looking at children with disabilities not as people who should be excluded, but as people who needed to be embraced by society. These were kids that society wanted to forget, and I felt that was wrong. We were able to generate so many services that are now commonplace today."

Scagnelli was instrumental in designing the first delinquency prevention program for ARC participants, and developed the first camp for mentally retarded children. He also built the Planned Lifetime Network, which enables parents to contribute to a community trust that provides services to their developmentally disabled children when the parents become too old to care for them. More than one hundred families contributed three million dollars to the trust to provide care for their children. "You'd have parents who were in their seventies or eighties who, before this trust was developed, had no way to provide care for their forty- or fifty-year-old retarded child," Scagnelli said. "I am very proud of that program."

Scagnelli spent twenty years with ARC, until he retired in 1990, and he continued his volunteer work thereafter, both with youth groups and as an active member of the Morris Plains community, where he served on the Recreation Commission, the Board of Education, the Board of Adjustment, YMCA, the United Way, and two Governor's Commissions on prevention and juvenile justice delinquency. Morris Plains is a picture-postcard township, with a railroad station in its center, and a main street lined with a breakfast diner, a drugstore, and attractive shops. Just outside the center is a state park with a beautiful pond that is perfect for hockey when it ices over in the winter, the *whoosh* of youngsters' skates and the *clack* of sticks on the puck reminiscent of a Currier & Ives picture from yesteryear. Bea and John Scagnelli live on a wide, tree-lined street in a neat two-story brick-front home, where they raised three children: John, Gail, and Robert. Morris Plains was home for John Scagnelli, and he threw his full energy and commitment into serving his town as he served those less fortunate, and before that, as he served his country during World War II.

And virtually his entire adult life—his commitment to family, to people less fortunate, and to community—was shaped by his experience on April 23, 1945. "It helped determine what my future was going to be," he would say later. "I had no idea whether I was going to survive, and no idea, if I *did* survive, which direction my life would go in. I look back on my life and there's the *Eagle 56* experience right in the center of my choices."

John Scagnelli did not dwell on the *Eagle 56* tragedy, but for fifty-six years this defining moment off the coast of Maine, and the events immediately afterward, had haunted his memories. In a folder that he tucked away safely, he had held onto all of the condolence letters that he wrote while in Washington, D.C., in the summer of 1945, the tissue-thin carbon copies more fragile for the passage of time, but their texture and content a powerful connection to his past and his country's history.

Now, with *The New York Times* story, that history came alive. Even more importantly, that history was being *changed*, rewritten so that it reflected the reality of what happened on April 23, 1945—not the inaccurate version of events which, for the first few years after the war, was nearly more than Scagnelli could bear or accept.

Scagnelli couldn't contain his excitement. His older son, John, was an attorney. He would know the best way for Scagnelli to go about contacting the historian, Paul Lawton, whom the *Times* said had been the catalyst behind the resurrection of the *Eagle* story. Lieutenant (jg) John Scagnelli wanted to let Lawton and the world know that there was a third *Eagle 56* survivor who had lived to see the truth revealed.

John Scagnelli reached for the phone and called his son.

One week after John Scagnelli and the rest of the country read *The New York Times* story, Islamic terrorists perpetrated the worst foreign attacks on American soil in her history, killing three thousand innocent people in New York City, Washington, D.C., and in a field in Shanksville, Pennsylvania. The terrible events of September 11, 2001, put the *Eagle 56* story and much of the country on hold throughout the fall.

It wasn't until December that Paul Lawton wrote two letters that would provide the exclamation point on the *Eagle 56* saga. One was his way of correcting the historical record on the other side of the Atlantic Ocean, in Germany, so that it was consistent with the revised U.S. record. He wrote to renowned German historian, Dr. Jürgen Rohwer, enclosing a CD-ROM of his research and the United States Navy's decision. "I hope you can make the German naval authorities [aware] of this correction of official naval history, crediting the *Kriegsmarine* and the *U-853*'s officers and crewmen, for this combat sinking," Lawton wrote.

The other letter was to his friend, archivist Jim Fahey, at the U.S. Navy Shipbuilding Museum aboard the USS *Salem* in Quincy, Massachusetts. Lawton informed Fahey that the Navy was attempting to expedite the issuance of Purple Hearts to the *Eagle* casualties, and that he would like to have an awards ceremony aboard the *Salem* sometime "near the anniversary of [the *Eagle*] loss . . ." For Paul Lawton, only such a ceremony would provide the reverence and gravitas to appropriately honor the memories of the *Eagle 56* crew. "The Navy was talking about mailing these Purple Hearts out to the family members with no ceremony of any kind, no event to memorialize the magnitude of this momentous decision after fifty-six years," he said. "It didn't seem right to me. These brave men deserved more."

As 2001 drew to a close, as Americans dealt with the full meaning and the broad spectrum of emotions produced by the events of September 11, Paul Lawton believed it was more important than ever to honor his nation's history, and pay homage to the men who had died making it.

45

January–March 2002
Annapolis, Maryland

Ginny Laubach Pettebone found herself "getting nervous" when she thought about the special Purple Heart ceremony planned aboard the USS *Salem*. After reading newspaper accounts of the Navy's decision, over-turning the 1945 Court of Inquiry, she had exchanged letters with Johnny Breeze and Paul Lawton, both of whom had informed her about the planned event, which she described as a "momentous occasion for all."

She was immensely grateful to Lawton for his "unselfish act of seek-ing the truth" in the face of enormous odds. She wrote her first letter to him on January 11, when she told him that she would be "honored to shake your hand and to say 'Well done.'"

Her only regret, as she mentioned to Johnny Breeze, was that Jack Barr did not live to learn the truth. "He felt the loss [of the *Eagle 56*] deeply," she wrote to Breeze. "He would have been so pleased to know of Paul Lawton's revelation. Jack Barr was a fine man and suffered over the loss." Peggy Barr Eastman had visited Ginny in early February, and Ginny gave her a copy of Lawton's CD to share with her mother. "She knew what the loss had meant to her dad," she wrote to Breeze. "He and Jack Laubach were good friends."

The new revelations about the *Eagle* stirred deep emotions in Ginny. Her connection to Jack, always present over the past fifty-six years, now seemed even stronger. She could see his face, his eyes, and his hair more clearly. She found herself longing to attend the USS *Salem* Purple Heart ceremony; her Christian faith would have comforted her with the knowledge that Jack would be looking down upon her and smiling as his former shipmates were accorded their long-overdue honor. She was in the process of lining up a friend to drive her to Quincy, Massachusetts, when the time was right.

Ginny also seemed happy to share her feelings with Johnny Breeze and Paul Lawton, writing to them as though she were speaking to Jack. "I thought I would die when the realization of the permanency of the separation set in," she said to Breeze. And to Lawton, she wrote: "You can never know how deeply all this has affected me. The tragedy changed my life forever. Jack and I had been friends from childhood and married almost seven years. Even though I am a widow for the second time, I have never gotten over losing my first love."

She told Paul Lawton that thanking him seemed "hardly adequate." Still, she was looking forward to meeting him in Quincy, where, after all these years, she would finally see her beloved Jack honored for his service, and she would quietly rejoice as the truth laid his soul to rest.

Rochester, New York

Even before the Massachusetts ceremony to honor the entire *Eagle 56* crew, western New York paid tribute to its favorite son, Harold Petersen, by awarding him the Purple Heart medal on February 21, 2002. At a ceremony at the federal building in downtown Rochester, Congresswoman Louise M. Slaughter pinned the medal to the left breast of Pete's blue blazer, while Pete's children, grandchildren, other family members, and friends looked on. "It's a beautiful thing," Pete said, gazing at the medal. Representative Slaughter replied: "It's a terrible thing to have to wait so long." Later, a friend of Petersen's, Ray Bliss, who knew the guilt Harold bore about the Court of Inquiry's initial ruling, said to Slaughter: "I want to thank you for taking a tremendous amount of guilt off Harold's shoulders."

As proud as he was, Pete deflected attention from himself, saying simply that he was glad the truth had finally emerged. "It's just helped everybody, all the families who lost sons," he said. "It's a terrible thing, thinking that your son died because of negligence."

Pete was "full of different emotions" on this day: exuberant that so many members of his family attended, yet somber that his wife, Mary, whose Alzheimer's had progressed rapidly, could not be there; grateful for the moving ceremony, yet resentful that the families of his fallen shipmates had to wait so long for the truth; proud to represent the *Eagle 56* family, but uneasy as the center of attention. Always gracious, however, Pete later wrote to Rep. Slaughter: "I want to thank you and your staff for the most perfect ceremony of the presentation of the Purple Heart that could be bestowed upon an individual. I felt very honored and happy about the whole ceremony."

Newspaper coverage in the days following the ceremony sparked congratulatory letters to Pete from veterans groups and well-wishers around the country, including a former teacher, now ninety years old, whom Pete had not heard from in sixty-one years. "We were all so proud of you," Rosemary Decker wrote in shaky cursive. "You always were a young man who stuck to the TRUTH. I'm proud to know you."

Yet, of all the messages, Harold Petersen most cherishes the letter he received from his daughter, Barbara Alice, on the evening of the February 21 ceremony. It accompanied another gift to her father, a set of wind chimes that featured a large eagle proudly and protectively hovering over four smaller eagles. Pete, who would reread the letter many times, said it "enters my heart and soul" and calls it his "most prized possession." Expressing a daughter's immense pride for both her father's military achievement and a lifetime of love, reprinted here are major portions of Barbara Alice's letter:

Dear Dad,

I want you to know how happy I am for you and how very proud I am of you. My goodness, do you know how many people are elated for you? The Purple Heart . . . after all these years. I always knew why I would get goose bumps and tears would sting my eyes when "The Star-Spangled Banner" was played. My first thought is you, Dad. You fought for our country, our freedom, and our flag. Thank God you made it when so many others did not. God bless all of them. My brothers and I would not be here today. How fortunate I was to have you and mom as my parents, how wonderful to have Ron and Rich for my brothers. Many years of love, happiness, respect, laughter, and great times growing together as the "best" family ever. Thank you, Dad.

Recently, I was talking to an elderly woman about your Purple Heart. We discussed what happen [sic] to you and all about the cover-up. I told her how a gentleman contacted you about your ship, the USS *Eagle PE-56*, and the sinking. I also stated you never pursued your Purple Heart—another person did for you. She said, and I quote, "A real hero never does." My reply was, "That's my dad," and she said, "Yes, that is your dad." Dad, you are a real hero, you always have been from the time I can remember.

I want you to think of wonderful thoughts whenever you hear your wind chimes. If you can't have them outside, keep them by a window wherever you may live. The eagle is what is important. This magnificent bird has his wings spread full to soar. The USS *Eagle PE-56* was sunk, you were in the water and survived. Dad, the instant you were pulled from the water, you too became an eagle. At that very moment, one eagle had gone under and a new eagle had emerged. You spread your wings and soared high above all of us. You were there to help everyone. You were there for my mother, your children, your mother and father, your sisters and brothers, your grandchildren, your nieces and nephews—the list can go on for ever. Remember me . . . and how much your daughter loves you today and always . . . I know that today, your special day, your wife, Alice, your mother Ruth, your father Clarence, your sister Ruthie are looking down on you with much love and pride. Dad, I too am looking at you the same way . . . I believe they are here with us in some special way every day of our lives. Isn't it wonderful, Dad?

Thank you, Dad, from the bottom of my heart. I love you with all my heart. My heart is filled with joy for you.

Congratulations, Harold Henry Petersen.

Pete's daughter signed the letter "Barbara Alice," her middle name after her mother. "She always gets that 'Alice' in there," Pete said. "Don't ever forget that 'Alice' when you talk to her."

Later, Pete would compile an autobiography, in words and pictures, which he entitled *My Life*. Barbara Alice's letter appears not in chronological order, but at the end. "I have left this most wonderful, most meaningful letter until last," Pete wrote.

The wind chimes hang inside Pete's house. "They are too beautiful and mean too much to leave outside," he said.

Brockton, Massachusetts

By March, Paul Lawton realized that the Navy's delay in issuing Purple Hearts for *Eagle 56* crew members who died on April 23, 1945, coupled with a few logistical and scheduling problems, would make it impossible to have the awards ceremony on the exact anniversary of the *Eagle* sinking.

He and Jim Fahey instead chose June 8, 2002, for the historic occasion. Dignitaries and VIPs would be invited, but Lawton knew the real guests of honor were the three *Eagle 56* survivors, and the family members whose loved ones were lost fifty-seven years earlier.

For that reason, he wanted the USS *Salem* ceremony to be special and memorable.

46

Ginny Laubach Pettebone died on May 21, 2002, at age eighty-seven, from complications from a massive heart attack, just eighteen days before the scheduled *Eagle 56* Purple Heart ceremony in Quincy, Massachusetts. Peggy Eastman told the gathering at Ginny's May 30 memorial service at St. Margaret's Church in Annapolis that "Ginny's death was gallant, as was her life." Ginny had decided against surgery or any life-extending treatments. Peggy Eastman recounted that when Ginny's cardiologist told her that she was making good decisions, Ginny remarked with characteristic humor: "I'm glad you're on my side."

Peggy recalled the kindness with which Ginny had cared for her husband, Elliott, before he died, and for her elder sister, Lena, who became bedridden shortly thereafter. "When people praised her or said something about the burdens she was carrying, she brushed aside both the praise and the concern," Peggy said. A subsequent broken hip slowed Ginny's walk, "but it didn't slow her mind, her sense of humor, or her appetite for reading and discussing the Scriptures in Bible study . . ." In a recent letter to Johnny Breeze, Ginny had written that she had had too many birthdays and was tired. "She knew exactly where she was going and she went in peace," Breeze said.

"Virginia Pettebone was a woman of grace and graciousness to those of us fortunate enough to have known her," Peggy Eastman said in her tribute to Ginny. "In her quiet, unassuming way, she embodied the Christian virtues of patience, forbearance, and compassion."

While Ginny did not live to attend the *Eagle 56* ceremony, she did receive Jack Laubach's Purple Heart medal in the mail just a few months before she died. "When the truth about the sinking was made known . . . a friend gave me a number to call to apply for the Purple Heart," she wrote to Paul Lawton. "I was sent a form . . . which I completed. Truthfully, I did not expect to hear from them [the government] after all these years. I certainly am sorry for any problem this might cause you. I will take the medal with me when I go to Quincy, Massachusetts."

The topics that occupied Ginny's thoughts in her final hours are not part of any historical record, but it is easy to imagine that the memories of Jack Laubach burned brightly even as her own life ebbed. Her best friend and her first love; gone for more than fifty years, yet the joy of his love and the pain of his loss always with her. Perhaps, as part of her last recollections, Ginny remembered the poems Jack's mother had penned in his memory. On the eve of the Korean War, Ginny's mother-in-law had written the last of those verses to honor her son. "I feel the time has come to have these verses printed, as they may be of some comfort to mothers who are facing again the sorrow and tragedies of war," she wrote. As Ginny neared death, strengthened by her faith in God and her love for Jack undiminished through the decades, she may have recalled her mother-in-law's last stanza of her final poem:

> *Truly, there is no armor against the love of God.*
> *When we let this truth sink deep within us, and open our hearts,*
> *Then, and then only, can this tired and weary world find peace.*
>
> *And so I close these written words with you, my dear,*
> *Asking always for a sense of your nearness, and the*
> *Courage to live so that when I go beyond to where you are,*
> *I will be able to see you and understand.*

Memorial Day 2002
Henrietta, New York, and Morris Plains, New Jersey

Fifty-seven years after they had nearly perished in the freezing North Atlantic water, John Scagnelli and Harold Petersen were the guests of honor at Memorial Day ceremonies in their respective hometowns.

In Henrietta, Petersen was honored as grand marshal of the parade. Dressed in tie, blazer, and wearing his American Legion cap, Petersen stood smiling next to the grand marshal car before the parade, medals—including his Purple Heart—gleaming on his chest. "It was a proud and colorful ceremony," he said. "I felt as though I was representing the USS *Eagle* and its crew."

More than three hundred miles away, on a sparkling day of sunshine and cool breezes, thousands of Morris Plains residents lined Mountain Way and Speedwell Avenue to view the parade that honored those veterans who had served and died for their country. Before the parade began, about five hundred people gathered for solemn ceremonies that were replicated in thousands of towns across America. Mayor Frank Druetzler saluted the courage of those who "died protecting our liberty" to give us "the gift of freedom." With the American flag at half-mast, the Morris Plains Borough School played the national anthem.

In this small New Jersey town, however, the morning services were highlighted by a presentation that brought cheers from a crowd that is normally subdued at Memorial Day ceremonies: Congressman Rodney Frelinghuysen awarded the Purple Heart medal to John Scagnelli, lone surviving officer of the USS *Eagle 56*. "I'm especially proud today because it gives me an opportunity to remember my shipmates who aren't here," Scagnelli told the *Daily Record* of Morris Plains. "It's a fitting day to remember them and the sacrifices they made." The *Daily Record* of Sunday, May 26, shows a close-up photo of Scagnelli's Purple Heart, and above it, a second photograph of Scagnelli after the medal was awarded. He is standing tall, a "USS *Eagle 56* survivor" cap perched on his head and a look of immense pride on his face, his medal and the congressman's proclamation under his left arm, and his right arm extended to the crowd in appreciative acknowledgment of their heartfelt cheers. "I will never forget that day," Scagnelli said later.

Several days later, on May 30, the *Daily Record* printed an opinion piece entitled IT'S NEVER TOO LATE FOR TRUTH TO COME OUT, in which the paper briefly recapped the *Eagle 56* story, recognized Scagnelli's role and Paul Lawton's efforts, and said Scagnelli was "fortunate enough to live to see" his long-overdue honor. The paper quoted Lawton as saying, "Their nation is finally acknowledging that they [*Eagle 56* victims] gave their lives in the line of duty in the face of enemy action in a time of war."

Eight days later, in Quincy, Massachusetts, relatives of the *Eagle 56* officers and crew members who died on April 23, 1945, would finally have *their* chance to acknowledge their loved ones' sacrifice.

47

Paul Lawton rose long before first light on this late spring Saturday, the June air still cool when he reached the USS *Salem* at 4:00 A.M. He, Jim Fahey, and a team of volunteers efficiently unloaded the chairs that would seat the honored guests and the ice that would cool the drinks in just a few hours. The U.S. Navy, which seemed reticent to extend help throughout the entire *Eagle 56* odyssey, offered no substantive assistance in organizing this special ceremony to honor forty-nine of her war dead. The use of the *Salem* was due to Fahey's influence. The chairs, the ice, the guest list, the agenda for the day, the programs for the event— all of it came together thanks to Lawton's dedication to detail and the personal stake he felt in honoring the *Eagle 56* crew members. He even distributed copies of his history of the *Eagle 56* story, entitled "The Sinking of the USS *Eagle PE-56*, Silent Victim of the *U-853*."

The day that he and the *Eagle* families had waited for had finally arrived, and Lawton wanted it to be perfect.

Nature did her part. By the time the ceremony began at 10:00 A.M., the *Salem* sparkled in the sunlight that drenched her decks. Honored guests and family members, who had been chatting and mingling and hugging the three survivors, took their seats for the playing of the national anthem and the invocation by U.S. Navy Chaplain Rev. Charles J. McCoy. Relatives had come from around the country, from as far away as Alaska, to honor their loved ones: widows, children, grandchildren and great-grandchildren, nephews and nieces, sisters and brothers. Phyllis Westerlund Kendrick, her three sons, and her daughter, Carol, sat quietly. Esta Smith was unable to make the trip, but her son, Bill Rollin, attended, and would later call it "a beautiful day." Alice Hultgren was there. Fred "Mike" Michelsen's son, Mick, was in the crowd also, as was George Vanderheiden, son of Lieutenant (jg) Ambrose Vanderheiden, for whom John Scagnelli stood as best man in Portland so many years ago. "He looked just like his father; I got a little filled up, lost my composure a bit," Scagnelli recalled as Vanderheiden's son approached him to say hello. "He asked me if I knew his dad—he had no idea I had been his father's best man."

Jim Fahey offered the introduction and Paul Lawton enlightened the crowd on the *Eagle 56* story and the path that had led the entire gathering to this point. Then came the presentation of the Purple Hearts to family members, the emotional moment most of them had been waiting for. Lawton called each deceased crew member's name, assisted by Thomas Kelley, Massachusetts Commissioner of Veterans' Services, a Medal of Honor and Purple Heart recipient himself. Sometimes an individual relative would step forward to receive the posthumous Purple Heart, but often, several members of a family would approach the podium, almost reverentially, to take possession of the medal and express their gratitude to Lawton.

When the medal ceremony concluded, it was time for Scagnelli, as the lone surviving officer, to read the solemn roll call of *PE-56* casualties, while Breeze and Petersen rang the ship's bell. Scagnelli started strong, his voice carrying across the *Salem*'s deck, but with each name and each toll of the bell, he saw with utter clarity in his mind's eye each of his former shipmates, their faces the faces of young men, and he simply could not get through the list. Petersen and Breeze continued to ring the bell as warm breezes blew in from the harbor.

Afterwards, a wreath was laid to honor the fallen *Eagle 56* sailors and the U.S. 2nd Marine Corps Color Guard fired a twenty-one-gun salute, the report from their weapons echoing around Quincy Bay. Trumpeter Vincent Macrina blew "Taps" before a moment of silence and Rev. McCoy's benediction concluded the formal ceremony.

But Scagnelli, Petersen, and Breeze weren't quite finished yet. They had a surprise for Paul Lawton, the man who had spent more than four years searching for and uncovering the truth, and in the process, unburdening them of their own guilt that festered any time they thought of the "boiler-explosion" theory. Now, the three survivors crowded around Lawton and presented him with a gold-trimmed cherrywood plaque of appreciation. The inscription, which also expressed gratitude to James Lawton, thanked Lawton "for the effort and dedication put forth to bring to the surface the forgotten disaster of the *PE-56* boat and crew after fifty-six years, from a mysterious explosion to the true facts, torpedoed and sunk in action."

And then, above the signatures of John Scagnelli, John Breeze, and Harold Petersen, the single line that Paul Lawton cherished above all others: "We thank you from the bottom of our hearts."

To Scagnelli, Breeze, and Petersen, the three remaining members of the Lucky Thirteen, Paul Lawton would always be one of the heroes of the *Eagle 56*. There would be no story without his remarkable efforts. Now, because of him, the *Eagle 56* crew members rest in peace, their families have found a measure of solace, and the three survivors—Petersen and Breeze, who were proud members of the Black Gang, and Scagnelli, who supervised the men belowdecks—have been vindicated. Today, all three of them still weep for their shipmates who were killed in 1945, but they know those brave men did not die as a result of carelessness or a terrible mistake.

For that, they thank Lawton.

Harold "Pete" Petersen summed up their feelings:

Paul brought out the truth. What's right is right. This took a long time to *get* right, but because of Paul, it finally happened. Every time I'd think of those poor guys [*Eagle* shipmates], and I did it often, I'd be sick to my stomach that the official word was "boiler explosion." Now, when I think of them, when I see their faces in my mind, I see guys who died as heroes serving their country. And that's because of Paul Lawton. It means something, not just to us, but to everyone. The truth is important to everyone.

48

On the eve of his grandson Timothy's graduation from the U.S. Army Military Academy, James Lawton was about to dress for the formal dinner for the Class of 2003 and their families, when his son Paul asked him what jacket he was going to wear.

"The blue blazer," James Lawton replied. "Why?"

Paul Lawton opened a small box he had brought to his father's room, from which he carefully withdrew a small bar upon which were mounted his father's World War II medals: the Purple Heart, the Bronze Star, the European Campaign medal, the Infantry badge, and his dad's paratrooper wings. Paul prepared to mount the medals on James Lawton's jacket.

"What are you doing?" James asked. "I'm not going to wear those."

"Oh yes, you are," Paul responded. "This is an historic event for our family; you're the grandfather of the graduate and a distinguished World War II veteran, and you are going to wear these medals whether you like it or not!"

James Lawton wore the medals proudly, but the point of this story is to illustrate his son's respect for military service and his reverence for those who served. "I never would have thought to wear those medals on my own," he said. "Paul planned it, it was very important to him to commemorate the event, and to connect the importance of my service with my grandson's." James Lawton also wore his medals to commencement the next day, and then up to Trophy Point, where Timothy received his lieutenant's bars. James Lawton pinned one shoulder, Timothy's father, Mark, pinned the other, and the West Point general pinned Timothy's bars to his cap. Paul Lawton captured the moment in a photograph, intent, as always, on honoring military achievement and ensuring the accuracy of the historical record—this time, his own family's.

Those values, James Lawton said, were the driving elements behind Paul Lawton's commitment to the *Eagle 56* story. "He felt for those men," James Lawton said. "On one level he wanted to set history straight, but on another, it was very personal to him. These sailors were the victims of an injustice, and that just didn't sit right with Paul. He's determined, he's thorough, and he wants things done the right way. And he never gives up. I knew better than to fight him on wearing the medals at West Point—the Navy should have known better than to fight him on the *Eagle* case."

June 2003
Henrietta, New York

Mary Petersen died on June 17 from the ravages of Alzheimer's, leaving Harold a widower for the second time. She had spoken her final words two months earlier, when, from her bed at the Monroe Community Hospital, she looked up at Harold and said: "Thank you for being so kind to me." Harold squeezed her hand and wept. Mary had not spoken for weeks previously, and somehow, she had the strength to utter the most special words he could ever hear.

Harold visited Mary every day, fed her dinner, and talked to her. Though she could not respond, she could hear him. He had nothing but praise for Monroe Community, and a month before her death, he penned a poem entitled "MCH Kindness" to pay tribute to the staff. "When I fed Mary her dinner, the staff always made sure I had something to eat, too," Harold said.

In the evening of Mary's last day, Harold sat by her bedside and held her hand. When her breathing became labored and "death started to come," Harold told her it was okay to take the journey into the Promised Land. "I knew she understood me and knew where those words were coming from." Seconds later, tears leaked from the corners of Mary's eyes and Harold wiped them, kissed her, and told her again that she could let go. "She gave her last sigh and very gently closed her eyes as if to say, 'I will do this for I know I will see you again someday,'"

Harold said. As Harold leaned over and kissed her for the last time, his own tears fell on Mary's face. " 'Mary, take these tears with you, they will take my place,' " he told her. " 'Death will take us apart from each other for a while, but our memories will always be there to have and to share and to keep.' "

When it came time for funeral arrangements, some of Mary's relatives first suggested that she be buried in Boston, near the family homestead. Harold gently, but firmly, said no. "I want Mary here with me," he said.

Mary's family agreed that Harold and Mary Petersen belonged together.

There is no doubt that Mary's death devastated Harold "Pete" Petersen. "It's a lonely and sorrowful life; I live alone and I have no Mary to go and see," he said. In a poem entitled "Conversation," Pete wrote about the need to talk to himself just to hear a voice. "I do have conversation, you see—even though it is only with me," he wrote. But even in his loneliness, Pete found humor: "I talk to my dog, he does not answer back. It's a good thing he doesn't—I would have a heart attack!"

Though memories are now his only companions in his Henrietta home, though he has endured the pain of losing Alice so suddenly and watching Mary suffer with a dreadful disease, Harold Petersen considers himself an immensely lucky man. He has lived into his eighties after narrowly escaping death on April 23, 1945. He has loved and laughed and worked for nearly sixty years, while his doomed *Eagle* shipmates never had that chance. The lesson is one he never forgot, and it is why he was so desirous for the Navy to correct the historical record.

"Look at my life," he said, not for the first time. "I have loved, and was loved by, two magnificent women. I have wonderful children and a wonderful family. The *Eagle 56* guys never had that. That means that no matter how tough my life has been, no matter what sad times I've had, I *owe* it to my shipmates to be grateful. *Nothing* I've gone through can compare to what they lost. I've lived to be an old man. Those guys—they died too young. I picture them almost every day, and they're all still young in my mind. They had no chance to grow old. That's why we owed it to them to uncover the truth. I hope a big cheer went up in heaven when the Navy finally revealed the truth."

Epilogue

Fifty-nine and a half years after the *Eagle 56* exploded and sank, most of her story has finally come to light. Yet, pieces are still missing in this World War II saga that has spilled over into the twenty-first century.

The mystery that first gripped Paul Lawton in 1998 won't let go, its pull as irresistible as a siren song for the Massachusetts military historian who resurrected the dormant tale from the archival cold-case file. Successful in convincing the Navy to rewrite history, Lawton, as of this writing, now wrestles with how to solve the story's greatest remaining question: Where is the submerged wreck of the torpedoed *PE-56*?

Lawton and his team have searched twice more after the hunt in 2000 that is detailed in this book, most recently in late summer 2004, yet the whereabouts of the *Eagle* remains a bewildering and frustrating riddle. It is as though the *Eagle* is a ghost-ship, or more accurately, a "ghost-wreck." The 2004 expedition was especially disappointing. Before the search, Gary Kozak called Lawton to say he had recalculated the *Eagle's* position at the time it went down, and he felt confident the new grid would yield at least one-half of the submerged *PE-56*. Deep-wreck divers John Chatterton and Richie Kohler—whose success in identifying the *U-869* off the coast of New Jersey was chronicled in the best-selling book, *Shadow Divers*—were on board with Lawton and Kozak, as was a documentary film crew. For ten hours they searched, leg by leg, painstakingly covering the entire grid, viewing the Atlantic bottom on a high-resolution flat-screen monitor, waiting . . . waiting . . . anticipating the sudden appearance of the *Eagle* wreck on the screen, poised to whoop and cheer and high-five when it did, then dive on her to *physically* confirm, once and for all, that a torpedo had ripped her apart.

But, again, they found nothing.

"We're trying to figure again what went wrong," Lawton declared. "Where is this thing? It *can't* disappear. It's not like this sinking was a fictitious event—this was an actual occurrence. The *Eagle 56 was sunk* on April 23, 1945. So where is she? Some of the world's top experts have used all the records available to us to pinpoint her location. It's frustrating, but we *will* find her. This story isn't over—I'm not giving up."

Finding the *Eagle 56* wreck would do more than add to the mountain of evidence to support the Navy's revised conclusion—it would also likely satisfy any remaining naysayers who have reviewed the case.

For, while Johnny Breeze, Harold Petersen, John Scagnelli, Bernard Cavalcante, Phyllis Westerlund, Esta Glenn, Paul Lawton, the United States Navy, and countless others believe that the *U-853* torpedoed the *Eagle 56* and was responsible for the deaths of forty-nine of her officers and crew members, not everyone is fully convinced.

Most notably, Horst Bredow, founder and director of the German U-boat archives, remains uncertain. Bredow acknowledges and appreciates the breadth and scope of Paul Lawton's work. Yet, in an April 2003 letter to this author, he wrote: "From the German side, there is no certainty that the *U-853* sank the USS *Eagle 56*. We only know that *U-853* was operating in this area. There is no radio message of *U-853* known that he [Froemsdorf] attacked the *Eagle*. But there is a short message that he attacked . . . *Black Point*. I cannot confirm with 100 percent certainty [that *U-853* sank the *Eagle*] so I will not do it. There are enough lies in our world—the *U-Boot-Archiv* has a good reputation [and] I do not want to loose [sic] it."

Is Bredow being unduly stubborn in the face of overwhelming documentary evidence, or simply reserving his historian's right to cautious skepticism? Is his unwillingness to embrace the U.S. Navy's rewrite of history based partly on a sense of professional disappointment that the evidence for that decision did not emanate from his own prestigious and authoritative U-boat archives? Before making an attempt to answer either of these two questions, it is necessary to consider, and weigh accordingly, the facts: Bredow's reputation is impeccable, and his integrity above reproach among historians and experts on both sides of the Atlantic.

It may take nothing less than Lawton's discovery and examination of the elusive *Eagle 56* wreck, along with photographs providing conclusive evidence that a German U-boat torpedo shattered her keel and broke her in half, to ultimately convince Bredow to revise the German archival record.

Elsewhere from the German side, renowned Battle of the Atlantic historian Jürgen Rohwer, in his response to Paul Lawton's voluminous research, seems to lean toward the American's conclusions, without explicitly saying so for the written record.

"I wish to thank you very much for sending me your CD about the sinking of the USS *Eagle 56* . . . I am very impressed by your intense research and all the details you could recover about this late event of the Battle of the Atlantic," Rohwer wrote to Lawton. "I think it may be best to present the CD to the *Marinearchiv* of the Library of Contemporary History in Stuttgart . . . There the information can be used by many researchers and does not lay only in my shelves!"

Thus, while Rohwer does not offer his unequivocal concurrence with Lawton's findings, his decision to include the American's research at the prestigious Stuttgart research facility is surely evidence of Rohwer's belief in its thoroughness and credibility.

Perhaps the last chapter of the *Eagle 56* story will finally be written upon the unquestioned acceptance of the *U-853*'s role by German historians.

The timing of that *final* chapter notwithstanding, Paul Lawton believes that an additional piece of the *Eagle* story must also be written—or more literally, must be permanently etched—into Portland, Maine's, history.

As this book went to press, he was planning a ceremony for April of 2005, to coincide with the sixtieth anniversary of the *Eagle 56* sinking, at Portland Head Light, the famous Maine lighthouse that the *Eagle 56* sailed past on the morning of April 23, 1945. Lawton's goal is to forever memorialize the *Eagle* story by ensconcing a permanent plaque on the lighthouse grounds at the mouth of Portland Harbor. Johnny Breeze, Harold Petersen, and John Scagnelli are all hopeful they can attend as invited guests of honor.

"We were successful in rewriting history—it's only fitting that we mark that history permanently and appropriately on the last outcropping of land that the *Eagle 56* went past on her way out to sea for the final time," Lawton said.

Finally, what about the players in the *Eagle 56* story, those whose lives and deeds fill the pages of this book, and are forever part of one of the longest-running and most unusual episodes in United States naval history? As the leaves turn color and the air chills in the fall of 2004, here is what we know:

KENNETH A. KNOWLES, who commanded the OP-20-G sub-tracking "Secret Room," went on to use his uncanny analytical abilities as an intelligence officer for the Central Intelligence Agency. He retired from the CIA in 1962 and received one of the nation's first National Intelligence Medals. Knowles died in 1986, one year before the National Security Agency declassified the Ultra records he fought so hard to keep secret during the Battle of the Atlantic in World War II. His son, Dr. Kenneth A. Knowles Jr.—whose recollections of his father aided in the development of this book—joined the Navy ROTC unit at the University of Virginia, spent seven years in the Navy, and served at four commands, including one in Vietnam. The younger Knowles worked at NASA, for the Trident submarine group, and is currently a professor at the U.S. Naval Academy in Annapolis in the weapons and systems engineering department. "My dad was proud of me when I came here to teach in 1975," Dr. Knowles said. "He loved the Academy."

ESTA GLENN SMITH lives in San Diego, California, and continues to battle against the terminal disease, COPD, that has left her housebound. Her memories of Harold Glenn and of the events of April 23, 1945, are amazingly comprehensive, almost photographic.

PHYLLIS WESTERLUND KENDRICK continues to live in North Carolina. Ever the fighter with the "good genes," she overcame a recent car accident (she was struck when crossing the street) and a serious stroke and has come through them both with few physical limitations. "The fact that she's walking at all is remarkable," said her daughter-in-law, Linda Westerlund. "At eighty-nine years old, she's still my hero."

PAULINE MICHELSEN TULLOCK CARLTON, who sobbed and held her son, Fredrick, close on August 6, 1945—"Hiroshima Day"— died on September 4, 2003, just before her eighty-eighth birthday. The widow of *PE-56* crew member Fredrick "Mike" Michelsen re-married on Christmas Eve of 1946 to Budge Tullock, who had been one of Fredrick's best friends. "For Mom, it started as a marriage of convenience," said her son, Fredrick Jr. (also known as "Mick"). "He loved and adored her, she needed help raising me . . . In 1955, she made the conscious decision to give her heart to him, and my sister Julie was born . . . Although Budge 'adopted' me as his own, it was never on the table for my name to be changed to Tullock." Following Budge Tullock's death in 1994, Pauline remarried again in 1996 to Irvin Carlton, because she "didn't want to grow old alone." Alas, Carlton passed away in 1999, much to Pauline's chagrin "for leaving her so soon," Mick said.

With Julie and Fredrick Jr. at her nursing home bedside, Pauline held Fredrick "Mike" Michelsen's Purple Heart just a few days be-fore she died. Though suffering from dementia, she was able, with minimal assistance from Julie, to recognize her first husband's photo-graph and the letter of condolence from the War Department. "She outlived three husbands who loved her dearly," Mick said. "She was a survivor; a strong-willed, tough, self-sufficient, sacrificing, God-fearing Depression kid who did what she had to do. Sister Julie and I miss her dreadfully. We are clearly seeing the passing of the Greatest Generation."

Mick and Harold Petersen, who had met at the Massachusetts Purple Heart ceremony, later exchanged letters about Mick's father. "It is my extreme sorrow that your dad . . . had to be the one to relieve me [on the watch]," Pete said. "I think of it often. Just remember what he and the others did and suffered [for] was a great part in keeping this country free and as proud as it is. The flag is still waving and he has contributed to that in a very big way. He is not forgotten and never will be." Mick responded: "It was an extreme pleasure to meet you . . . and finally make contact with a shipmate of my father['s] . . . this was made even more special to find out that he relieved you from your post shortly before the attack. I was extremely impressed and moved by the words you spoke and the time you spent with me. I will always remember that."

ALICE HEYD HULTGREN, the former Navy WAVE and court stenographer during the *Eagle 56* Court of Inquiry who provided sworn testimony to Paul Lawton in 1998, lives with her husband in Reading, Massachusetts. Following the Purple Heart ceremony aboard the USS *Salem,* she wrote to Paul Lawton: "I talked to several families and they were so happy to be sharing their stories at last . . . You really have done a wonderful thing. It was a pleasure for me to be involved and to see this to the proper conclusion . . ."

JAMES LAWTON, Paul's father and the World War II medal-winner who assisted his son on the *Eagle 56* case, lives in Brockton, Massachusetts, and as of this writing is recovering from a serious heart attack. One additional story from World War II that illustrates the whims of fate: In 1995, at the fiftieth reunion of the 513th Parachute Infantry of the 17th Airborne Division, Lawton was reunited with the medic who had treated him as he lay wounded in Wesel, Germany, the man Lawton believed was killed when a shell exploded near them and blew him backward. "I just assumed he had been killed," Lawton said. "Fifty years later, we got reintroduced. When someone first told me 'The medic who treated you is standing over there,' I didn't believe it. I said, 'No way, I saw him die.' But he didn't die—I met him half a century later. Isn't that amazing?"

EDWARD J. MELANSON, the retired Navy captain whose phone call dislodged the *Eagle 56* Court of Inquiry records from the Navy JAG office, continues to live in Virginia.

THE WESTERLUND BROTHERS—Bob, Paul, and Fred, Ivar's and Phyllis's sons—continue to live in Brockton, Massachusetts, follow news about the *Eagle 56* case, and keep in touch with Paul Lawton. It is likely they will be aboard the vessel that conducts the next search mission for the *Eagle* wreck.

DIANNA WOODS-MURRAY, daughter of *Eagle* crew member Ralph William Woods, whose aunt Johnny Breeze wrote condolences to in

June of 1945, lives in Mount Pleasant, South Carolina. She did not
find out about the *Eagle 56* story until early 2004, when she came
across the story on the Internet. Later, she dug through some of her
father's papers and found the records from 1945, including Breeze's
letter, which she forwarded to the author. "What an amazing week
this has been for me and my family," she wrote. "I still find it hard
to believe . . . I spoke to my father's cousin in Anniston, Alabama,
and he told of the long battle they had to get my father's name on
the WWII monument."

BERNARD CAVALCANTE continues his work as senior archivist at
the Naval Historical Center in Washington, D.C. After more than
forty years of service, he shows no signs of slowing down. He still
knows the Battle of the Atlantic records better than anyone.

PEGGY EASTMAN, John Barr's daughter and Ginny Laubach's dear
friend, lives in Chevy Chase, Maryland. A journalist and writer, she
wrote movingly about Ginny and Jack Laubach in her book, *Godly
Glimpses: Discoveries of the Love That Heals*, delivered the eulogy
at Ginny's funeral, and shared the poems that Jack Laubach's mother
wrote in memory of her son. Peggy's mother, Isabelle, John Barr's
wife, is alive and well at age eighty-eight. Tragedy struck the family
in February of 2004, when Peggy's only sibling, her brother Jack,
who delivered the eulogy at his father's funeral, died of cancer. In
February of 2002, Peggy wrote to Paul Lawton: "My father was always convinced that a German submarine had caused the ship's explosion. He knew the ship and the crew, and he trusted Jack Laubach
. . . totally. You have set the record straight, and, on behalf of my father, I thank you for all your hard work and persistence."

PAUL LAWTON, the military historian and attorney most knowledge-
able about the *Eagle 56* case, and the man most responsible for the
unprecedented rewriting of naval history, continues to live, teach,
and practice law in Brockton, Massachusetts. No one is betting
against his finding the submerged *Eagle 56* wreckage at the bottom
of the North Atlantic.

Since the *Eagle 56* story became public, JOHN SCAGNELLI, HAROLD
PETERSEN, and JOHNNY BREEZE have formed a bond with each other

and with many descendants of their long-dead shipmates. They also believe it is their responsibility to further spread the truth about the *Eagle 56* when they have the opportunity, in salute of their comrades who died on April 23, 1945. Scagnelli in Morris Plains, New Jersey, and Breeze, in Seattle, draw great love and support from their wives and best friends, Bea Scagnelli and Betty Breeze; in Henrietta, New York, Pete derives his strength from his children, grandchildren, extended family, and the memory of Alice's and Mary's love. All three men remember their shipmates well and can visualize their faces as clearly as bright stars against the curtain of a black winter sky.

They occasionally exchange letters and chat on the phone, yet their loyalty runs deep. When it became clear that Johnny Breeze would not be eligible for the Purple Heart, Pete threatened to refuse his own medal. Breeze told him to forget it, that Pete *had* to accept the Purple Heart as a way to honor his fallen shipmates. Both Pete and Scagnelli believe Breeze deserves the Purple Heart for the hypothermia he suffered, and both think the Navy's refusal to award the medal to Breeze is the final miscarriage of justice in the *Eagle* case. Whether that decision is ever changed remains to be seen.

Ultimately, all three men are grateful they have lived long enough to see the truth become public and their shipmates honored. They cannot find the appropriate words to praise Paul Lawton, and they are thankful they have had the opportunity to reconnect with each other after a half-century without contact. Petersen summed it up for all of them: "It was like meeting members of your family that you didn't know existed," he said.

They have also gone to great lengths to help with the development of this book, agreeing unhesitatingly to personal interviews in their homes and countless follow-up questions. Breeze and Petersen shared autobiographies they had penned, and Scagnelli turned over the precious stack of condolence letters he wrote in 1945. All three men willingly shared letters and photographs, stories and memories, to add to the accuracy and richness of this book. They did this for their *Eagle 56* shipmates, brave sailors who died too young, but who died as heroes.

Scagnelli, Petersen, and Breeze would agree that the words Jack Laubach's mother expressed on the title page of her poetry collection apply to the entire *Eagle 56* crew:

"A country can live only as long as she has men who are ready to die for her."

Each day for sixty years, the three living survivors have remembered the men who were ready, and who died, on April 23, 1945.

They now have honored that memory in full.

Author's Afterword

It's a good thing that Paul "Pete" Priestas had his television on while he prepared dinner one evening in mid-November of 2004. Otherwise, you would be holding this book in your hands without knowing about the final remarkable turn in the sixty-year-old *Eagle 56* story.

Specifically, you wouldn't know about Paul's brother, Joseph Charles Priestas, who is eighty-three years old, living in Latrobe, Pennsylvania, and who forevermore will be known as the fourth living *Eagle 56* survivor.

Scagnelli. Breeze. Petersen. And now—just as this book went to press—Priestas, the fourth member of the Lucky Thirteen still alive sixty years later.

Nobody knew Joe Priestas was still alive; not Paul Lawton, not the United States Navy, not Scagnelli, Breeze, or Petersen. Priestas had missed the many newspaper articles and the television documentaries about the *Eagle 56* story.

But on that November evening, his brother was preparing dinner in the kitchen and the television was on in the living room, set to the History Channel. Paul Priestas heard a narrator's voice mention the *Eagle 56* "out of Portland, Maine," and ran into the living room just in time to see a photo of the rescued sailors clustered in the hospital after their rescue (and published in this book). He recognized his brother Joe immediately. "I called him up and said, 'You were just on television,' and he thought I was crazy," Paul said. "He couldn't believe people were talking about the *Eagle* after all these years."

Paul Priestas contacted Paul Lawton to tell the military historian that a fourth survivor, Joe Priestas, was still alive, though not in the best of health, living in Latrobe. Lawton called me and I spoke with both Priestas brothers the following day. It was clearly too late to weave Joe into the narrative of *Due to Enemy Action*, but he had come forward just in time for his story to be told in this afterword.

Joe Priestas was a twenty-three-year-old Water Tender 3rd Class who had just finished the 8:00 A.M. to noon watch in the *Eagle 56*'s boiler room, and had ventured topside to get some air, when the *U-853*'s torpedo slammed into the subchaser. "Something made me go up on deck to catch some air," he said. "I must have had a guardian angel that day." When the explosion lifted the *Eagle 56* into the air, Priestas was thrown to the deck and then scrambled into the freezing water. He grabbed a two-by-six piece of shoring that floated by him and hung on for dear life.

"My God, that water was so cold, cold like you wouldn't believe," he recalled sixty years later. "I still shiver today thinking about it. When they took us to the dispensary later, all I can remember is how I was shivering uncontrollably. Another five minutes, the doctor said; another five minutes and we would have all been gone."

Clinging to the shoring in the freezing water, Priestas watched in horror as his shipmates "were dying all around him, and I couldn't do anything to help them. I tried a couple of times to reach for guys, but I couldn't do it. All my buddies went down that day." Priestas thought he was next, until he saw the *Selfridge*'s lifeboat "coming right toward me. Then I blacked out and I don't remember anything until I woke up in the hospital bed with hypothermia." Like Johnny Breeze, Joe Priestas said he had no other injuries—"just a couple of scratches"—and therefore is doubtful he is eligible for a Purple Heart, either. "If the Navy said no to Breeze, then they'll say no to me," he said. "Although I have to admit, when I heard about the Purple Heart medals, I said, 'What about me?'"

In his 1945 Court of Inquiry testimony, Priestas told his questioners that the *Eagle 56* was "rocked with a terrific explosion . . . the guys I was with got knocked down . . . first thing we did was get off as fast as we could. My first thought was that a depth charge had exploded and torn the ship in half."

Priestas discounted the "boiler-explosion" theory in 1945, and did so again in 2004. "Those boilers were working fine, I had just left them," he said. "There was nothing wrong with them. There would never even

have been enough pressure for a boiler to cause the damage we suffered."
He said the Court of Inquiry's initial ruling "didn't sit well with me . . .
it made us [Black Gang members] all look bad, like we did something
wrong, and it kept those other family members [of the men who died]
from finding out the truth."

After the war, Priestas returned to Latrobe, married, and had three
children. He worked for thirty-six years in a steel manufacturing plant
and missed two days of work during the entire time. His wife, Emma,
died in 1973, and today Joe lives with his daughter. Joe Priestas recently
suffered a mild stroke, and in January of 2004, he had a tumor removed
from his heart and triple bypass surgery. "I'm still a little wobbly," he
said eleven months later, "and I can't drive anymore. That's tough. I'm
pretty much stuck in the house."

Priestas said he was shocked that the Navy changed its decision; indeed, he was amazed the *Eagle 56* story was even in the news after so
many years. "I thought for sure they had forgotten all about us," he
said. "There was even a time when I tried to push it from my mind, but
I never really could. Sometimes I dream about that day [April 23, 1945],
and sometimes when I'm just lying in bed, awake, I can see my buddies
in the water and I can feel how cold that water was. I'll never forget that
day and I'll never forget those guys."

How does he feel about the reversal of naval history?

"I think it's fabulous," he said. "I can't believe it's happened. I thought
it was all buried and forgotten. My health has been shaky lately—who
knows how much time I have left? I thank God I got to see this."

Joe Priestas, the fourth living survivor, is present and accounted for.
All the members of the *Eagle 56* family have finally come home.

Appendix 1:
Casualties and Survivors

USS *Eagle 56 (PE-56)*

Officers and Enlisted Men Killed

OFFICERS (5)

Lt. James G. Early (Commander), USNR

Lt. (jg) John R. Laubach, USNR

Lt. (jg) Ambrose G. Vanderheiden, USNR

Ensign Seth E. Chapin, USNR

Ensign Roy F. Swan, USNR

ENLISTED MEN (44)
(Bodies Not Recovered)

John J. Alexander, USNR

James O. Brown, USN

Robert G. Coleman, USNR

Percy Collins, USNR

James O. Cunningham, USNR

Robert L. Davies, USNR

Joseph P. Gegan, USNR

Harold S. Glenn, USNR

Walter W. Goe, USNR

John R. Gonzales, USNR

Arthur A. Grosch, USNR

William L. Harden, USNR

James P. Johnson, USN

Norris W. Jones, USNR

Robert V. Kessler, USNR

Joseph A. Lydon, USNR

Maurice J. Manning, USNR

Edwin F. Mathys, USN

J. H. McKenzie, USNR

John C. Merk, USNR

Fredrick Michelsen, USNR

Willie B. Morgan, USNR

Zug C. Phelps, USNR

Christopher C. Phillips, USNR

Jasper D. Pulley, USN

Virgil Quinn Jr., USNR

Harold R. Rodman, USNR

Archibald Ronald, USNR

George Sabatino, USNR
Edwin J. Schneider, USNR
Joseph F. Setzer, USNR
Eliott M. Shinn, USNR
James Hutchnes Smith, USNR
Nathan C. Stafford, USNR
Leonard J. Surowiec, USNR
James F. Talley, USNR
Raymond R. Wallace, USNR
Henry L. Wengert, USNR
Ivar A. Westerlund, USNR
Ellis E. Whitcomb, USNR
Ralph W. Woods, USNR
Earle E. Young, USNR

(Bodies Recovered)
Paul J. Knapp, USNR
George W. Neugen, USNR

SS *Black Point*

U.S. Navy Armed Guard Killed (1)
Lonnie L. Whitson, USN

Merchant Crewmen Killed (11)
William Antilley
George P. Balser
Leo H. Beck
Laurel F. Clark
Cleo Hand
Robert L. Korb
Reino Lindstrom
Milton Matthews
Marvin A. Mertinek
Ansey L. Morgan
Richard C. Shepson

Survivors: "The Lucky Thirteen"
OFFICER (1)
Lt. (jg.) John P. Scagnelli, USNR

ENLISTED MEN (12)
John L. Breeze, USNR
Oscar F. Davis, USNR
Lawrence L. Edwards, USNR
Cletus J. Frane, USNR
John A. Happoldt, USNR
Daniel E. Jaronik, USNR
Edward G. Lockhart, USNR
John E. Luttrell, USNR
Harold H. Petersen, USNR
Joseph Priestas, USNR
William A. Thompson, USNR
John A. Wisniewski, USNR

Survivors (34)
U.S. NAVY ARMED GUARD SURVIVORS
Harry T. Berryhill, USN
Alcester R. Colella, USN
Stephen Svetz, USN
Gustav A. Vogelbacher, USN

CAPTAIN AND MERCHANT CREWMEN SURVIVORS
Master: Captain Charles E. Prior
Clair V. Berry, 1st Mate
Calvin Baumgartner
Earl Campbell
Francis E. Curran

James Davis
Joseph R. Desourdy
Lawrence Drayton
Argvris P. Economou
James C. Fowlkes
Abel Gomes
Francis L. Kelley
Joseph W. Kelley
James N. Lane
Patrick N. Leary
Howard A. Locke
Thomas P. Mello
Rufus K. Nash

Sanford Nauha
Richard Nehls
Gordon Nelson
L. Roland Pelletier
Joseph S. Pires
Marcus L. Rowe
Glennen W. Ryan
John E. Shoaff Jr.
Homer P. Small
John N. Smith
Joseph R. Tharl
Stewart M. Whitehouse

U-853
German Navy Officers and Crewmen Killed (55)

U-BOOT-ARCHIV: EHRENTAFEL
DER GEFALLENEN (HONOR
ROLL OF THOSE KILLED)
Hans-Ulrich Abele
Eugen Bartsch
Arthur Bereskin
Egon Bohm
Siegfried Brdlik
Hermann Buhler
Anton Corbach
Paul Dorwald
Herbert Elder
Helmut Fehrs
Helmut Froemsdorf
Oskar Gari
Heinz GeiBler
Werner Grahl
Rudolf Greiner
Kurt Heiligtag
Rudolf Herbert

Herbert Hoffmann
Herbert Holzer
Heinrich Kistner
Joseph Klein
Rudolf Lehmann
Willibald Liebscher
Gunter Luckei
Johann Lyhs
Willi Maker
Erich Mazallik
Helmut Meier
Helmut Mieschliwietz
Helmut Mruck
Franz Nasse
Walter Pokel
Gotthart Poorten
Franz Porstner
Rgon Rauch
Berthold Reister
Heinrich Roseman

Helmut Rosenmuller
Erich Schaadt
Wolfgang Schancke
Lothar Schanz
Kurt Schmidt
Werner Schumann
Helmut Schwarz
Theo Schwenk
Herbert Suchy
Alfred Trotz
Freidrich Volk

Christian Wilde
Herbert Winkler
Nicolaus Wolf
Willibald Wulle
Karl Wurster
Karl Wust
Karl-Heinz Zacher

(No U-853 officers or crew members survived)

Appendix 2:
Vessels and Aircraft Involved in the
USS *Eagle 56/U-853* Incident

U.S. Navy Warships (37)

USS *Acme*

USS *Action*

USS *Adamant*

USS *Amick*

USS *Atherton*

USS *Baldwin*

USS *Barney*

USS *Blakeley*

USS *Booth*

USS *Breckenridge*

USS *Brunswick*

USS *Card*

USS *Craven*

USS *Croatan*

USS *Dale W. Peterson*

USS *Eagle 56*

USS *Earle*

USS *Eberle*

USS *Ericsson*

USS *Evarts*

USS *Frankford*

USS *Gleaves*

USS *Muskegon*

USS *Nelson*

USS *Newport*

USS *Penguin*

USS *Restless*

USS *Rinehart*

USS *SC-1022*

USS *SC-1301*

USS *Selfridge*

USS *Semmes*

USS *Sturtevant*

USS *Uniontown*

USS *Wingfield*

USS *Woolsey*

USS *YMS-74*

U.S. Coast Guard Vessels (6)

USCGC *Dione*
USCGC *Hibiscus*
USCGC *Hornbeam*
USCGC *Moberly*
USCGC *Nantucket*
USCGC 92004

Merchant Vessels (3)

SS *Black Point*
SS *Karmen*
SS *Scandinavia*

U.S. Navy Aircraft (10)

1   Grumman F6F "Hellcat" fighter
2   Lockheed Vega-37 "Ventura" PV-1
    patrol bombers
4   Consolidated PBY "Catalina"
    flying boats

3   ZNP Type Blimps: *K-16*, *K-38*,
    K-58

Enemy Warship (1)

U-853 German U-boat

Vessels Destroyed and Sunk (3)

USS *Eagle 56 (PE-56)*
SS *Black Point*
U-853

Casualties

U-853
    55 killed, 0 survivors
USS *Eagle 56*
    49 killed, 13 survivors
SS *Black Point*
    12 killed, 34 survivors

Total Killed 116

Bibliographic Essay

The essential core of narrative historical nonfiction is a sturdy foundation of rich primary and secondary source material upon which to build the story's drama, pacing, and real-life characters. Even more so than conventional historical writing (and perhaps contrary to conventional thinking), I believe the narrative style often requires a *broader* array of sources to satisfy the story's expanded breadth and the reader's desire for a more in-depth and intimate portrayal of the characters.

Due to Enemy Action comprises a plethora of primary source material, which forms the heart of the book's narrative, thanks to numerous contributions: Paul Lawton's voluminous government and military document collection and his meticulous record-keeping; Bernard Cavalcante's invaluable knowledge and assistance; the generosity of Peggy Barr Eastman, Dr. Kenneth A. Knowles Jr., and the three *Eagle 56* living survivors, John Scagnelli, Harold Petersen, and Johnny Breeze; the thoroughness of Horst Bredow and the German U-boat archives; and the cooperation of many widows, relatives, descendants, and friends of the *Eagle 56* crew.

Throughout this book, I have built the dramatic narrative and drawn conclusions based upon a combination of these primary and secondary sources; I have taken no "poetic license." In sections that obviously call for speculation—examples that include Helmut Froemsdorf's state of mind, whether he received Dönitz's cease-fire order, why crew members of the *U-853* deployed a life raft—I have done so based on the best available source material, and my knowledge of the characters' background and related events. I limited any speculation or conjecture to those matters for which no known documentation exists, and have tried to make those few instances clear to the reader. Otherwise, the narrative of each scene in *Due to Enemy Action* is drawn from primary and secondary source documents, written correspondence, or personal interviews.

Like all good primary sources, the documents used in *Due to Enemy Action* provide more than information; their physical presence and texture actually conjure a sense of time, place, and drama. As I read through the Ultra dispatches from Kenneth Knowles's "Secret Room" and the intercepted messages from Admiral Dönitz to his U-boat commanders, it was as though I had been transported to 1945 and landed in the middle of this high-stakes and deadly cat-and-mouse game. Poring through John Scagnelli's condolence letters, I felt like I was sitting next to him in the Washington heat as he struggled to find the right words to convey his feelings to his shipmates' loved ones in July 1945. Jack Laubach's mother's anguish seemed to leap off the dog-eared pages of her poetry collection and grab hold of me. When an infirm Esta Smith, her voice wistful and melancholy, related her memory of Harold Glenn bounding back up their apartment house front stairs to kiss her good-bye on April 23, 1945, I envisioned myself *in the scene*, standing at the bottom of the same steps in Portland, Maine, looking up at a young and beautiful Esta, who was at first perplexed, and then pleased, by her husband's gesture.

These, and others, are special sources, and I was privileged to have access to them. My fervent hope is that this book does justice to their powerful and timeless authenticity, and the visceral connection they establish between past and present.

For the benefit of readers, I have divided the sources in this essay into primary/unpublished and secondary, and have grouped them further into subcategories that I hope are most helpful.

Primary and Unpublished Sources
U.S. MILITARY AND GOVERNMENT RECORDS

Record Group 457, Records of the National Security Agency, Special Research Histories and Studies (Formerly Classified), including "Ultra" Enigma intercepts:

- SRMN-032, "COMINCH File of Memoranda Concerning U-boat Tracking Room Operations, 2 January 1943–6 June 1945" (Formerly Secret)

- SRMN-033, "COMINCH File of Messages on U-boat Estimates and Situation Reports, September 1944–June 1945." (Formerly Secret)
- SRMN-037, "COMINCH File of U-boat Intelligence Summaries, January 1943–May 1945." (Formerly Secret)
- SRMN-038, "Functions of the 'Secret Room' (F-211) of COMINCH Combat Intelligence, Atlantic Section, Anti-Submarine Warfare, WWII," Undated. (Formerly Secret)
- SRMN-054, "OP-20-G Special Studies Relating to U-boat Activity, 1943–1945." (Formerly Secret)
- Formerly Ultra Top Secret memorandum from Kenneth A. Knowles to Admiral Low, "A Brief Report on A/S [Anti-Submarine] Operations West of the Cape Verde Islands," 26 May 1944.
- Formerly Ultra Top Secret memorandum from Kenneth A. Knowles to Admiral Low, "Passing Ultra Material to CINCLANT," 29 June 1944.

Deck Logs, Action Reports, War Diaries, Anti-Submarine Action by Surface Ship Reports, Depth-Charge and Hedgehog Attack Plots (Formerly Classified):

- April 23, 1945 Action Reports and Deck Log Entries of USS *Craven.*
- April 23, 1945 Action Reports and Deck Log Entries of USS *Earle.*
- April 23, 1945 Action Reports and Deck Log Entries of USS *Evarts.*
- April 23, 1945 Action Reports and Deck Log Entries of USS *Tenacity.*
- April 23, 1945 Action Reports and Deck Log Entries of USS *Woolsey.*
- April 23, 1945 Extract from Deck Log of USS *Nantucket.*
- April 23, 1945 Action Reports, Deck Log Entries, "Report on Sinking of USS *Eagle (PE-56)* and Rescue Operations," Anti-Submarine Action Reports and Depth-Charge Attack Plot of USS *Selfridge.*
- April 24 and April 25, 1945 Action Reports, Deck Log Entries, Anti-Submarine Action by Surface Ship Reports, Depth-Charge and Hedgehog Attack Plots and War Diary of USS *Muskegon.*
- April 24 and April 25, 1945 Action Reports, Deck Log Entries, Anti-Submarine Action by Surface Ship Reports, Depth-Charge and Hedgehog Attack Plots and War Diary of U.S. Coast Guard Cutter *92004.*
- May 5/6, 1945 Action Reports, Deck Log Entries, Anti-Submarine Action Report, and Depth-Charge and Hedgehog Attack Plot of USS *Atherton.*
- May 5/6, 1945 Action Report and Deck Log Entries of USS *Ericsson.*
- May 5/6, 1945 Action Report, Deck Log Entries, Anti-Submarine Action Reports, and Depth-Charge and Hedgehog Attack Plot of USS *Moberly.*
- May 7, 1945 Deck Log Entries of USS *Acme.*

Commander Eastern Sea Frontier, "War Diary Eastern Sea Frontier: Activity Prior 24 April 1945 (RE: EAD 1215/23) COMINCH evaluation," 1945. (Formerly Classified)

Commander Eastern Sea Frontier, "War Diary Eastern Sea Frontier, April, 1945," 1945. (Formerly Classified)

"Records of a COURT OF INQUIRY Convened on Board the U.S. Naval Station Portland, Maine, By Order of Commandant, First Naval District and Navy Yard, Boston, Massachusetts, to inquire into all the circumstances connected with the loss of the USS *Eagle (PE-56)* off Portland Harbor, Maine, at about 12:17 P.M., 23 April 1945," April 26–May 2, 1945. (Formerly Classified)

U.S. Navy Court of Inquiry, "Loss of USS *Eagle 56 (PE-56)*, Argument of the Judge Advocate, Findings of Fact & Opinion, June 1, 1945." (Formerly Confidential)

Eastern Sea Frontier, "Activity Report of 29 April 1945" (Formerly Classified)

Letter of Felix Gygax (USN) Rear Admiral, Commander, First Naval District and Navy Yard, Boston, Massachusetts, June 1, 1945. (Formerly Confidential)

First Naval District War Diary, "U.S. Coast Guard Operations Section, 16 to 30 April, 1945." (Formerly Confidential)

Eastern Sea Frontier, "Surface Control Log 'Flag File' Records of Naval Operating Forces, May, 1945." (Formerly Secret)

Letter of E. M. Ellis, Commander (USN), U.S. Naval Air Station, Brunswick, Maine, April 26, 1945.

Letter of Lieutenant (jg) John P. Scagnelli (USNR), Surviving Senior Officer of *PE-56*, August 2, 1945, to Navy Department Board of Decorations and Medals, seeking posthumous Purple Hearts for deceased *Eagle 56* crew members.

Various letters, telegrams, and notes from navy chaplains, officers, and Secretary of the Navy to relatives of *Eagle 56* deceased crew members, 1945.

Various Navy personnel records (induction notices, discharges, etc.) for numerous *Eagle 56* crew members, including John Scagnelli, Harold Petersen, Johnny Breeze, Fredrick Michelsen, Oscar Davis, Ralph Woods, and Ivar Westerlund.

Various Navy personnel records for Commander Kenneth A. Knowles.

Letter of Captain H. G. Patrick, USN (Ret.) Navy Department Board of Decorations and Medals, to Lt. (jg) John P. Scagnelli, April 3, 1946.

U.S. War Department, "Harbor Defense Projects for Harbor Defenses in the Portland–Cape Cod Area, Parts 1 to IV," 1932; revised September 18, 1942; revised April 11, 1945.

Letter of the Director of Naval History, through the Office of the Chief of Naval Operations, for the Correction of Naval History and the posthumous issuance of Purple Heart Medals to the casualties of the USS *Eagle 56*, signed by the Secretary of the Navy Gordon England on June 26, 2001.

GERMAN MILITARY RECORDS

German U-boat archival records (Cuxhaven-Altenbruch) on Helmut Froemsdorf and the *U-853*, including Froemsdorf's biographical information, the U-boat's mission dates, samples of the "trotting horse and shield" insignia on the boat's conning tower, and other *U-853* records.

Other Primary and Unpublished Sources

Lt. John P. Scagnelli, Collection of Condolence Letters written to family members of deceased *Eagle 56* crew members, July 1945.

Jack Laubach's mother (first name unknown), "So Lovingly Remembered," a collection of poems in tribute to Jack Laubach, 1945–1950.

Paul Lawton, extensive collection of letters and correspondence, 1998–2002, in the matter of the USS *Eagle 56 (PE-56)*.

James Lawton, letters to Congressman Joseph Moakley and White House Chief of Staff Andrew Card.

Bureau of Ships, Construction and Repair Statistics Division, Information Sheet No. 1, USS *Eagle 56*.

Ford Motor Company Eagle Boat blueprints, diagrams, and technical specifications, Henry Ford Museum, Dearborn, Michigan.

Letter of Robert L. Ferree, helmsman, USS *Selfridge*, letter dated April 4, 1995.

Letter of Richard I. DuBurg, former sonarman aboard the U.S. Coast Guard Cutter *Moberly*, letter dated September 9, 2001.

Letters from United States Senator Hillary Rodham Clinton and Rep. Louise Slaughter on behalf of Harold Petersen.

Letters from Esta Glenn Smith, Ginny Laubach Pettebone, and Phyllis Westerlund Kendrick to various recipients, including Paul Lawton, John Breeze, and the author.

Letters from children and family members of *Eagle 56* crew members to Paul Lawton and to the author.

Sworn Statement of John L. Breeze, October 5, 1998.

Sworn Statement of Alice (Heyd) Hultgren, October 5, 1998.

Sworn Affidavit of John L. Breeze, December 28, 1998.

Paul Lawton's *The Sinking of the USS* Eagle PE-56: *Silent Victim of the* U-853, 2003.

PERSONAL INTERVIEWS

John P. Scagnelli, *Eagle 56* survivor.

Harold "Pete" Petersen, *Eagle 56* survivor.

Johnny Breeze, *Eagle 56* survivor.

Joseph Priestas, *Eagle 56* survivor.

Esta Glenn Smith, widow of Harold Glenn, *Eagle 56* crew member killed on April 23, 1945.

Phyllis Westerlund Kendrick, widow of Ivar Westerlund, *Eagle 56* crew member killed on April 23, 1945.

Lorraine Luttrell, widow of John Luttrell, *Eagle 56* crew member.

Robert, Paul, and Fred Westerlund, sons of Ivar Westerlund.

Dr. Kenneth A. Knowles Jr., son of "Secret Room" Commander Kenneth Knowles.

James Lawton, World War II veteran and father of Paul Lawton.

Sharon Atkins, daughter of Oscar Davis, surviving Eagle 56 crew member.

Lorraine Tracy, wife and widow of Oscar Davis.

Bernard Cavalcante, Senior Archivist, U.S. Naval Historical Center.

Horst Bredow, founder and director of German U-boat archives (written correspondence).

Peggy Eastman, daughter of former *Eagle 56* commander, Captain John Barr, and close friends with Ginny Laubach Pettebone, widow of *Eagle 56* executive officer Jack Laubach.

Dianna Woods-Murray, daughter of Ralph Woods, *Eagle 56* crew member who was killed on April 23, 1945.

Fred "Mick" Michelsen, son of *Eagle 56* crew member Fredrick Michelsen, who was killed on April 23, 1945, and Pauline Michelsen.

Paul Lawton, attorney and military historian who presented the *Eagle 56* evidence to the Navy.

Alice Hultgren, Navy WAVE stenographer during the *Eagle 56* Court of Inquiry.

Captain (Ret.) Edward J. Melanson, Alice Hultgren's friend who obtained the first copy of the *Eagle 56* Court of Inquiry records.

Secondary Sources

Throughout the book, on virtually every subject, I consulted hundreds of pages of newspapers and magazines, including the *Portland (Maine) Press Herald*, *The New York Times*, the *Brockton (MA) Enterprise*, *The Boston Globe*, the *Boston Herald*, the *Rochester Democrat*, the *Daily Record* of Morris Plains, New Jersey, *Time* magazine, and others. Most of the specific citations are included within the text; thus, in the interest of space, I have not listed here every individual newspaper issue I consulted. It is worth noting that one of the finest World War II newspaper compilations has been organized by the Brockton, Massachusetts, Library, which has organized hundreds of articles from the *Brockton Enterprise* into a collection entitled, "Brockton's Part in the War," upon which I relied heavily.

Let me offer a brief word on the remainder of the secondary sources. Esteemed military historian John Keegan has claimed that the definitive history of the Second World War has not yet been written, that more time needed to pass before historians could gain true perspective. Perhaps he is correct. Nonetheless, while *the* definitive history of World War II may not yet have been written, it is safe to say that more has been written about the world's greatest conflict than virtually any other historical subject, with the possible exception of Abraham Lincoln and the Civil War; and the John F. Kennedy presidency and assassination. The World War II literature is vast in terms of general histories, and it has generated numerous subcategories of literature that have become major areas of study and analysis in and of themselves; the Holocaust and the fascination with Hitler's life and death are among the two best known in this category. Within the last ten years, as World War II veterans pass on, a focus on what Tom Brokaw called the "Greatest Generation" has spawned an even greater emphasis on their stories, including this book.

Yet, one area has been overlooked. Despite several fine works on the U-boat war and the Battle of the Atlantic, these subjects fall mostly within the purview of military historians and remain largely unknown to the general reader, even those with a strong interest in World War II. Most are shocked to learn that German U-boats sunk hundreds of merchant ships scant miles from America's East Coast in the first six months of 1942. This book is an attempt to bring some of that remarkable story to general readers; additional work needs to be done in this fertile area.

What follows is a list of the secondary sources that I consulted for background, or works that I referenced in the text, grouped according to categories that I believe are most beneficial to the reader.

THE BATTLE OF THE ATLANTIC AND THE U-BOAT WAR

The literature for this category is extensive, well researched, and compelling, but—as I mentioned—needs to find a wider audience. Among the most helpful general works were Clay Blair's excellent two-volume compendium and analysis, *Hitler's U-boat War: The Hunters, 1939–1942* and *Hitler's U-boat War: The Hunted, 1942–1945* (New York, Random House, 1996 and 1998, respectively); Edwin P. Hoyt's *The Death of the U-boats* (New York, McGraw Hill, 1988); *To Die Gallantly: The Battle of the Atlantic,* Timothy J. Runyan and Jan M. Copes, eds., (San Francisco: Westview Press, 1994); Peter Padfield's *War Beneath the Sea: Submarine Conflict During World War II* (New York: John Wiley & Sons, 1995); Dan van der Vat's *The Atlantic Campaign: World War II's Great Struggle at Sea* (New York: Harper & Row, 1988); Samuel Eliot Morison's *The Battle of the Atlantic: September 1939–May 1943* (Boston: Little, Brown, 1966); Nathan Miller's *War At Sea: A Naval History of World War II* (New York: Oxford Press, 1995); *Battle Report: The Atlantic War,* prepared from official sources by Commander Walter Karig, USNR (New York: Farrar & Rinehart, 1946); and, from the British point of view, Captain S. W. Roskill's *The War At Sea: 1939–1945, Volume III, The Offensive, 1st June 1944–14th August 1945* (London: Her Majesty's Stationery Office, 1961).

Michael Gannon's *Operation Drumbeat: The Dramatic True Story of Germany's First U-boat Attacks Along the American Coast in World War II* (New York: Harper & Row, 1990) focuses on the harrowing first six months of 1942, while Homer Hickam's *Torpedo Junction: U-boat War off America's East Coast, 1942* (Annapolis: United States Naval Institute, 1989) primarily details the merchant ship killing ground off Cape Hatteras, North Carolina. Peter Kemp examines the controversy surrounding Admiral King's approach to convoys in *Decision at Sea: The Convoy Escorts* (New York: Elsevier-Dutton, 1978).

To understand the battle from the perspective of the U-boat commanders and crews, please see Jordan Vause's *Wolf: U-boat Commanders in World War II* (Annapolis: Naval Institute Press, 1997); Herbert A. Werner's *Iron Coffins: A Personal Account of the German U-boat Battles of World War II* (New York: Holt, Rinehart and Winston, 1969); Jak P. Mallmann Showell's *U-boat Warfare: The Evolution of the Wolf Pack* (Annapolis: Naval Institute Press, 2002); and *Countermeasures Against U-boats During World War II: The Monthly Reviews, November 2002,* Jak P. Mallmann Showell, ed., (Cuxhaven-Altenbruch, Germany and Bletchley Park: Her Majesty's Stationery Office, 2002). Eugene Rachlis's *They Came to Kill: The Story of Eight Nazi Saboteurs in America* (New York: Random House, 1961) and Michael Dobbs's *Saboteurs: The Nazi Raid on America* (New York: Alfred A. Knopf, 2004) provide information about the U-boats while telling the full story of the German saboteurs who came ashore in New York and Florida in 1942.

Jürgen Rowher's *Axis Submarine Successes, 1939–1945* (Annapolis: Naval Institute Press, 1983) and Rowher's and Gerhard Hummelchen's *Chronology of the War at Sea, 1939–1945: The Naval History of World War II* (Annapolis: Naval Institute Press, 1992) are indispensable to understanding the Battle of the Atlantic, as are Henry C. Keatts's and George C. Farr's *Diving Into History* books, *Volume 1, Warships* and *Volume 3, U-boats* (Houston: Pisces Books, 1990 and 1994, respectively). Finally, for a full accounting of the U-boats, please see Kenneth Wynn's *U-boat Operations of the Second World War*, comprised of *Volume 1: Career Histories, U-1 to U-510 and Volume 2: Career Histories, U 511 to U-1225* (Annapolis, Naval Institute Press, 1997 and 1998, respectively).

KENNETH KNOWLES, "ULTRA" RECORDS, CODE BREAKING

I am deeply indebted to David Kohnen for his excellent analysis of Kenneth Knowles's role in the Battle of the Atlantic in *Commanders Winn and Knowles: Winning the U-boat War with Intelligence 1939–1943* (Krakow, Poland: The Enigma Press, 1999). Kohnen's work, and my interviews with Dr. Kenneth Knowles Jr., assisted me greatly in developing the character of Commander Kenneth Knowles, one of the true unsung American heroes of World War II. It was the senior Knowles himself who provided insight into the Tenth Fleet's aggressive philosophy to use Ultra information as an offensive weapon in his article, "Ultra and the Battle of the Atlantic: The American View," in Robert W. Love, Jr., ed. *Changing Interpretations and New Sources in Naval History: Papers from The Third United States Naval Academy History Symposium* (New York: Garland, 1980).

Other works that I found helpful in this category included: Hervie Haufler's *Codebreakers' Victory: How the Allied Cryptographers Won World War II* (New York: New American Library, 2003); F. H. Hinsley's and Alan Stripp's *Codebreakers: The Inside Story of Bletchley Park* (Oxford, England: Oxford Press, 1993); David Kahn's *Seizing the Enigma: The Race to Break the German U-boat Codes, 1939–1943* (Boston: Houghton Mifflin, 1991); and Philip Gerard's *Secret Soldiers: The Story of World War II's Heroic Army of Deception* (New York: Dutton, 2002).

EISENHOWER, CHURCHILL, ROOSEVELT, AND TRUMAN

These four giants have inspired some of the finest World War II writing ever, with readers unable to get enough of fresh interpretations and analyses of the leadership that steered the United States and England through the Second

World War. While their names are mentioned prominently in every volume about the war, the following books provided insights for *Due to Enemy Action*:

For the Supreme Commander of the Allied Forces that orchestrated the victory over Nazi Germany, I relied on Carlo D'Este's magnificent in-depth wartime biography, *Eisenhower: A Soldier's Life* (New York: Henry Holt, 2002). Stephen Ambrose's *Eisenhower: Soldier and President* (New York: Simon & Schuster, 1990), a condensation of his two-volume biography of Eisenhower, remains the best and most readable one-volume examination of Ike's life (in war and as president), and was invaluable to me. While written from a grandson's perspective, David Eisenhower's *Eisenhower: At War, 1943–1945* (New York: Random House, 1986) is also objective, compelling, and far-reaching. Ike's own *Crusade in Europe* (Baltimore: The Johns Hopkins University Press, 1948) is required reading as a first-person account of the most successful military campaign in history; its publication just a few years after the war ended also heightens the contemporaneous drama of the events it describes.

Roosevelt and Churchill are legends unto themselves; their words, actions, and motives have been examined more thoroughly than any other wartime figures. For this book, I looked at Conrad Black's stunningly comprehensive biography, *Franklin Delano Roosevelt: Champion of Freedom* (New York: Public Affairs, 2003); FDR scholar Frank Freidel's fine one-volume biography, *Franklin D. Roosevelt: A Rendezvous with Destiny* (Boston: Little, Brown, 1990); and Eric Larrabee's *Commander in Chief: Franklin Delano Roosevelt, His Lieutenants and Their War* (New York: Harper & Row, 1987). I relied on Roy Jenkins's *Churchill: A Biography* (New York: Farrar, Straus, and Giroux, 2001) for insights into England's prime minister, as well as Churchill's classic six-volume history, *The Second World War*, written between 1949 and 1953. Two books that helped me understand the complex and trusting relationship between FDR and Churchill were Jon Meacham's *Franklin and Winston: An Intimate Portrait of an Epic Friendship* (New York: Random House, 2003) and David Stafford's intriguing *Roosevelt and Churchill: Men of Secrets* (New York: The Overlook Press, 2000), which focused on both leaders' involvement in secret intelligence activities.

The outstanding standard-bearing biography about FDR's successor, David McCullough's *Truman* (New York: Simon & Schuster, 1992), provided me with all I needed to recount the scenes about the atomic bomb. Michael Beschloss's *The Conquerors: Roosevelt, Truman and the Destruction of Hitler's Germany, 1941–1945* (New York: Simon & Schuster, 2002) was an invaluable source in linking the two presidents' commitment to the doctrine of "unconditional surrender" for Germany. Such a policy was necessary to avoid the ambiguity that existed at the end of World War I, festered, and ultimately spawned Hitler's rise;

yet, "unconditional surrender" also resulted in Dönitz's final desperate U-boat attacks late in the war and the destruction of the *Eagle 56* in April of 1945.

HITLER, DÖNITZ, GERMANY

Ian Kershaw's epic two-volume biography, *Hitler: 1889–1936, Hubris* and *Hitler: 1936–1945, Nemesis* (New York: W.W. Norton, 1998 and 2000 respectively), offer the most fascinating portraits of the man who sought to dominate the world. Joachim Fest's *Inside Hitler's Bunker: The Last Days of the Third Reich* (New York: Farrar, Straus and Giroux, 2002) described the final hours of desperation and madness for Hitler and the German High Command. Michael Burleigh's *The Third Reich: A New History* (New York: Farrar, Straus and Giroux, 2000) is a comprehensive examination of Hitler's movement. Antony Beevor's *The Fall of Berlin 1945* (New York: Viking, 2002) is required reading to understand the terror and brutality that swept the German capital in the days and weeks before her demise. For my insights into Dönitz, I relied on Samuel W. Mitcham Jr.'s and Gene Mueller's *Hitler's Commanders: Officers of the Wehrmacht, the Luftwaffe, the Kriegsmarine, and the Waffen-SS* (Lanham, Maryland: Scarborough House, 1992) and Ann and John Tusa's *The Nuremberg Trials* (New York: Scribner, 1983).

THE AMERICAN HOME FRONT IN WORLD WAR II

Two of the finest works on this topic were invaluable to this book: David M. Kennedy's *Freedom From Fear: The American People in Depression and War, 1929–1945* (New York: Oxford University Press, 1999) and Doris Kearns Goodwin's *No Ordinary Time: Franklin & Eleanor Roosevelt and the Home Front in World War II* (New York: Simon & Schuster, 1994). For a fascinating look at Franklin Roosevelt's connection with the American people during wartime, see Lawrence and Cornelia Levine's *The People and the President: America's Conversations with FDR* (Boston: Beacon Press, 2002). Similarly, the relationship between a town, its servicemen, and their sacrifice is movingly told in Alex Kershaw's *The Bedford Boys* (Cambridge, Mass.: Da Capo Press, 2003).

OTHER WORKS CONSULTED

For a general one-volume, international discussion of the Second World War, see Gerhard Weinberg's *A World at Arms: A Global History of World War II* (New York: Cambridge University Press, 1994). The Allied perspective is analyzed shrewdly in Richard Overy's *Why the Allies Won* (New York: W.W. Norton, 1995), and for a comprehensive one-volume operational history of the Second World War, see Williamson Murray's and Allan R. Millett's *A War to be*

Won: Fighting the Second World War (Cambridge, Mass.: Harvard University, 2000). I learned a great deal about America's premier war correspondent in James Tobin's *Ernie Pyle's War: America's Eyewitness to World War II* (New York: The Free Press, 1997).

For background about John Scagnelli's town, I consulted Virginia Dyer Vogt's and Daniel B. Myers's *Morris Plains* (Charleston, S.C.: Arcadia: 2000); for information about the Merchant Marine, of which he was a member, I found helpful John Bunker's *Heroes in Dungarees: The Story of the American Merchant Marine in World War II* (Annapolis: Naval Institute Press, 1995). For a history of Harold Petersen's community, I relied on Eleanor Kalsbeck's *Henrietta Heritage* (Henrietta, New York: Henrietta Town Historian, 1977).

Finally, I am grateful to Peggy Barr Eastman for writing so movingly about Ginny Laubach Pettebone in *Godly Glimpses: Discoveries of the Love That Heals* (Huntington, Indiana: Our Sunday Visitor Publishing, 1999).

Acknowledgments

I first met Paul Lawton on June 8, 2002, immediately following the *Eagle 56* Purple Heart ceremony aboard the USS *Salem* in Quincy, Massachusetts. We had a brief conversation that marked the beginning of my involvement in this enormously gratifying project. Lawton was celebrating the culmination of his years of work when I came into the picture, yet he graciously agreed to the idea of a book. Later, he shared with me hundreds of pages of research and dozens of photographs that he had compiled over more than four years, documents and images that provided me with the tools to turn the kernel of an idea into a full-length work. *Due to Enemy Action* would not have been possible without Paul Lawton: first, there would have been no *Eagle 56* story at all without his determination to learn the truth and reverse U.S. naval history; and second, the documents he collected—most of which were previously classified—form the foundation for this book. I am profoundly grateful to Paul for entrusting me with our shared goal of bringing the *Eagle* story to a wide audience, and hope this book does justice to his efforts and his expectations.

I am deeply indebted to three of the living *Eagle 56* survivors, who opened their hearts and their homes to me to make this book possible. I was honored that John Scagnelli, Harold "Pete" Petersen, and Johnny Breeze shared memories they've held for more than a half-century, and described 1945 events as though they happened yesterday. These are men of great character and immense pride. Throughout the *Eagle 56* saga, they sought neither redemption nor notoriety, but when both were thrust upon them, they reacted with grace and graciousness. More importantly, they took up the mantle for their deceased shipmates, never forgetting their sacrifice on April 23, 1945, always emphasizing that the truth was essential to allow those men to rest in peace. More than fifty-six years after their buddies had died in the freezing waters of the North Atlantic, Scagnelli, Petersen, and Breeze continually expressed their love for their former shipmates each time we spoke or corresponded.

These three survivors have shared boundless love with their wives, too, women who came into their lives after the *Eagle 56* tragedy, yet fully embraced their husbands' need and desire to correct the historical record in their twilight years. I had the pleasure of meeting and talking with Bea Scagnelli and Betty Breeze, two strong women whose love, friendship, and support through the decades have provided the inspiration for their husbands' hopes and dreams. I was not fortunate enough to have met Mary Petersen before she died, though Pete insists I would have liked her. Knowing him, I have no doubt.

Throughout this project, I was rewarded with cooperation and encouragement each time I contacted and spoke with the far-flung members of the *Eagle 56* "family." Each person was anxious to reveal what they knew about the *Eagle* story—not once did I encounter an individual reluctant to share their thoughts and remembrances, or their documents, letters, and photographs, all of which deeply enriched this book.

My deepest thanks go to the widows, Esta Glenn Smith and Phyllis Westerlund Kendrick, who described to me their short-lived time with Harold and Ivar in remarkable detail, and with the yearning that can only accompany the memories of a first love lost too soon. I was stunned at Phyllis's clear and vivid recollection, nearly sixty years after the fact, of the raindrops falling into the pails while she read Ivar's poems in 1945. I was equally astounded by Esta's detailed description of her feelings when Harold returned to the top front step of their Portland apartment house to kiss her good-bye on the morning of April 23, 1945. Ginny Laubach Pettebone died before I had an opportunity to speak to her; however, I felt I knew Ginny well thanks to her poignant letters to Paul Lawton and Johnny Breeze, her mother-in-law's poetry collection, and especially, thanks to Peggy Eastman, who generously shared her writings and recollections of Ginny with me. Pauline Michelsen's poor health made it impossible for me to speak with her, either. However, interviews with her son, Mick—to whom I'm deeply indebted—and a cache of letters from his father, provided me with more than enough information about the widow who became a mother on

Hiroshima Day, August 6, 1945, just a few months after her husband died in the torpedo attack on the *Eagle*.

Other members of the *Eagle 56* family who were instrumental in contributing to this story include: Ivar Westerlund's sons, Bob, Fred, and Paul, and Linda Westerlund (Paul's wife); Sharon Atkins (Oscar Davis's daughter) and Lorraine Tracey (Oscar's widow); Dianna Woods-Murray, daughter of *Eagle 56* crew member Ralph Woods, who was killed on April 23, 1945; Lorraine Luttrell, widow of Lucky Thirteen crew member John Luttrell; and Alice Heyd Hultgren, the Navy WAVE stenographer during the *Eagle 56* Court of Inquiry.

Captain (Ret.) Edward Melanson, Alice Hultgren's friend who obtained the Court of Inquiry records, was generous with his time in recounting his role and providing his impressive background. Dr. Kenneth A. Knowles Jr. took time out from his teaching responsibilities at the United States Naval Academy to contribute invaluable information about his father's life, character, and pivotal role in the Battle of the Atlantic. Horst Bredow, founder and director of the German U-boat archives, provided background on Froemsdorf and the *U-853*, as well as his own opinions on the *Eagle 56* story. Bernard Cavalcante— "Cal"—senior archivist at the U.S. Naval Historical Center, graciously submitted to full-length interviews and my repeated requests for additional documents, especially pertaining to the "Secret Room," as well as details about his role in convincing the Navy to overturn the 1945 Court of Inquiry.

I'm grateful to Judge (Ret.) James Lawton, who described his own World War II experiences, and his role in the *Eagle 56* story, with the self-effacing modesty that I associate with virtually all members of the Greatest Generation. In honor of his service, this book is partially dedicated to him. Further, I appreciated his insights about Paul Lawton that only a father could offer about his son.

In addition to the remarkable assistance I received from people involved directly in the *Eagle 56* story, I was also the beneficiary of outstanding personal support and encouragement from dozens of friends and family members whose interest and enthusiasm in this project provided me with the energy to bring it to completion. In addition, many of these individuals have supported me by attending my previous book signings and presentations, writing letters of encouragement, and recommending and purchasing my first book. Space prohibits me from listing all these wonderful folks here, but they know who they are; I hope they also know that I am forever grateful and appreciative for all they have done.

I would like to single out a few people.

As she has with my previous writing projects (and indeed, with projects of any kind), my dear friend, Ellen Keefe, offered her full support, guidance, and encouragement on all aspects of *Due to Enemy Action*, from assisting with the early research to reading the final manuscript, and virtually every step in between. No amount of thanks seems sufficient. I took pause while writing these words to realize that Ellen and I have been friends for nearly thirty years; if a man's fortune can be measured by his friendships, I've been a rich man these past three decades for knowing Ellen.

It is hard to describe how grateful I am to my agent, Joy Tutela, of the David Black Literary Agency. Let me try by keeping with the World War II theme of this book (using an Army rather than a Navy example): If I were in a foxhole, I would want Joy right beside me. She fights hard and never gives up. She remains undaunted and unflappable when the going gets tough. She never panics, even if I do. She is strong and steady and very good at what she does. Joy wears the many hats of an agent with skill, confidence, honesty, and grace—whether she's acting as editor, adviser, negotiator, drill sergeant, booster, coach, or (unsparing) critic. Best of all for me, she always keeps the "friend hat" within easy reach. Thanks, Joy.

I'm thankful to George Donahue at The Lyons Press, for his enthusiasm for the *Eagle 56* story and this book, and his willingness to add *Due to Enemy Action* to the publisher's prestigious list of military and history titles. I'm also grateful to my editor, Holly Rubino, for providing steady direction and careful stewardship to guide this book to publication under a tight deadline.

My parents, Rose and Tony Puleo, have lent their unwavering love, support, and encouragement throughout this project, and as always, I am humbled by all they have done for me. This book is particularly special to them, I think, because of their visceral generational connection to the people in this story, and my father's own World War II service. My parents, my wife Kate, and I attended the World War II Memorial dedication in Washington, D.C., on Memorial Day of 2004, a wondrous and emotional weekend for all of us; I believe my mom and dad view this book as an extension of that experience. In fact, as much as this book honors the contributions of the *Eagle 56* crew, it indirectly pays tribute to every member of the World War II generation. For that reason, *Due to Enemy Action* is partially dedicated to my father, a Purple Heart recipient himself, for his wartime service.

This brings me to Kate, my wife and best friend. I suppose there are many people who write books quite capably without the support and generosity of someone who loves them above all, but I don't know how they do it. Kate's love *always* strengthens and inspires me, but its profoundness strikes me most deeply when I'm in the midst of a project as time-consuming as this book. When I'm searching through records at the library or staring at the computer monitor, I may be by myself, but I am never alone—Kate's rock-solid support is always with me, the irrepressible constant that keeps me going and helps me realize that anything is possible. She listens, advises, and encourages; she criticizes gently and praises enthusiastically. She has an editor's instinct for language and a proofreader's eye for detail. I say "thank you" to Kate all the time, but I can never *really* thank her. In 2005 we celebrate our twenty-fifth wedding anniversary, and I can only hope she knows that, each and every day, I am overwhelmed and honored by the blessing of her love and friendship.

Finally, I want to remember and acknowledge the contributions and sacrifice of the *Eagle 56* crew members who were killed on April 23, 1945, men whose voices were stilled in an instant, men who died far too young. This story is their story. For the laughter they never enjoyed, the memories they never experienced, the loved ones they never held—this book is also dedicated to them.

Stephen Puleo
November 2004

Index

About the Author

Stephen Puleo is the author of *Dark Tide: The Great Boston Molasses Flood of 1919*, a critically-acclaimed Boston-area bestseller, an Associated Press round-up selection, and a finalist for the Boston Authors Club's prestigious Julia Ward Howe prize given to books of literary merit. He has a master's degree in history and has contributed feature stories and book reviews to *American History* magazine. Formerly an award-winning newspaper reporter, he currently works as a corporate communications and public relations consultant. He and his wife, Kate, live in the Boston area. To learn more, visit www.stephenpuleo.com.

Stephen donates a portion of his book proceeds to the Juvenile Diabetes Research Foundation. JDRF is the leading charitable funder and advocate of juvenile (type 1) diabetes research worldwide. To learn more, visit www.JDRF.org.